THE PENGUIN BOOK OF WITCHES

KATHERINE HOWE, the direct descendant of three accused Salem witches, is the *New York Times* bestselling author of the novels *The Physick Book of Deliverance Dane, The House of Velvet and Glass,* and the young-adult novel *Conversion,* a modern-day retelling of *The Crucible* set in a Massachusetts prep school. She teaches in the American Studies program at Cornell University in Ithaca, New York.

The Penguin Book of Witches

Edited by
KATHERINE HOWE

PENGUIN BOOKS

PENGUIN BOOKS

Published by the Penguin Group
Penguin Group (USA) LLC
375 Hudson Street
New York, New York 10014

USA I Canada I UK I Ireland I Australia I New Zealand I India I South Africa I China
penguin.com
A Penguin Random House Company

First published in Penguin Books 2014

Introduction and selection copyright © 2014 by Katherine Howe

ISBN 978-0-14-310618-0

Printed in the United States of America
1 3 5 7 9 10 8 6 4 2

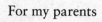
For my parents

Contents

THE PENGUIN BOOK OF WITCHES

English Antecedents

The Early Colonies

Salem

After Salem

Introduction

Marblehead, Massachusetts, is a bedroom community in suburban Boston, a comfortable seaside enclave of historic houses. It has good public schools, intermittent bus service, and a weekly newspaper that is read mainly for the juicy names-naming police log. It is not the sort of place where one would expect to find a witch.

But a witch did live there, though she is not buried there. Wilmot Redd, or sometimes Reed, was one of the more than one hundred people who was accused during the Salem witch crisis of 1692, and, like the other condemned witches, her body was thrown into a shallow ditch at the base of a rocky ledge to the west of Salem Town after being cut down from the gallows. At that time, the area at the foot of the hill where the gallows stood was flooded with brackish water at high tide, and so Wilmot Redd, after resting uneasily in the rocky earth of coastal Essex County, was most likely carried out to sea. Today the ditch she was thrown into is hidden under a pharmacy parking lot.

Redd, like the other North American witches who have left impressions—sometimes lasting, sometimes glancing—in the historical record, presents something of a conundrum. How can the English colonists who settled North America, who were relatively literate compared with their European cousins, who were reasonably thoughtful and self-examining, who lived in tightly interconnected communities dependent on collective effort for success, have believed in witches? And not just believed in witches, but also put them to death? The historical fact of witchcraft weighs uneasily in our current culture, particularly given how much symbolic, nation-building weight the colonists are required to bear in the realms of popular history.

Histories of witchcraft have often revealed more about the time in which the historian was writing than about witchcraft itself. Within each all-encompassing theory of witchcraft in the English Atlantic world came a new set of contemporary biases and prerogatives, obscuring the fact that, to the individual living in the early modern world, from the sixteenth through the middle part of the eighteenth centuries, witchcraft was a legitimate, but dangerous, category for explaining reality. Witchcraft intersected, contained, and sometimes overwrote other important social questions—most notably of gender, class, inequality, and religion—but to treat it merely as a proxy for those other ideas, because those other ideas have persisted into our own time while witchcraft has not, strips away the explanatory power that witchcraft held for the people who were touched by it.[1] An idea, even today, does not have to be empirically verifiable for it to matter.

A surer way to access the meaning and function of witchcraft in the early modern world is to peel back the layers of popular myth and academic historiography and to look with fresh eyes at the primary sources. What ultimately emerges is a complicated picture. The witch appears first, in biblical terms, as the Other, as that which is not doctrinaire. Witchcraft is less a set of defined practices than a representation of the oppositional, as the intentional thwarting of the machinery of power, whether that power lies with the church, with the king, or with the dominant cultural group. Under the heavy guidance of English theologians, witches and witchcraft assume a set of identifiable principles and practices, though those practices remain distilled from oppositional definitions. Witches pervert the generative properties of womanhood in their suckling of imps and their copulations with devils; they subvert the church's authority by turning Christian rituals on end; and they undermine class hierarchy by claiming unearned power for themselves.

The English abstraction of who a witch is, and what she is likely to do, travels with the colonists to North America. While primarily a Puritan phenomenon on North American shores, witchcraft penetrates deeper into colonial life than might initially be suspected. The majority of witch trials were held in New England, though the cultural content of witchcraft finds expression throughout the colonies, and in ongoing dialogue with England. The use of English precedent as template and justification for the conduct of the Salem trials underscores the fact that Salem, rather than being an aberration, was instead the most intense, and perhaps the most defining, expression of North American religious, cultural, and legal thought.

Whereas nineteenth-century historians treated colonial-era belief in witchcraft as a faintly embarrassing holdover of medieval thought that was quickly purged, the belief in and pursuit of witches must instead be seen as a central concept informing a shifting North American identity. Even after Salem forever changed the way that witchcraft would (and, soon enough, would not) be prosecuted, belief in witchcraft persisted well into the Enlightenment. Witches served as both literal and figurative scapegoats for frontier communities under profound economic, religious, and political pressure. The figure of the witch, the idea of the witch, and the need to flush her out of her hiding place and into the light served as a binding agent among fragile communities that were subject to waves of arrival and departure, living with uncertain rights in unsecured territories. The witch—ever the embodiment of the oppositional—served a vital role in the formation of what would eventually be a new united nation. That's one of the reasons that she and the events of Salem persist in our political discourse and in our popular culture. We need her in order to know who we are *not* so that we can begin to imagine who we are.

This book argues for witchcraft's presence in the mainstream of thought in colonial North American culture, extending beyond passing fits of unreason or hysteria. Belief in witchcraft was not an anomalous throwback to late medieval thought by provincial colonists, nor was it an embarrassing blip in an otherwise steady march to an idealized nationhood. It was not a disease. It was not a superstition. Witchcraft's presence or absence was constitutive to the colonial order. It was a touchstone that reinforced what was normal and what was aberrant. For upper echelons of society—in the world of the Protestant church and the court system—prosecution of witchcraft allowed for the consolidation of power and the enforcement of religious and social norms. For common people, belief in witchcraft explained away quotidian unfairness and misfortune. These two circles of belief intersected in the bodies of individuals, usually women, who were out of step with their society, and who were thought to have pledged themselves to the Devil in exchange for the power to work their will through invisible means.

The Penguin Book of Witches is an annotated volume of primary source documents about witchcraft in English North America that is designed for readers interested in learning about the reality behind the fiction. Its goal is to assemble a broad array of sources, chosen for their representative value as well as their narrative power, which, taken as a whole, will leave a reader with a solid command of the meaning of witchcraft in early American life. The first chapter focuses on the legal and cultural beliefs about witchcraft in precolonial England, as the region that made the greatest contribution to the beliefs about witchcraft in colonial North America. The second chapter presents selected records of witchcraft cases from North America before the Salem panic, from the earliest hints of witch suspicion to the first confirmed witch trial in Massachusetts. This chapter does not limit its scope to New England, also looking at the few witch trials outside the Puritan settlements of northern Massachusetts. The third chapter focuses on the unique events of Salem, which, in addition to being the most infamous North American witch trial, was also the most widespread, and the most deadly. The final chapter investigates witchcraft after Salem, when witchcraft was decriminalized but remained an enduring part of American culture. Witchcraft did not vanish from North American consciousness in a sudden burst of reason and Enlightenment. It persisted as a shadowy reminder of an intellectual world that had faded but had never fully disappeared.

Witchcraft continues to fascinate us today, a fact evidenced by the ongoing popularity of witches in fiction, tourism, history, popular religion, and historical writing. Much of what we think we know about witchcraft is actually cribbed from popular culture. When we talk about witches, we imagine a Halloween stereotype of a woman with a pointy hat, broom, and cat, blended with the magic-using housewife of *Bewitched*, who could wiggle her nose to make a pot roast. But the real witches of early modern England and North America are not cackling cartoon characters in pointy hats. The reality of witchcraft in English North America is much more fascinating—and terrifying.

On a chilly spring day not too long ago, I lined up with my gossiping neighbors outside a modest antique house in Marblehead, Massachusetts, that dated from the late 1600s. The occupant had lived there her entire life and had lately passed away. The line was for admission to a tag sale to dispose of the belongings the occupant's family didn't want. Inside, the house was tiny—possibly eight hundred square feet—its walls stained with tobacco smoke, every corner crammed with the flotsam of a long and often difficult life within view of the sea. For extra space, the occupant had expanded into her unfinished basement, where one corner had been set up for sewing projects, another for laundry. One wall was filled, somewhat unnervingly, with shelves of homemade dolls. A far wall held a small spice rack of herbs next to several photographs of women pasted up, at first glance, at random.

Or not at random. The photographs were arrayed around a cutout of the earth from a science magazine. On closer inspection, the pictures of women seemed to be generations of the former occupant's family. Next to the altar—for that is what the wall of devotional pictures proved to be—stood a bookshelf packed with well-thumbed texts about witchcraft, mostly of the contemporary post–New Age variety that dated back to the 1970s. The neighbors rooted through her belongings, bartering for candlesticks, haggling over Federal-style end tables, unaware that a witch had been living next door for three decades.

I took home her dusty mantel clock, a simple table that became my desk, and the well-loved witchcraft books. But my real joy lay in knowing that my neighbor had found a connection to history that was meaningful to her, and from which she drew empowerment. Even after witchcraft disappeared as a deadly legal problem, the belief in witchcraft persists, continuing to do its cultural work, hiding in plain sight in the staid bedroom communities of Boston.

KATHERINE HOWE

Suggestions for Further Reading

Archives

Cornell University Witchcraft Collection, Division of Rare Books, Kroch Library, Ithaca, NY
Essex County Court Archives Collection
Essex Institute Archive
Houghton Library, Harvard University, Cambridge, MA
Massachusetts Archives Collection
Massachusetts Historical Society, Boston, MA
Massachusetts Judicial Archives Collection
Massachusetts State Archives, Boston, MA
New York Public Library, Manuscripts and Archives Division
Peabody Essex Museum, Salem, MA
University of Virginia Salem Witch Trials Documentary Archive and Transcription Project

Books and Articles

Adler, Margot. *Drawing Down the Moon: Witches, Druids, Goddess-Worshippers, and Other Pagans in America.* New York: Penguin Books, 1979.

Anglo, Sydney, ed. *The Damned Art: Essays in the Literature of Witchcraft.* London and Boston: Routledge & K. Paul, 1977.

Baker, Emerson W. *The Devil of Great Island: Witchcraft and Conflict in Early New England.* New York: Palgrave Macmillan, 2007.

Behringer, Wolfgang. *Witches and Witch-Hunts: A Global History.* Cambridge, UK, and Malden, MA: Polity Press, 2004.

Boyer, Paul S., and Stephen Nissenbaum. *Salem Possessed: The Social Origins of Witchcraft*. Cambridge, MA: Harvard University Press, 1974.

Breslaw, Elaine G. *Tituba, Reluctant Witch of Salem: Devilish Indians and Puritan Fantasies*. New York: New York University Press, 1996.

Clark, Stuart. *Thinking with Demons: The Idea of Witchcraft in Early Modern Europe*. Oxford: Clarendon Press; New York: Oxford University Press, 1997.

Cross, Tom Peete. *Witchcraft in North Carolina*. Chapel Hill: University of North Carolina, 1919.

Davies, Owen. *Popular Magic: Cunning-Folk in English History*. New York: Bloomsbury, 2007.

Demos, John Putnam. *Entertaining Satan: Witchcraft and the Culture of Early New England*. New York: Oxford University Press, 1982.

Gibson, Marion. *Witchcraft Myths in American Culture*. New York: Routledge, 2007.

Godbeer, Richard. *The Devil's Dominion: Magic and Religion in Early New England*. Cambridge; New York: Cambridge University Press, 1992.

Goss, K. David. *Daily Life During the Salem Witch Trials*. Santa Barbara, CA: Greenwood, 2012.

Hall, David D. *Worlds of Wonder, Days of Judgment: Popular Religious Belief in Early New England*. New York: Knopf, 1989.

Hansen, Chadwick. *Witchcraft at Salem*. New York: G. Braziller, 1969.

Hutton, Ronald. *The Triumph of the Moon: A History of Modern Pagan Witchcraft*. Oxford, New York: Oxford University Press, 1999.

Karlsen, Carol F. *The Devil in the Shape of a Woman: Witchcraft in Colonial New England*. New York: Norton, 1987.

Levack, Brian P. *The Witch-Hunt in Early Modern Europe*. 3rd ed. Harlow, England, New York: Pearson Longman, 2006.

Macfarlane, Alan. *Witchcraft in Tudor and Stuart England: A Regional and Comparative Study*. Prospect Heights, IL: Waveland, 1991.

Matossian, Mary K. "Ergot and the Salem Witchcraft Affair." *American Scientist* 70 (1970): 355–57.

Mixon Jr., Franklin G. "Weather and the Salem Witch Trials." *The Journal of Economic Perspectives* 19, no. 1 (2005): 241–42.

Norton, Mary Beth. *In the Devil's Snare: The Salem Witchcraft Crisis of 1692*. New York: Alfred A. Knopf, 2002.

Parke, Francis Neal. *Witchcraft in Maryland.* Baltimore: 1937.

Purkiss, Diane. *The Witch in History: Early Modern and Twentieth-Century Representations.* New York: Routledge, 1996.

Ray, Benjamin. "The Geography of Witchcraft Accusations in 1692 Salem Village." *The William and Mary Quarterly* 65, no. 3 (2008): 449–78.

Roach, Marilynne K. *The Salem Witch Trials: A Day-by-Day Chronicle of a Community Under Siege.* New York: Cooper Square Press, 2002.

Rosenthal, Bernard. *Salem Story: Reading the Witch Trials of 1692.* Cambridge, UK: Cambridge University Press, 1993.

Rosenthal, Bernard, Gretchen A. Adams, et al., eds. *Records of the Salem Witch-Hunt.* Cambridge, UK: Cambridge University Press, 2009.

Thomas, Keith. *Religion and the Decline of Magic.* New York: Scribner, 1971.

Trask, Richard B. *The Devil Hath Been Raised: A Documentary History of the Salem Village Witchcraft Outbreak of March 1692: Together with a Collection of Newly Located and Gathered Witchcraft Documents.* Danvers, MA: Yeoman Press, 1997.

Weisman, Richard. *Witchcraft, Magic, and Religion in 17th-Century Massachusetts.* Amherst: University of Massachusetts Press, 1984.

A Note on the Text

Spelling, capitalization, and punctuation have been modernized for ease of comprehension. In some instances, line breaks and italics have been added for clarity of the speakers and events described in a trial transcript.

Redactions in running text are indicated by an ellipsis.

Confusing vocabulary or usage is clarified in the endnotes.

Occasional problems in transcription of the original document, such as losses or illegible words, are indicated in brackets.

Acknowledgments

My deepest thanks to my patient and excellent editor, John Siciliano at Penguin Classics, for his thoroughgoing vision and support, to his editorial assistant Douglas Clark, and to my agent, Suzanne Gluck at William Morris Endeavor, for her unflagging friendship and brilliance. Thank you also to the friends and colleagues who have believed in my work on this project, with particular gratitude to David Hall, Patricia Hills, Bruce Holsinger, Virginia Myhaver, Mary Beth Norton, Brian Pellinen, Benjamin Ray, and Bruce Schulman. Rebecca Goetz did yeoman's labor reading drafts and providing commentary, and I am so grateful to her for her guidance and support. My particular gratitude also to Katerina Stanton for making order out of chaos, and to the librarians and archivists at Houghton Library, Cornell Special Collections, the Huntington Library, and the Massachusetts State Archives for their work preserving the heritage of witchcraft in North America for generations of scholars to come. The online Salem archive maintained by the University of Virginia is a boon to scholars of Salem that is hard to overstate, and I am grateful to UVA for maintaining that initiative.

Thank you to all the book clubs and individual readers I have encountered over the years whose hunger for history inspires me every day, and to my students at Boston University and Cornell for keeping me passionate about the life of the mind.

Finally, my most ardent thanks to Louis Hyman, whose love, support, guidance, counsel, research assistance, and psychoanalysis made the completion of this project a reality.

The Penguin Book
of Witches

ENGLISH
ANTECEDENTS

WITCHES IN THE BIBLE

When thinking about witches today, a certain standard image comes to mind: she is an old crone with a warty nose, a black pointed hat, raggedy clothes, and a black cat by her side. Though our contemporary picture of the witch has evolved away from the Puritan conception, the American colonists too had a set of assumptions about who a witch was likely to be, and how she—for it was almost always a "she"—was able to conduct her devilish doings. But where did these assumptions come from? How did the colonists define what a witch was?

We might assume that the early modern conception of a witch derived from a description in the King James Bible. This version of the Bible, which was begun in 1604 in response to Puritan criticisms of earlier English translations, became the most widely read translation of the Bible in English during the early modern period. Printing was expensive, but then, as now, the most commonly available printed object was a Bible.

And yet the Bible is strangely quiet about witchcraft. It confirms that witches exist, but most of the telltale details—the identifying characteristics that set a witch apart from a run-of-the-mill person, and the powers that a witch is supposed to have—do not appear.

In fact, witches, as a category of their own, rather than as wizards or sorcerers, are mentioned fewer than a dozen times in the King James Bible. The first appearance comes early, in Exodus 22:18, "Thou shalt not suffer a witch to live." This command forms the justification for capital punishment of witches, but it appears without any illumination or commentary, wedged between a guideline *about dowry payment and a prohibition against bestiality. Witches are declared not allowed, and yet all of Exodus 22 remains silent on the definition of what or who a witch is, or on what activities might constitute witchcraft. Even a witch's gender is, at least according to this translation, undefined.*

A bit more detail emerges with the next mention, in Deuteronomy 18:10–12:

> There shall not be found among you any one that maketh his son or his daughter to pass through the fire, or that useth divination, or an observer of times, or an enchanter, or a witch. Or a charmer, or a consulter with familiar spirits, or a wizard, or a necromancer. For all that do these things are an abomination unto the LORD: and because of these abominations the LORD thy God doth drive them out from before thee.

This passage appears as part of the advice to the tribe of Levi, so that their priests will not pick up any of the unsanctioned religious practices that they will encounter in the lands to which God will send them. Deuteronomy places witches in a context with other deviant forms of religion: "necromancers" who attempt to practice magic, astrologers, and diviners who claim to see the future.

The principal dangers of witchcraft in this context are twofold: first, witchcraft as a practice stands outside of sanctioned religious structure. Witchcraft is that which we, the chosen tribe of God, ought not to do. Defining witchcraft as a negative quality (that which we do not do) rather than by a set of affirmative qualities (divining, say, which is a concrete activity), Deuteronomy opens the possibility of a language to describe witchcraft that can be molded to suit any number of witch-hunters working within different contexts, and toward different goals. In this passage the signal quality of witchcraft is difference, specifically difference from those who hold religious power.

Deuteronomy does supply a few details about witchlike behavior that would be important in early modern accusations against suspected witches, in particular the mention of "familiar spirits." This obscure signifier will eventually morph into the Hollywood witch's black cat, but the idea of familiar spirits will come to play a substantial role in the thinking about, and prosecution of, early modern witchcraft in Europe and North America.

The proscription against witchcraft in Deuteronomy reappears in the story of Manasseh, in 2 Chronicles 33:6:

And he caused his children to pass through the fire in the valley of the son of Hinnom: also he observed times, and used enchantments, and used witchcraft, and dealt with a familiar spirit, and with wizards: he wrought much evil in the sight of the LORD, to provoke him to anger.[1]

Manasseh makes himself worse than the heathens, for in theory he ought to know better than to question the practices that God has set forth for him. Fortunately Manasseh, in the course of his affliction, humbled himself before God and saw the error of his ways. Witchcraft in this context appears as more a question of adherence or rejection of orthodoxy, rather than as a specific set of deviant practices. The degree of God's disapproval becomes clarified, including what is truly at risk for a person practicing witchcraft, and yet we still have only the vaguest sense of what a "witch" really is.

If the Bible could not provide clarity on how to identify a witch, and how to deal with her once identified, academic theologians appointed themselves equal to the task. By the early modern period in England, the religious and intellectual landscape that would predominate in initial waves of North American settlement, there was no shortage of theologians willing to do just that.

TRIAL OF URSULA KEMP, ST. OSYTH, ENGLAND 1582

The first witchcraft act in England was passed in 1542, and the last antiwitchcraft statute was not officially repealed until 1736. During that two-hundred-year span, witch trials in England occurred sporadically and tended to be clustered in Essex County, England, much as their North American counterparts would be clustered in Essex County, Massachusetts, a century later. English witch-hunting reached its peak in the 1580s, when witch cases made up 13 percent of all criminal hearings, an impressive number, even considering the high rates of acquittal.[1]

One of the most notable early modern English witch trials occurred in February and March of 1582, when Justice of the Peace Brian Darcy of St. Osyth, Essex, charged one Ursula Kemp with witchcraft. Darcy pursued Kemp under the antiwitchcraft statute of 1563, holding hearings to determine if there was sufficient evidence to present the case to the Chelmsford assizes. The trial of Ursula Kemp demonstrates a remarkable consistency with later North American witch cases, both in terms of the character of the suspected witch, and the context of her trial.[2]

The author of the ensuing text, given as "W.W.," has not been conclusively identified. It could be a pseudonym for Darcy himself. Much of the evidence appears recorded in the first person, including statements that had been delivered with no one but Darcy present to hear them. The tract depicts Darcy as a committed witch-hunter, but also shows a small community under pressure, with long-standing grudges and quarrels unearthed for fresh consideration, a pattern that will be echoed in North America.[3]

St. Osyth, *like many early modern English villages, was a poor society whose members depended on barter and trade, a sometimes fraught social relationship that often resulted in squabbling. The amount of begging represented in the Kemp trial indicates how widespread poverty was at the time, and how begging could instill resentment in neighbors.*

Another contributing factor to suspicions of witchcraft in the early modern period was the inexplicable sudden onset of ailments in both persons and cattle.[4] *Sickness from unhygienic conditions made for a high infant mortality rate, but those deaths were easier to bear if they could be blamed on someone else. Harder to understand than the desire to assign blame is Ursula's confession, however— was she insane? Did she enjoy the attention, however negative? Or did she really think she had witchly powers?*[5]

Ursula Kemp's witch trial establishes a pattern for witch trials to come. Her marginal status within the community, her alleged crimes, the use of children as witnesses, her familiar spirit, the promise of lenience in exchange for confession, and the search of her body for a so-called witch's teat all reappear in North American witch trials a century later.

At the St. Osyth trial, one woman, Joan Pechey, was acquitted, but Ursula Kemp was executed after trial at the Chelmsford Lent Assizes.[6] *The injustice of this particular case likely inspired Reginald Scot's* The Discoverie of Witchcraft *of 1584, which is the most explicit skeptical account of witchcraft in England and which in many cases attacks Darcy by name.*[7]

THE TRIAL OF URSULA KEMP[8]

[The Information of Grace Thurlowe]

The 19th Day of February the 24th year of the reign of our Sovereign Lady Queen Elizabeth. The information of Grace

Thurlowe, the wife of John Thurlowe, taken before me, Brian Darcy, the day and year above said, against Ursula Kemp, alias Grey, as followeth.

[· · ·]

The said Grace saith also that about three quarters of a year ago she was delivered of a woman child, and saith that shortly after the birth thereof, the said Ursula fell out with her, for that she would not suffer her to have the nursing of that child; at such times as she the said Grace continued in work at the Lord Darcy's place. And saith that she, the said Grace nursing the said child, within some short time after that falling out, the child lying in the cradle, and not above a quarter old, fell out of the said cradle, and broke her neck, and died. The which the said Ursula hearing to have happened, made answer it maketh no matter. For she might have suffered me to have the keeping and nursing of it.[9]

And the said Grace saith that when she lay in,[10] the said Ursula came unto her, and seemed to be very angry for that she had not the keeping in of the said Grace, and for that she answered unto her that she was provided. And thereupon they entered further into talk, the said Grace saying that if she should continue lame as she had done before, she would find the means to know how it came, and that she would creep upon her knees to complain of them to have justice done upon them. And to that she the said Ursula said, "It were a good turn." Take heed (said Grace) Ursula, thou hast a naughty name. And to that Ursula made answer, though she could unwitch she could not witch,[11] and so promised the said Grace that if she did send for her privately,[12] and send her keeper away, that then she would show the said Grace how she should unwitch herself or any other at any time.

And the said Grace further saith that about half a year past she began to have a lameness in her bones, and specially in her legs, at which time the said Ursula came unto her unsent for and without request and said she would help her of her lameness if she the said Grace would give her twelve pence, [then] which the said Grace speaking her fair, promised her so to do, and thereupon for the space of five weeks after, she was well and in good case as she was before. And then the said Ursula came unto the said Grace, and asked her the money she promised to her. Whereupon the said Grace made answer that she was a poor and a needy woman, and had no money. And then the said Ursula requested of her cheese for it but she said she had none. And she the said Ursula, seeing nothing to be had of the said Grace, fell out with her and said that she would be even with her and thereupon she was taken lame, and from that day to this day hath so continued.

And she saith that when she is anything well or beginneth to amend, then her child is tormented, and so continueth for a time in a very strange case, and when he beginneth to amend then she the said Grace becommeth so lame, as without help she is not able to arise or to turn her in her bed.

[The Information of Annis Letherdall]

The information of Annis Letherdall, wife of Richard Letherdall, taken by me, Brian Darcy, Esquire, against Ursula Kemp, alias Grey, the 19th day of February.

The said Annis saith that before Michaelmas[13] last, she the said Ursula sent her son to the said Letherdall's house to have scouring sand and sent word by the said boy that his mother would give her the dyeing of a pair of women's hose for the sand.[14] But the said Annis knowing her to be a naughty[15] beast sent her none. And after she the said Ursula, seeing her girl[16] to carry some to one of her neighbors' houses, murmured as the said child said, and presently after her child was taken as it lay very big with a great swelling in the bottom of the belly and other private parts. And the said Annis saith that about the tenth day of February last she went unto the said Ursula, and told her that she had been forth with a cunning body, which said, that she the said Ursula had bewitched her child.[17] To that the said Ursula answered that she knew she had not so been, and so talking further she said that she would lay her life that she the said Annis had not been with any, whereupon she requested a woman being in the house a-spinning with the said Ursula to bear witness what she had said. And the next day the child was in most piteous case to behold, whereby she thought it good to carry the same unto mother Ratcliffe, for that she had some experience of her skill. The which when the said mother Ratcliffe did see, she said to the said Annis that she doubted she should do it any good, yet she ministered unto it, et cetera.

[The Information of Thomas Rabbet]

The information of Thomas Rabbet, of the age of 8 years or thereabouts, base son to the said Ursula Kemp, alias Grey, taken before me, Brian Darcy, Esquire, one of Her Majesty's justices, the 25th day of February, against his said mother.

The said Thomas Rabbet saith that his said mother Ursula Kemp, alias Grey, hath four several spirits, the one called Tyffin, the other Tittey, the third Pigeon, and the fourth Jack and being asked of what colors they were, saith that Tittey is like a little gray cat, Tyffin is like a white lamb, Pigeon is black like a toad, and Jack is black like a cat. And he saith he hath seen his mother at times to give them beer to drink, and of a white loaf of cake to eat, and saith that in the nighttime the said spirits will come to his mother, and suck blood of her upon her arms and other places of her body.[18]

This examinant being asked whether he had seen Newman's wife to come unto his mother, saith that one morning he being in a chamber with his mother, his Godmother Newman came unto her, and saith that then he heard her and his mother to chide, and to fall out. But saith before they parted they were friends and that then his mother delivered an earthen pot unto her, in the which he thinketh her spirits were, the which she carried away with her under her apron.

And this examinant saith that within a few days after the said Newman's wife came unto his mother, and that he heard her to tell his mother that she had sent a spirit to plague Johnson to the death and another to plague his wife.

[···]

[The Examination of and Confession of Ursula Kemp, alias Grey]

The examination and confession of Ursula Kemp, alias Grey, taken at St. Osyth, and brought before me, Brian Darcy, Esquire, one of Her Majesty's justices of the peace, the 20th day of February, 1582.

Condemned.

The said Ursula Kemp saith that about ten or eleven years past, she this examinant was troubled with a lameness in her bones, and for ease thereof, went to one Cocke's wife of Weley, now deceased, who telled this examinant that she was bewitched, and at her entreaty taught her to unwitch herself. And hath her take hogs' dung and charcoal and put them together and hold them in her left hand, and to take in the other hand a knife, and to prick the medicine three times, and then to cast the same into the fire, and to take the said knife and to make three pricks under a table, and to let the knife stick there. And after that to take three leaves of sage, and as much of herb John (alias herb grace[19]) and put them into ale, and drink it last at night and first in the morning, and that she taking the same had ease of her lameness.

The said examinant saith that one Page's wife and one Gray's wife, being either of them lame and bewitched, she being requested and sent for to come unto them, went unto them. And saith that she knew them to be bewitched, and at their desires did minister unto them the foresaid medicine, whereupon they had speedy amendment.

The said Brian Darcy then promising to the said Ursula that if she would deal plainly and confess the truth, that she should have favor. And so by giving her fair speeches she confessed as followeth.

The said Ursula bursting out with weeping, fell upon her knees, and confessed that she had four spirits, whereof two of them were hes, and the other two were shes. The two he spirits were to punish and kill unto death, and the other two shes were to punish with lameness and other diseases of bodily harms, and also to destroy cattle.

And she this examinant, being asked by what name or names she called the said spirits, and what manner of things or color they were of, confesseth and saith that the one is called Tittey, being a he, and is like a gray cat; the second called Jack, also a he, and is like a black cat; the third is called Pigeon, being a she, and is like a black toad; the fourth is called Tyffin, being a she, and is like a white lamb.

This examinant being further asked which of the said spirits she sent to punish Thurlowe's wife and Letherdall's child, confessed and said that she sent Tittey to punish Thurlowe's wife, and Pigeon Letherdall's child.

And this examinant, without any asking of her own free will at that present, confessed and said that she was the death of her brother Kemp's wife, and that she sent the spirit Jack to plague her, for that her sister had called her whore and witch.

And this examinant further confessed that upon the falling out between Thurlowe's wife and her, she sent Tyffin the spirit unto her child, which lay in the cradle, and willed the same to rock the cradle over, so as the child might fall out thereof, and break the neck of it.

These foresaid 5 last recited matters, being confessed by the said Ursula privately to me the said Brian Darcy, were afterward (supper being ended, and she called again before me, the said Brian) recited and particularly named unto her all which she confessed, as before in the presence of us, whole names he hereunder subscribed.

Also after this examinant's aforesaid confession, the said Thurlowe's wife and Letherdall's wife being then in my house, and she the said Letherdall's wife having her child there also, were brought in my presence before this examinant, who, immediately after some speeches had passed between them, she this examinant burst out in tears and fell upon her knees, and asked forgiveness of the said Letherdall's wife, and likewise of Thurlowe's wife, and confessed that she caused Newman's wife to send a spirit to plague the child, asking the said Letherdall's wife, if she were not afraid that night that the spirit came unto the child, and telled her about the same hour, and said that she herself by reason thereof was in a great sweat. And this examinant confesseth that she caused the said Newman's wife to send a spirit to Thurlowe's wife to plague her where that thought good, et cetera.

The said Letherdall's child (being a woman child) at the time of this examination appeared to be in most piteous sort consumed, and the private and hinder parts thereof to be in a most strange and wonderful[20] case, as it seemed to very honest women of good judgment, and not likely to live and continue any long time.

Note also that it is specially to be considered, that the said child being an infant and not a year old, the mother thereof carrying it in her arms, to one mother Ratcliffe's, a neighbor of hers, to have her to minister unto it, was to pass by Ursula this examinant's house, and passing by the window, the infant cried to the mother, wo, wo, and pointed with the finger to the window wards. And likewise the child used the like as she passed homeward by the said window, at which she confessed her conscience moved her, so as she went shortly after and talked with the said Ursula, whereupon she used such speeches as moved her to complain.

[The Second Confession and Examination of Ursula Kemp]

The second confession and examination of Ursula Kemp, taken the 21st day of February.

The said Ursula, being committed to the ward and keeping of the constable that night, upon some speeches that she had passed, said that she had forgotten to tell Mr. Darcy one thing, whereupon the next day she was brought before Brian Darcy, and the second time examined, who confessed and said.

That about a quarter of a year last past, one Alice Newman, her near neighbor, came unto this examinant's house and fell out with her, and said she was a witch, and that she would take away her witchery, and carry the same unto Mr. Darcy. But this examinant saith she thought she did not mean it, but after they had children they became friends, and so she departed carrying away with her her spirits in a pot, as this examinant saith.

And she further saith that about Christmas last, she went to the said Alice Newman, and declared to her that Thurlowe's wife and she were fallen out, and prayed the said Newman's wife, to send the spirit called Tittey, unto her to plague the said Thurlowe's wife, where that thought good. The which this examinant saith she did, and at the return of the said spirit it told this examinant that it had punished Thurlowe's wife upon her knee. And then it had a reward by sucking blood of this examinant, and so returned as she saith to the said Alice Newman.

This examinant saith that about three months past, she and one John Stratton fell out, and the said John called her whore and gave her other evil speeches, whereupon this examinant saith that shortly after she sent her boy for spices unto the wife of the said John. But she saith she sent her none, whereupon this examinant saith she went unto the said Newman's wife, and told her of the falling out between Stratton and her, and requested the said Newman's wife to send Jack the spirit unto Stratton's wife to plague her, the which the said Alice Newman promised this examinant to do the next night, as this examinant saith she did. And the spirit told this examinant when it returned, that it had plagued her in the back even unto death. And the spirit did suck of this examinant upon the left thigh, the which when she rubbeth (she saith) it will at all times bleed.

And she saith that then the spirit did return to the said Newman's wife again, and had the like reward of her as she thanketh.

This examinant saith, that about Friday was seeneight[21] being about the ninth of February, she went unto the said Alice Newman, and did show her that one Letherdall's wife and she were fallen out, and saith that she prayed her to send one of the spirits unto her young child. Whereunto she the said Alice answered well, she would. And this examinant saith that at that time she could have no longer talk with her, for that her husband was then present in the house. And this examinant saith that the said Alice sent the spirit Pigeon to plague the said child where that thought good, and after that it had sucked of this examinant. She saith it returned to the said Newman's wife, and more at that time the said examinant confessed not.[22]

REGINALD SCOT,
THE DISCOUERIE OF
WITCHCRAFT
1584

*To the modern reader, Reginald Scot might sound like
a beacon of reason in a wilderness of early modern fear
and superstition. Though relatively little is known about
Scot, he nevertheless serves as one of the strongest skeptical voices to emerge in opposition to the common attitudes toward witches and witchcraft in early modern
England. His only other known work is a well-regarded
horticultural guidebook,* A Perfite Platforme of a Hoppe
Garden *of 1574. In the decade between these two publi-
cations, witch trials in England had picked up remarkably in pace; Scot himself may have been witness to the
St. Osyth witch trial. Scot appears to be a man appalled
by the apparent prejudice within the legal structure of
witch trials, while pitying the type of woman so often
accused of such a crime. His religious belief suggests
that any pretense of magic or doings outside the realm
of nature is false, unprovable, invented, or worse.[1] In
effect, Scot argued that contemporary witch mongers
were suffering from a failure of faith, ascribing powers
to individuals that should be reserved only for God.*

*To prove his case, Scot argued from biblical interpre-
tation and evidence, claiming that modern translations
of the Scriptures collapsed several different categories
of malefactors—soothsayers, cheats, poisoners, and so
forth—into the single category of "witch."[2] More than
even biblical authority, however, Scot relied on empir-
ical reason. He looked at the sort of women typically*

accused of witchcraft and recognized them for what they were: often poor or mentally ill, uneducated, objects of fear and disgust within their communities, and unable to defend themselves. Scot argued that these women should be shown Christian charity and compassion. Interestingly, Scot also grappled with the problem of those like Ursula Kemp, who had confessed. In that regard, Scot addressed not only those witches as understood in the ecclesiastical sense, but also those so-called cunning folk, purveyors of folk magic and charms, widespread throughout the British countryside. Scot was concerned with separating the deluded and weak members of society from the charlatans, and with revealing the errors in reason and judgment that he perceived among witchhunters. A relatively straightforward task, it would seem, and yet Scot would remain the most ardent skeptic throughout the active period of English and North American witchcraft, serving as the inspiration for King James I's subsequent spirited defense of witch trials in Daemonologie *(1597).*[3]

THE DISCOUERIE OF WITCHCRAFT[4]

Booke 1.
Chapter 1.

An impeachment of witches' power in meteors and elementary bodies tending to the rebuke of such as attributed too much unto them.

The fables of witchcraft have taken so fast hold and deep root in the heart of man that few or none can (nowadays) with patience endure the hand and correction of God. For if any adversity, grief, or sickness, or loss of children, corn, cattle, or liberty happen unto them, by and by they exclaim upon witches. As though there were no God in Israel that ordereth all things according to his will,[5] punishing both just and unjust with griefs, plagues, and afflictions in manner and form as he thinketh good, but that certain old women here on earth, called witches, must needs be the contrivers of all men's calamities, and as though they themselves were innocents, and had deserved no such punishments. Insomuch as they stick not to ride and go to such, as either are injuriously termed witches, or else are willing so to be accounted, seeking at their hands comfort and remedy in time of their tribulation, contrary to God's will and commandment in that behalf, who bids us resort to him in all our necessities.[6]

Such faithless people (I say) are also persuaded that neither hail nor snow, thunder nor lightning, rain nor tempestuous winds come from the heavens at the commandment of God, but are raised by the cunning and power of witches and conjurers; insomuch as a clap of thunder, or a gale of wind is no sooner heard, but either they run to ring bells, or cry out to burn witches, or else burn consecrated things, hoping by the smoke thereof to drive the Devil out of the air, as though spirits could be frightened[7] away with such external toys. Howbeit, these are right enchantments, as Brentius affirmeth.[8]

But certainly, it is neither a witch, nor devil, but a glorious God that maketh the thunder. I have read in the scriptures that God maketh the blustering tempests and whirlwinds, and I find that it is the Lord that altogether dealeth with them, and that they blow according to his will.[9] But let me see any of them all rebuke and still the sea in time of tempest, as Christ did, or raise the stormy wind, as God did with his word, and I will believe in them. Hath any witch or conjurer or any creature entered into the treasures of the snow or seen the secret places of the hail, which God hath prepared against the day of trouble, battle, and war? I for my part also think with Jesus, Sir, that at God's only commandment the snow falleth, and that the wind bloweth according to his will, who only maketh all storms to cease and who (if we keep his ordinances) will send us rain in due season and make the land to bring forth her increase and the trees of the field to give their fruit.

[· · ·]

Chapter 2.

The inconvenience growing by men's credulity herein, with a reproof of some churchmen, which are inclined to the common conceived opinion of witches' omnipotency, and a familiar example thereof.

But the world is now so bewitched and overrun with this fond error, that even where a man should seek comfort and counsel, there shall he be sent (in case of necessity) from God to the Devil and from the physician to the cozening[10] witch, who will not stick to take upon her, by words to heal the lame (which was proper only to Christ and to them whom he assisted with his divine power). Yea, with her familiar and charms she will take upon her to cure the blind, though in the tenth of Saint John's gospels it be written that the Devil cannot open the eyes of the blind.[11] And they attain such credit as I have heard (to my grief) some of the ministry affirm, that they have had in their parish at one instant, seventeen or eighteen witches, meaning such as could work miracles supernaturally. Whereby they manifested as well their infidelity and ignorance in conceiving God's word, as their negligence and error in instructing their flocks. For they themselves might understand and also teach their parishioners that God only worketh great wonders and that it is he which sendeth such punishments to the wicked and such trials to the elect. According to the saying of the prophet Haggai, "I smote you with blasting and mildew, and with hail, in all the labors of your hands; and yet you turned not unto me, saith the Lord."[12] And therefore saith the same prophet in another place, "You have sown much, and bring in little." And both in Joel and Leviticus, the like phrases and proofs are used and made.

[· · ·]

But I will rehearse an example whereof I myself am not only Oculatus testis[13] but have examined the cause and am to justify the truth of my report, not because I would disgrace the ministers that are godly, but to confirm my former assertion, that this absurd error is grown into the place, which should be able to expel all such ridiculous folly and impiety.

At the assizes holden at Rochester, anno 1581, one Margaret Simons, the wife of John Simons, of Brenchlie in Kent, was arraigned for witchcraft at the instigation and complaint of diverse fond[14] and malicious persons and specially by the means of one John Ferrall, vicar of that parish, with whom I talked about that matter and found him both fondly assotted in the cause and enviously bent toward her and (which is worse) as unable to make a good account of his faith as she whom he accused. That which he, for his part, laid to the poor woman's charge, was this.

His son (being an ungracious boy and apprentice to one Robert Scotchford clothier, dwelling in that parish of Brenchlie) passed on a day by her house, at whom by chance her little dog barked. Which thing the boy taking in evil part, drew his knife, and pursued him therewith even to her door, whom she rebuked with some such words as the boy disdained and yet nevertheless would not be persuaded to depart in a long time. At the last he returned to his master's house and within five or six days fell sick. Then was called to mind that fray betwixt the dog and the boy: insomuch as the vicar (who thought himself so privileged, as he little mistrusted that God would visit his children with sickness) did so calculate; as he found, partly through his own judgment, and partly (as he himself told me) by the relation of other witches, that his said son was by her bewitched. Yea, he also told me, that this his son (being as it were past all cure) received perfect health at the hands of another witch.[15]

He proceeded yet further against her, affirming that always in his parish church, when he desired to read most plainly, his voice so failed him as he could scant be heard at all. Which he could impute, he said, to nothing else but to her enchantment. When I advertised the poor woman hereof as being desirous to hear what she could say for herself she told me that in very deed his voice did much fail him, especially when he strained himself to speak loudest. How be it, she said, that at all times his voice was hoarse and low, which thing I perceived to be true. But sir, said she, you shall understand, that this our vicar is diseased with such a kind of hoarseness, as diverse of our neighbors in this parish, not long since, doubted that he had the French pox[16] and in that respect utterly refused to communicate with him until such time as (being thereunto enjoined by M.D. Lewen the Ordinary[17]) he had brought from London a certificate, under the hands of two physicians, that his hoarseness proceeded from a disease in the lungs. Which certificate he published in the church, in the presence of the whole congregation. And by this means he was cured, or rather, excused of the shame of his disease. And this I know to be true by the relation of diverse honest men of that parish.[18] And truly, if one of the jury had not been wiser than the other, she had been condemned thereupon, and upon other as ridiculous matters as this. For the name of a witch is so odious and her power so feared among the common people, that if the honestest body living chance to be arraigned thereupon, she shall hardly escape condemnation.[19]

Chapter 3.

Who they be that are called witches, with a manifest declaration of the cause that moveth men so commonly to think, and witches themselves to believe, that they can hurt children, cattle, et cetera, with words and imaginations, and of cozening witches.

One sort of such as are said to be witches are women which be commonly old, lame, bleary-eyed, pale, foul, and full of wrinkles; poor, sullen, superstitious, and papists; or such as know no religion, in whose drowsy minds the Devil hath bought[20] a fine seat. So as, what mischief, mischance, calamity, or slaughter is brought to pass, they are easily persuaded the same is done by themselves, imprinting in their minds an earnest and constant imagination hereof. They are lean and deformed, showing melancholy in their faces to the horror of all that see them. They are doting, scolds, mad, devilish, and not much differing from them that are thought to be possessed with spirits. So firm and steadfast in their opinions, as whosoever shall only have respect to the constancy of their words uttered would easily believe they were true indeed.

These miserable wretches are so odious unto all their neighbors and so feared, as few dare offend them or deny them anything they ask. Whereby they take upon them, yea, and sometimes think, that they can do such things as are beyond the ability of human nature. These go from house to house and from door to door for a pot full of milk, yeast, drink, pottage,[21] or some such relief, without the which they could hardly live,[22] neither obtaining for their service and pains nor by their art nor yet at the Devil's hands (with whom they are said to make a perfect and visible bargain) either beauty, money, promotion, wealth, worship, pleasure, honor, knowledge, learning, or any other benefit whatsoever.

It falleth out many times, that neither their necessities nor their expectation is answered or served in those places where they beg or borrow, but rather their lewdness is by their neighbors reproved.

And further, in tract of time the witch waxeth odious and tedious to her neighbors, and they again are despised and despited of her, so as sometimes she curseth one and sometimes another and that from the master of the house, his wife, children, cattle, et cetera to the little pig that lieth in the sty. Thus in process of time they have all displeased her, and she hath wished evil luck unto them all, perhaps with curses and imprecations made in form. Doubtless (at length) some of her neighbors die or fall sick or some of their children are visited with diseases that vex them strangely, as apoplexies,[23] epilepsies, convulsions, hot fevers, worms, et cetera. Which by ignorant parents are supposed to be the vengeance of witches. Yea, and their opinions and conceits are confirmed and maintained by unskillful physicians, according to the common saying *Inscitiæ pallium maleficium & incantation.*[24] Witchcraft and enchantment is the cloak of ignorance, whereas indeed evil humors, and not strange words, witches, or spirits are the causes of such diseases. Also some of their cattle perish either by disease or mischance. Then they, upon whom such adversities fall, weighing the fame that goeth upon this woman (her words, displeasure, and curses meeting so justly with their misfortune) do not only conceive, but also are resolved, that all their mishaps are brought to pass by her only means.

The witch, on the other side, expecting her neighbor's mischances and seeing things sometimes come to pass according to her wishes, curses, and incantations (for Bodin himself confesseth that not above two in a hundred of their witchings or wishings take effect), being called before a justice, by due examination of the circumstances is driven to see her imprecations and desires, and her neighbors' harms and losses to concur, and as it were to take effect. And so confesseth that she (as a goddess) hath brought such things to pass. Wherein, not only she, but the accuser and also the justice are foully deceived and abused; as being thorough her confession and other circumstances persuaded (to the injury of God's glory) that she hath done, or can do, that which is proper only to God himself.

Another sort of witches there are, which be absolutely cozeners.[25] These take upon them, either for glory, fame, or gain, to do anything, which God or the Devil can do, either for foretelling of things to come, betraying of secrets, curing of maladies, or working of miracles. But of these I will talk more at large hereafter.

GEORGE GIFFORD, *A DIALOGUE CONCERNING WITCHES AND WITCHCRAFTES* 1593

One of the earliest writers dealing with the question of witchcraft in English was Puritan minister George Gifford of Maldon, Essex. His best known, and most entertaining, work is the Dialogue Concerning Witches and Witchcraftes *of 1593, a lively discussion not only of the nature of witchcraft, but of the implications that witchcraft and witch trials held for the common Christian believer. Gifford's dialogue was meant to be easily understood, and addressed itself to widespread cultural practices, such as seeking the counsel of cunning folk in cases of suspected bewitchment. Some historians have argued that Gifford's approach was at root an anthropological one.[1] Instead of treating witchcraft as an intellectual problem, as Reginald Scot did, or as a theological problem, as King James I would, Gifford explored witchcraft as a pastoral challenge: how could Christians be persuaded to give up their cultural beliefs in magic and turn their trust entirely over to God?[2]*

The dialogue opens with a troubled man named Samuel, who is convinced that his family has been bewitched. The family suffered the sudden unexplained death of a valuable hog, and then his wife lost a number of chickens shortly afterward. Samuel considered making some sort of sacrifice to free himself from these unwelcome diabolical incursions, and was on the point of visiting a village cunning man for help, when he encountered his godly friend Daniel along the highway. Daniel suggested that the problems in Samuel's life derived not from the malefaction of a witch, but from the Devil himself. Samuel invites Daniel back to his house to discuss the situation further, with the help of an intellectually pretentious schoolmaster.

Gifford was concerned primarily with helping the average person, and it was for this reason he used Samuel as a mouthpiece for mainstream early modern English beliefs about witches. Samuel thought that witches had power over physical bodies and property. Gifford, by way of Daniel, wanted to persuade Samuel that witches may exist, but are deluded if they think that any power lies with them. All witchly power derives from Satan himself, and so the best defense against witches is not legal or intellectual, but spiritual. According to Gifford, most actions against witches were motivated by greed, anger, fear, and hate, rather than by desire to grow in the eyes of God.[3] Nothing makes Satan happier, Gifford suggested, than a rollicking witch trial in which neighbors turned against each other. Instead of worrying about witches out in the world, Gifford would rather his flock eradicated Satan's influence over and presence in their own souls.[4]

A DIALOGUE CONCERNING WITCHES AND WITCHCRAFTES[5]

The Speakers.
Samuel, Daniel, the wife of Samuel, M. B., Schoolmaster, the good wife R.

[· · ·]

Dan. What is the matter man? Do you take thought and care for the world? Take heed of that, for the scripture saith, worldly sorrow worketh death. 2. Corinthians 7–.10.[6] It is a great sin rising from unbelief, and distrust in God's providence, when men be over-pensive for the world.

Sam. Indeed my mind is troubled, but not for that which you say, for I hope in God I shall not want so long as I live.

Dan. Is it any trouble of conscience for sin? If it be, that may turn to good.

Sam. O, no, no. I know no cause why.

Dan. Why, what is it then? If I may be so bold, I pray you tell me. I think you take me for your friend.

Sam. Indeed I have always found you my very good friend, and I am sure you will give me the best counsel you can. Truly we dwell here in a bad country. I think even one of the worst in England.

Dan. Is it so? I think you dwell in a fine country, in a sweet wholesome air, and fruitful grounds.

Sam. Air, man? I find no fault with the air; there be naughty people.

Dan. Naughty people? Where shall a man dwell, and not find them? Swearers, liars, railers,[7] slanderers, drunkards, adulterers, riotous, unthrifts, dicers,[8] and proud high-minded persons, are everywhere to be found in great plenty.

Sam. Nay, I do not mean them. I care not for them. These witches, these evil-favored old witches do trouble me.

Dan. What? Do you take yourself to be bewitched?

Sam. No, no, I trust no evil spirit can hurt me, but I hear of much harm done by them. They lame men and kill their cattle. Yea, they destroy both men and children. They say there is scarce any town or village in all this shire, but there is one or two witches at the least in it. In good sooth, I may tell it to you as to my friend, when I go but into my closes, I am afraid, for I see now and then a hare; which my conscience giveth me is a witch, or some witch's spirit, she stareth so upon me. And sometimes I see an ugly weasel run through my yard, and there is a foul great cat sometimes in my barn, which I have no liking unto.

Dan. You never had no hurt done yet, had you, by any witch?

Sam. Trust me, I cannot tell, but I fear me I have, for there be two or three in our town which I like not, but especially an old woman. I have been as careful to please her as ever I was to please mine own mother, and to give her ever anon one thing or other, and yet methinks she frowns at me now and then. And I had a hog which eat his meat with his fellows and was very well to our thinking overnight, and in the morning he was stark dead. My wife hath had five or six hens even of late dead. Some of my neighbors wish me to burn something alive, as a hen or a hog.[9] Others will me in time to seek help at the hand of some cunning man, before I have any further harm. I would be glad to do for the best.

Dan. Have you any cunning man hereabout, that doth help?

Sam. There is one, they say, here a twenty miles off at T. B., which hath helped many. And thus much I know, there was one of mine acquaintance but two miles hence, which had great losses. He lost two or three kin; six hogs, he would not have took fifteen shillings a hog for them; and a mare. He went to that same man, and told him he suspected an old woman in the parish. And I think he told me, that he showed him her in a glass,[10] and told him she had three or four imps, some call them puckerels,[11] one like a gray cat, another like a weasel, another like a mouse. A vengeance take them. It is great pity the country is not rid of them, and told him also what he should do. It is half a year ago, and he never had any hurt since. There is also a woman at R. H. five and twenty miles hence, that hath a great name, and great resort there is daily unto her. A neighbor of mine had his child taken lame, a girl of ten years old, and such a pain in her back, that she could not sit upright. He went to that woman. She told him he had some bad neighbor. The child was forespoken, as he suspected. Marry, if he would go home, and bring her some of the clothes which the child lay in all night, she would tell him certainly. He went home, and put a table napkin about her neck all night, and in the morning took it with him, and she told him the girl was bewitched in deed, and so told him what he should do, and he had remedy. The girl is as well at this day, and a pretty quick girl. There was another of my neighbors had his wife much troubled, and he went to her, and she told him, his wife was haunted with a fairy. I cannot tell what she bade him do, but the woman is merry at this hour. I have heard, I dare not say it is so, that she weareth about her Saint John's Gospel, or some part of it.[12]

Dan. If you have such cunning men and women, what need you be so much afraid?

Sam. Alas man, I could time it to go and some counsel me to go to the man at T. B. and some to the woman at R. H. And between them both I have lingered the time, and fear I may be spoiled before I get remedy. Some wish me to beat and claw the witch until I fetch blood on her, and to threaten her that I will have her hanged. If I knew which were the best I would do it.

Dan. I perceive your danger is between two stools.[13]

Sam. It is very true. If I had heard but of one, I should have gone ere this time, and I am glad that I met with you. I pray you let me have your best counsel. I trust you bear me good will.

Dan. Truly I will give you the best counsel I can, which I am sure shall do you good, if you will follow it, for indeed I pity your case, it is most certain you are bewitched.

Sam. Bewitched? Do you think I am bewitched? I feel no harm in my body. You make me more afraid.

Dan. Nay, I do not think that the old woman hath bewitched you, or that your body is bewitched, but the Devil hath bewitched your mind, with blindness and unbelief, to draw you from God, even to worship himself, by seeking help at the hands of devils. It is a lamentable case to see how the Devil hath bewitched thousands at this day to run after him: and even to offer sacrifice unto him.[14]

Sam. I defy the Devil. Worship him? Fie upon him. I hate him with all my heart. Do you think any seek help at his hands? We seek help against him. I think he never doth good. He hurteth, but he never helpeth any.

Dan. It is not in these matters to be taken as we imagine, but as the word of God teacheth. What though a man think he worshippeth not devils nor seeketh not help at their hands, as he is persuaded, nor hath any such intent, is he ever the near, when as yet it shall be found by God's word, that he doth worship them, and seek unto them for help?

Sam. Do you think then that there be no witches? Doth not God suffer wicked people to do harm? Or do you think that the cunning men do help by the Devil? I would be glad to reason with you, but I have small knowledge in the scriptures. We have a schoolmaster that is a good pretty scholar, they say, in the Latin tongue, one M. B. He is gone to my house even now. I pray you let me entreat you to go thither. You two may reason the matter, for you are learned.

Dan. I could be content, but it will ask some time, and I am going to such a place upon special business.

Sam. I pray you let me entreat you: four or five hours is not so much.

Dan. Well, I will go with you.

Sam. Wife, I have brought an old friend of mine. I pray thee bid him welcome.

The wife.[15] He is very welcome. But truly man, I am angry with you, and half out of patience, that you go not to seek help against yonder same old beast. I have another hen dead this night. Other men can seek remedy. Here is M. B. tells me, that the good wife R. all the last week could not make her butter come.[16] She never rested until she had got her husband out to the woman at R. H. and when he came home, they did but heat a spit red hot, and thrust into the cream, using certain words, as she willed him, and it came as kindly as any butter that ever she made. I met the old filth this morning. Lord, how sourly she looked upon me, and mumbled as she went. I heard part of her words. Ah (quoth she), you have an honest man to your husband. I hear how he doth use me. In truth, husband, my stomach did so rise against her, that I could have found in my heart to have flown upon her, and scratched her, but that I feared she would be too strong for me. It is a lusty old queen. I wished that the good wife R. had been with me. I pray you, good husband, let me entreat you to go to that same good woman. You may ride thither in half a day.

Sam. Wife, I pray thee be content. I have entreated this, mine old friend, to reason with M. B. for he tells me that we be in a very foul error.

M. B. I suppose, so far as my learning and capacity do extend, that small reasoning may serve. The word of God doth show plainly that there be witches and commandeth they should be put to death. Experience hath taught too many, what harms they do. And if any have the gift to minister help against them, shall we refuse it? Shall we not drink when we are a thirst? Shall we not warm us when we are a cold? It is pity that any man should open his mouth any way to defend them, their impiety is so great.

Dan. For my part, I go not about to defend witches. I deny not but that the Devil worketh by them and that they ought to be put to death. We ought also to seek remedy against them. But as I told my friend, the Devil doth bewitch men by means of these witches, and lead them from God, even to follow himself, to offer sacrifice unto him to worship him, to obey his will, to commit many grievous sins, and to be drowned in manifold errors.

[· · ·]

M. B. I heard you say, if I did not mistake your speech, that there be witches that work by the Devil. But yet I pray you tell me, do you think there be such? I know some are of opinion there be none.[17]

Dan. It is so evident by the scriptures, and in all experience, that there be witches which work by the Devil, or rather, I may say, the Devil worketh by them, that such as go about to prove the contrary, do show themselves but cavilers.[18]

M. B. I am glad we agree in that point. I hope we shall in the rest. What say you to this? That the witches have their spirits. Some hath one; some hath more, as two, three, four, or five, some in one likeness, and some in another, as like cats, weasels, toads, or mice, whom they nourish with milk, or with a chicken, or by letting them suck now and then a drop of blood, whom they call when they be offended with any, and send them to hurt them in their bodies; yea, to kill them, and to kill their cattle.

Dan. Here is great deceit, and great illusion. Here the Devil leadeth the ignorant people into foul errors, by which he draweth them headlong into many grievous sins.

M. B. Nay, then I see you are awry, if you deny these things, and say they be but illusions. They have been proved, and proved again, even by the manifold confessions of the witches themselves.[19] I am out of all doubt in these, and could in many particulars lay open what hath fallen out. I did dwell in a village within these five years, where there was a man of good wealth, and suddenly within ten days' space, he had three kine[20] died, his gelding worth ten pounds fell lame, he was himself taken with a great pain in his back, and a child of seven years old died. He sent to the woman at R. H. and she said he was plagued by a witch, adding, moreover, that there were three women witches in that town, and one man witch,[21] willing him to look whom he most suspected. He suspected one old woman, and caused her to be carried before a justice of the peace and examined. With much a doe at the last she confessed all. Which was this, in effect: that she had three spirits: one like a cat, which she called Lightfoot, another like a toad, which she called Lunch, the third like a weasel, which she called Makeshift. This Lightfoot, she said, one mother Barlie of W. sold her above sixteen years ago, for an oven cake and told her the cat would do her good service. If she would, she might send her of her errand. This cat was with her but a while, but the weasel and the toad came and offered their service. The cat would kill kine, the weasel would kill horses, the toad would plague men in their bodies. She sent them all three (as she confessed) against this man: She was committed to the prison, and there she died before the assizes. I could tell you of many such. I had no mind to dwell in that place any longer.

Dan. You mistake me. I do not mean that the things are not. But my meaning is, that the Devil by such things both beguiles and seduces ignorant men, and leads them into errors and grievous sins.

KING JAMES I,
DAEMONOLOGIE
1597

Written in Edinburgh in 1597, King James I's Daemon-
ologie has been called "neither original nor profound,"
a text that, taken on its own merits without regard to
its royal authorship, would be of interest only because
it promotes the Continental understanding of witchcraft
in England (and, crucially, in English).[1] However, the
fact that Daemonologie *was written by an individual not*
only with a unique ability to promote witchcraft pros-
ecutions, but who was also a sitting monarch, makes it a
worthwhile read. James I set out to refute noted skeptics
of the time, in particular Reginald Scot, and in so doing
addressed himself to several familiar questions. He first
examined whether witches were real, basing his affirma-
tive argument on scriptural evidence. He also described
the means by which the Devil is able to work through
individuals, lingered lovingly on the details of the
witches' Sabbath, remarked on the ability of witches to
work magic with wax figures, and even touched upon the
fact that the majority of suspected witches were women.

However, James I's task extended beyond a restate-
ment of widespread Continental witchcraft beliefs. Dae-
monologie provided James I with an opportunity to
demonstrate his intellectual and theological rigor to a
wide audience, thereby consolidating both the mandates of
his kingship with his position as the head of the Church
of England. This expression of competence and author-
ity was in keeping with the kind of monarch that James I
desired to be: a benevolent patriarch.[2] The Devil is the
first cause of ungovernability and disorder; James I's

ability to explain, and so thwart, devilish influences on earth reinforced his authority to rule over men. The same religious and political position informed not only the writing of Daemonologie *but also the production of the Bible translation that bears his name.*

The quarto is structured as a dialogue between Epistemon, a demonologist, and Philomathes, who voices the dominant skeptical objections to witchcraft. The dialogue is divided into three parts, the first of which deals with magic and necromancers, or people who consciously choose to persuade the Devil to do their bidding. The second part, reproduced below, deals with witchcraft. Witches, we are given to understand, differ from magicians in that the Devil enacts his will through them, and not the other way around. The third book describes the realm of spirits and ghosts, which Epistemon argues are real, and werewolves, which are delusions.[3]

Most striking to a contemporary reader will be the conflation of the pseudoscientific with the imaginary. In fact, James I was at pains to explain the difference between what was possible through witchcraft and what was merely a mental delusion. He also must have grappled with the continually vexing question of why God permits the Devil to have such power. James I's theodicy took a number of tacks, including the possibility that witchcraft could challenge those with flagging faith to rekindle their belief, but ultimately he resorted to the story of Job to justify the continual ability of Satan to tempt us into sin.[4]

THE SECOND BOOK OF *DAEMONOLOGIE*

Argument: *the description of sorcery and witchcraft in special.*

Chapter 1 Argument

Proved by the scripture that such a thing can be. And the reasons refuted of all such as would call it but an imagination and melancholic humor.[5]

Philomathes. NOW Since ye have satisfied me now so fully, concerning magic or necromancy, I will pray you to do the like in sorcery or witchcraft.[6]

Epistemon. That field is likewise very large, and although in the mouths and pens of many, yet few knows the truth thereof, so well as they believe themselves, as I shall so shortly as I can, make you (God willing) as easily to perceive.

Phi. But I pray you before ye go further, let me interrupt you there with a short digression, which is that many can scarcely believe that there is such a thing as witchcraft.[7] Whose reasons I will shortly allege unto you, that ye may satisfy me as well in that as you have done in the rest. For first, whereas the scripture seemed to prove witchcraft to be, by diverse examples, and specially by sundry of the same, which you have alleged, it is thought by some that these places speak of magicians and necromancers only and not of witches. As in special, these wise men of pharaohs, that counterfeited Moses' miracles were magicians, say they, and not witches. As likewise that Pythoness that Saul consulted with. And so was Simon Magus in the New Testament, as that very stile imports.[8] Secondly, where thee would oppose the daily practice and confession of so many, that is thought likewise to be but very melancholic imaginations of simple raving creatures.[9] Thirdly, if witches had such power of witching of folks to death (as they say they have), there had been none left alive long since in the world, but they, at the least, no good or godly person of whatsoever estate could have escaped their devilry.

Epi. Your three reasons, I take, are grounded the first of them negative upon the scripture, the second affirmative upon physick,[10] and the third upon the certain proof of experience. As to your first, it is most true indeed that all these wise men of Pharaoh were magicians of art. As likewise it appears well that the Pythoness, with whom Saul consulted was of that same profession and so was Simon Magus. But ye omitted to speak of the law of God, wherein are all magicians, divines, enchanters, sorcerers, witches, and whatsoever of that kind that consults with the Devil, plainly prohibited, and alike threatened against. And besides that, she who had the spirit of Python, in the Acts, whose spirit was put to silence by the apostle, could be no other thing but a very sorcerer or witch, if thee admit the vulgar distinction to be in a manner true, whereof I spake in the beginning of our

conference.[11] For that spirit whereby she conquested such gain to
her master was not at her raising or commanding, as she pleased
to appoint, but spake by her tongue as well publicly as privately.
Whereby she seemed to draw nearer to the sort of Demoniacs
or possessed, if that conjunction betwixt them had not been
of her own consent, as it appeared by her, not being tormented
therewith, and by her conquesting of such gain to her masters
(as I have already said). As to your second reason grounded
upon physick, in attributing their confessions or apprehensions
to a natural melancholic humor: any that pleases physically to
consider upon the natural humor of melancholy, according to all
the physicians that ever writ thereupon, they shall find that that
will be over short a cloak to cover their knavery with. For as the
humor of melancholy in the self is black, heavy, and terrene,[12]
so are the symptoms thereof in any persons that are subject
thereunto, leanness, paleness, desire of solitude, and if they come
to the highest degree thereof, mere folly and mania. Whereas by
the contrary, a great number of them that ever have been convict
or confessors of witchcraft, as may be presently seen by many
that have at their time confessed, they are by the contrary, I
say, some of them rich and worldly wise, some of them fat or
corpulent in their bodies, and most part of them altogether given
over to the pleasures of the flesh, continual haunting of company,
and all kind of merriness, both lawful and unlawful, which are
things directly contrary to the symptoms of melancholy, whereof
I spake, and further experience daily proves how loath they are to
confess without torture, which witnesseth their guiltiness, where
by the contrary, the melancholics never spare to betray themselves
by their continual discourses, feeding thereby their humor in that
which they think no crime.[13] As to your third reason, it scarcely
merits an answer. For if the Devil their master were not bridled, as
the scriptures teacheth us, suppose there were no men nor women
to be his instruments, he could find ways enough without any
help of others to wrack all mankind, whereunto he employs his
whole study, and goeth about like a roaring lion (as Peter saith)
to that effect, but the limits of his power were set down before
the foundations of the world were laid, which he hath not power
in the least jot to transgress.[14] But beside all this, there is over
great a certainty to prove that they are, by the daily experience of
the harms that they do, both to men and whatsoever thing men

possesses, whom God will permit them to be the instruments, so to trouble or visit, as in my discourse of that art, ye shall hear clearly proved.

[· · ·]

Chapter 3 Argument

The witches' actions divided in two parts: the actions proper to their own persons and their actions toward others. The former of the conventions, and adoring of their master.

Phi. Ye have said now enough of their initiating in that order. It rests then that the discourse upon their practices, for they be passed apprentices, for I would faine hear what is possible to them to perform in very deed. Although they serve a common master with the necromancers (as I have before said), yet serve they him in another form. For as the means are diverse which allures them to these unlawful arts of serving of the Devil, so by diverse ways use they their practices, answering to these means, which first the Devil used as instruments in them, though a tending to one end. To wit, the enlarging of Satan's tyranny and crossing of the propagation of the kingdom of Christ, so far as lieth in the possibility, either of the one or other sort, of the Devil their master. For where the magicians, as allured by curiosity in the most part of their practices, seeks principally the satisfying of the same, and to win to themselves a popular honor and estimation, these witches on the other part, being enticed either for the desire of revenge or of worldly riches, their whole practices are either to hurt men and their goods[15] or what they possess, for satisfying of their cruel minds in the former, or else by the wrack in whatsoever sort, of any whom God will permit them to have power off, to satisfy their greedy desire in the last point.

Epi. In two parts their actions may be divided: the actions of their own persons and the actions proceeding from them towards any other. And this division being well understood will easily resolve you what is possible to them to do. For although all that they confess is no lie upon their part, yet doubtlessly in my opinion, a part of it is not indeed according as they take it to be. And in this I mean by the actions of their own persons. For as I said before, speaking of magic, that the Devil eludes the sense of these scholars of his[16] in many things, so say I the like of these witches.

Phi. Then I pray you, first to speak of that part of their own persons, and syne[17] ye may come next to their actions towards others.

Epi. To the effect that they may perform such services of their false master, as he employs them in, the Devil as God's ape, counterfeits in these servants this service and form of adoration that God prescribed and made his servants to practice. For as the servants of God, publicly uses to convene for serving of him, so makes he them in great numbers to convene (though publicly they dare not) for his service. As none convenes to the adoration and worshipping of God, except they be marked with his seal, the sacrament of baptism. So none serves Satan and convenes to the adoring of him that are not marked with that mark[18] whereof I already spake. As the minister sent by God teacheth plainly at the time of their public conventions how to serve him in spirit and truth, so that unclean spirit in his own person teacheth his disciples at the time of their convening how to work all kind of mischief. And craves compt[19] of all their horrible and detestable proceedings passed for advancement of his service.[20] Yea, that he may the more vilely counterfeit and scorn God, he oft times makes his slaves to convene in these very places which are destined and ordained for the convening of the servants of God (I mean by churches). But this far, which I have yet said, I not only take it to be true in their opinions, but even so to be indeed. For the form that he used in counterfeiting God amongst the Gentiles makes me so to think. As God spake by his oracles, spake he not so by his? As God had as well bloody sacrifices, as others without blood, had not he the like? As God had churches sanctified to his service, with altars, priests, sacrifices, ceremonies and prayers, had he not the like polluted to his service? As God gave responses by urim and thummim, gave he not his responses by the entrails of beasts, by the singing of fowls, and by their actions in the air?[21] As God by visions, dreams, and ecstasies revealed what was to come and what was his will unto his servants, used he not the like means to forewarn his slaves of things to come? Yea, even as God loved cleanness, hated vice, and impurity, appointed punishments therefore, used he not the like (though falsely I grant, and but in eschewing the less inconvenient, to draw them upon a greater) yet dissembled he not I say, so far as to appoint his priests to keep their bodies clean and undefiled before their asking responses of him? And feigned he not God to be a protector of every virtue, and a just revenger of the contrary? This reason then moves me, that as he is that same Devil and as crafty now as he was then, so will he not spare as prettily in these actions that I have spoken of concerning the witches' persons. But further, witches oft times confesses not only his convening in the church with them, but his occupying the pulpit. Yea, their form of adoration, to be the kissing of his hinder parts.[22] Which though it seem ridiculous, yet may it likewise be true, seeing we read that in Calicute, he appearing in form of a goat buck,[23] hath publicly that un-honest homage done unto him, by every one of the people. So ambitious is he and greedy of honor (which procured his fall) that he will even imitate God in that part, where it is said, that Moses could see but the hinder parts of God, for the brightness of his glory. And yet that speech is spoke but [Greek interjection].[24]

[· · ·]

Chapter 5 Argument

Witches' actions toward others. Why there are more women of that craft nor men. What things are possible to them to effectuate by the power of their master. The reasons thereof. What is the surest remedy of the harms done by them?

Phi. For sooth your opinion in this seems to carry most reason with it, and since ye have ended, then, the actions belonging properly to their own persons, say forward now to their actions used towards others.

Epi. In their actions used towards others, three things ought to be considered. First, the manner of their consulting thereupon. Next, their part as instruments. And last, their master's part, who puts the same in execution. As to their consultations thereupon, they use them oftest in the churches, where they convene for adoring, at what time their master enquiring at them what they would be at. Every one of them propones unto him what wicked turn they would have done, either for obtaining of riches or for

revenging them upon any whom they have malice at. Who, grant-
ing their demand as no doubt willingly he will, since it is to do
evil, he teacheth them the means whereby they may do the same.
As for little trifling turns that women have ado with, he causeth
them to joint dead corpses and to make powders thereof, mixing
such other things there amongst, as he gives unto them.

Phi. But before ye go further, permit me I pray you to interrupt
you one word, which you have put me in memory of, by speaking
of women. What can be the cause that there are twenty women
given to that craft, where there is one man?[25]

Epi. The reason is easy, for as that sex is frailer then man is,
so is it easier to be entrapped in these gross snares of the Devil,
as was over well proved to be true, by the serpents deceiving to
Eve at the beginning, which makes him the homelier with that
sex sensine.[26]

Phi. Return now where ye left.

Epi. To some others at these times he teacheth how to make pictures of wax or clay. That by the roasting thereof, the persons that
they bear the name of may be continually melted or dried away by
continual sickness.[27] To some he gives such stones or powders as
will help to cure or cast on diseases. And to some he teacheth
kinds of uncouth poisons, which mediciners understand not (for
he is far cunninger than man in the knowledge of all the occult
properties of nature) not that any of these means which he
teacheth them (except the poisons, which are composed of things
natural) can of themselves help anything to these turns that they
are employed in, but only being God's ape, as well in that as in all
other things.[28] Even as God by his sacraments which are earthly
of themselves works a heavenly effect, though no ways by any
cooperation in them. And as Christ by clay and spittle wrought
together, eyes of the blind man, suppose there was no virtue in
that which he outwardly applied, so the Devil will have his outward means to be shows, as it were, of his doing, which hath no
part of cooperation in his turns with him, how far that ever the
ignorant be abused in the contrary. And as to the effects of these
two former parts, to wit, the consultations and the outward
means, they are so wonderful as I dare not allege any of them
without joining a sufficient reason of the possibility thereof.[29] For
leaving all the small trifles among wives, and to speak of the principal points of their craft. For the common trifles thereof, they

can do without converting well enough by themselves. These principal points I say are these: they can make men or women to love
or hate other, which may be very possible to the Devil to effectuate, seeing he being a subtle spirit, knows well enough how to persuade the corrupted affection of them whom God will permit him
so to deal with:[30] They can lay the sickness of one upon another,
which likewise is very possible unto him. For since by God's permission, he laid sickness upon Job, why may he not far easier lay
it upon any other. For as an old practician, he knows well enough
what humor dominates most in any of us, and as a spirit he can
subtly waken up the same, making it picante, or to abound, as he
thinks meet for troubling of us, when God will so permit him.[31]
And for the taking off of it, no doubt he will be glad to relieve
such of present pain, as he may think by these means to persuade
to be catched in his everlasting snares and fetters. They can
bewitch and take the life of men or women by roasting of the pictures,[32] as I spake of before, which likewise is very possible to
their master to perform, for although (as I said before) that instrument of wax have no virtue in that turn doing, yet may he not
very well even by that same measure that his conjured slaves melt
that wax at the fire, may he not, I say, at these same times, subtly
as a spirit so weaken and scatter the spirits of life of the patient, as
may make him on the one part, for faintness to sweat out the
humor of his body. And on the other part, for the not concurrence
of these spirits, which causes his digestion, do debilitate his stomach, that his humor radical continually, sweating out on the one
part, and no new good suck being put in the place thereof, for
lack of digestion on the other, he at last shall vanish away, even as
his picture will do at the fire.[33] And that knavish and cunning
workman, by troubling him only at some times, makes a proportion so near betwixt the working of the one and the other, that
both shall end as it were at one time. They can raise storms and
tempests in the air, either upon sea or land, though not universally, but in such a particular place and prescribed bounds, as
God will permit them so to trouble. Which likewise is very easy to
be discerned from any other natural tempests that are meteors, in
respect of the sudden and violent raising thereof, together with the
short enduring of the same. And this is likewise very possible to
their master to do, he having such affinities with the air as being a
spirit, and having such power of the forming and moving thereof,

as you have heard me already declare; for in the scripture, that stile of the prince of the air is given unto him.[34] They can make folks to become frantic or maniac, which likewise is very possible to their master to do, since they are but natural sicknesses. And so he may lay on these kinds as well as any others. They can make spirits either to follow and trouble persons or haunt certain houses and affray oftentimes the inhabitants, as hath been known to be done by our witches at this time. And likewise they can make some to be possessed with spirits, and so to become very demoniacs. And this last sort is very possible likewise to the Devil their master to do, since he may easily send his own angels to trouble in what form he pleases, any whom God will permit him to use.

Phi. But will God permit these wicked instruments by the power of the Devil their master, to trouble by any of these means, any that believes in him?

Epi. No doubt, for there are three kind of folks whom God will permit so to be tempted or troubled: the wicked for their horrible sins to punish them in the like measure; the godly that are sleeping in any great sins or infirmities and weakness in faith, to waken them up the faster by such an uncouth form; and even some of the best, that their patience may be tried before the world, as Job's was.[35] For why may not God use any kind of extraordinary punishment, when it pleases him; as well as the ordinary rods of sickness or other adversities.

Phi. Who then may be free from these devilish practices?

Epi. No man ought to presume so far as to promise any impunity to himself. For God hath before all beginnings preordained as well the particular sorts of plagues as of benefits for every man, which in the own time he ordains them to be visited with,[36] and yet ought we not to be the more afraid for that, of anything that the Devil and his wicked instruments can do against us? For we daily fight against the Devil in a hundred other ways. And therefore as a valiant captain, afraid no more being at the combat, not stays from his purpose for the rummishing[37] shot of a cannon nor the small clack of a pistolet. Suppose he be not certain what may light upon him. Even so ought we boldly to go forward in fighting against the Devil without any greater terror, for these his rarest weapons, nor for the ordinary whereof we have daily the proof.

Phi. Is it not lawful then by the help of some other witch to cure the disease that is casted on by that craft?

Epi. No ways lawful. For I gave you the reason thereof in that axiom of theology, which was the last words I spake of magic.

Phi. How then may these diseases be lawfully cured?[38]

Epi. Only by earnest prayer to God, by amendment of their lives, and by sharp pursuing every one, according to his calling of these instruments of Satan, whose punishment to the death will be a salutary sacrifice for the patient. And this is not only the lawful way, but likewise the most sure. For the Devil's means can never the Devil be casted out, as Christ saith.[39] And when such a cure is used, it may well serve for a short time, but at the last, it will doubtlessly tend to the utter perdition of the patient, both in body and soul.

WILLIAM PERKINS, A DISCOURSE OF THE DAMNED ART OF WITCHCRAFT 1608

Concern about witches was not limited to the Catholic mind nor was it restricted to the doctrinaire branches of the Church of England. Puritan theologians had much to say on the subject of witchcraft, and Cambridge Puritan William Perkins was no exception.

A moderate in his religious positions, Perkins received an unusually high level of renown during his lifetime, which almost exactly corresponded with the length of Elizabeth I's reign. He can be credited with importing widespread Continental beliefs about witchcraft to England.[1] Perkins's thoughts on witchcraft, and specifically on the means of prosecuting witches, were widely read among religious Puritans in the North American colonies. Historian Larry Gragg, in his biography of Salem minister Samuel Parris, alludes to a footnote in the Proceedings of the Massachusetts Historical Society in 1892, which suggests that a copy of Perkins's Discourse of the Damned Art of Witchcraft had been inscribed to Samuel Parris on March 1, 1692, the day before Parris's slave Tituba confessed.[2] In the selection excerpted below, Perkins suggests that the word of a confessed witch holds particular weight when she then goes on to accuse someone else. Tituba confessed and went on to name other witches in her community, laying the groundwork in Salem for a conspiracy among an unknown number of *people, thus contributing to the unprecedented spread of accusations into the surrounding towns.*

Though Parris's timely ownership of Perkins's witch-hunting manual is impossible to verify with complete accuracy, the wide reach of Perkins's scholarship is not in question. Perkins argued for the necessity of taking legal recourse to combat witchcraft, moving it from the purely religious or cultural domain to the official.[3] Perkins's thinking would have profound impact on witch-hunting not only in England but in North America as well.[4]

[TO THE READER]

Exodus 22. 18. Thou shalt not suffer a Witch to live.

This text containeth one of the judicial laws of Moses touching the punishment of witchcraft, which argument I have chosen to entreat of, for these causes:

First, because witchcraft is a rife and common sin in these our days, and very many are entangled with it, being either practitioners thereof in their own persons, or at the least, yielding to seek for help and counsel of such as practice it.[5]

Again, there be sundry men who receive it for a truth that witchcraft is nothing else but a mere illusion, and witches nothing but persons deluded by the Devil. And this opinion takes place not only with the ignorant, but is holden and maintained by such as are learned, who do avouch it by word and writing that there be no witches but as I said before.[6]

Upon these and such like considerations, I have been moved to undertake the interpretation of this judicial law, as a sufficient ground of the doctrine which shall be delivered. In handling whereof, two things are distinctly to be considered. The first, what is a witch. The second, what is her due and deserved punishment.[7] And both these being opened and handled, the whole meaning of the law will the better appear.

For the first. To give the true description of a witch is a matter of great difficulty because there be many differences and diversities of opinions touching this point; and therefore that we may properly and truly define a witch, we must first pause a while in opening the nature of witchcraft, so far forth as it is delivered in the books of the Old and New Testament, and may be gathered out of the true experience of learned and godly men.

Touching witchcraft, therefore, I will consider three points:

What witchcraft is.

What is the ground of the whole practice thereof?

How many kinds and differences there be of it?

Chapter 1

Of the Nature of Witchcraft.

To begin with the first. According to the true meaning of all the places of holy scripture which treat of this point, it may be thus described:

Witchcraft is a wicked art, serving for the working of wonders, by the assistance of the Devil, so far forth as God shall in justice permit.

Section 1

I say it is an art, because it is commonly so called and esteemed among men, and there is reason why it should be thus termed. For as in all good and lawful arts, the whole practice thereof is performed by certain rules and precepts, and without them nothing can be done; so witchcraft hath certain superstitious grounds and principles whereupon it standeth, and by which alone the feats and practices thereof are commonly performed.[8]

If it be demanded what these rules be and whence they had their beginning, considering that every art hath reference to some author by whom it was originally taught and delivered, I answer that they were devised first by Satan and by him revealed to wicked and ungodly persons of ancient times, as occasion served, who, receiving them from him, became afterward, in the just judgment of God, his instruments to report and convey them to others from hand to hand.[9]

For manifestation whereof, it is to be considered that God is not only in general a sovereign Lord and king over all his creatures, whether in heaven or earth, none excepted, no, not the devils themselves; but that he exerciseth also a special kingdom, partly of grace in the church militant upon earth, and partly of

glory over the saints and angels, members of the church trium-
phant in heaven. Now in like manner the Devil hath a kingdom,
called in scripture the kingdom of darkness, whereof himself is
the head and governor, for which cause he is termed the prince of
darkness,[10] the God of this world,[11] ruling and effectually working in the hearts of the children of disobedience.

Again, as God hath enacted laws whereby his kingdom is
governed, so hath the Devil his ordinances whereby he keep-
eth his subjects in awe and obedience, which generally and for
substance, are nothing else but transgressions of the very law of
God. And amongst them all, the precepts of witchcraft are the
very chief and most notorious. For by them especially he holds
up his kingdom, and therefore more esteemeth the obedience of
them than of other. Neither doth he deliver them indifferently to
every man, but to his own subjects, the wicked; and not to them
all, but to some special and tried ones, whom he most betrust-
eth with his secrets, as being the fittest to serve his turn, both in
respect of their willingness to learn and practice, as also for their
ability to become instruments of the mischief which he intendeth
to others.[12]

If it be here asked whence the Devil did fetch and conceive his
rules, I answer, out of the corruption and depravation of that
great measure of knowledge he once had of God, and of all the
duties of his service. For that being quite depraved by his fall, he
turned the same to the inventing and devising of what he is possibly able, against God and his honor. Hereupon, well perceiving
that God hath expressly commanded to renounce and abhor all
practices of witchcraft, he hath set abroach this art in the world,
as a main pillar of his kingdom, which notwithstanding is flatly
and directly opposed to one of the main principal laws of the
kingdom of God, touching the service of himself in spirit and
truth.

Again, the reason why he conveys these ungodly principles and
practices from man to man is because he finds in experience that
things are far more welcome and agreeable to the common nature
of mankind which are taught by man like unto themselves than if
the Devil should personally deliver the same to each man in special. Hereupon, he takes the course at first to instruct some few
only, who being taught by him, are apt to convey that which they

know to others. And hence in probabilities this devilish trade had his first original and continuance.

Section 2

In the second place, I call it a wicked art to distinguish it from all good and lawful arts taught in schools of learning, which as they are warrantable by the word of God, so are they no less profitable and necessary in the church. Again, to show the nature and quality of it, that it is a most ungracious and wicked art, as appeareth by the scriptures. For when Saul had broken the express commandment of God in sparing Agag and the best things, Samuel tells him that rebellion and disobedience is as the sin of witchcraft, that is, a most horrible and grievous crime, like unto that wicked, capital, and mother sin.[13]

Section 3

Thirdly, I add, tending to the working or producing of wonders, wherein is noted the proper end of this art, whereby I put a further difference between it and others that are godly and lawful.

Now if question be moved, why man should desire by witchcraft to work wonders, I answer, the true and proper cause is this: the first temptation, whereby the Devil prevailed against our first parents, had enclosed within it many sins. For the eating of the forbidden fruit was no final or single offence, but as some have taught, contained in it the breach of every commandment of the moral law. Among the rest, Satan labored to bring them to the sin of discontentment, whereby they sought to become as gods, that is, better than God had made them, not resting content with the condition of men.[14] This sin was then learned, and could never since be forgotten, but continually is derived from them to all their posterity, and now is become so common a corruption in the whole nature of flesh and blood, that there is scarce a man to be found who is not originally tainted therewith as he is a man.

This corruption shows itself principally in two things, both of which are the main causes of the practices of witchcraft.

First, in man's outward estate, for he being naturally possessed with a love of himself and an high conceit of his own deserving, when he lives in base and low estate, whether in regard of poverty, or want of honor and reputation, which he thinks by right is due unto him, he then grows to some measure of grief and sorrow within himself. Hereupon, he is moved to yield himself to the Devil to be his vassal and scholar in this wicked art,[15] supporting that by the working of some wonders, he may be able in time to relieve his poverty and to purchase to himself credit and countenance amongst men.

It were easy to show the truth of this by examples of some persons, who by these means have risen from nothing to great places and preferments in the world. Instead of all, it appeareth in certain popes of Rome, as Sylvester the second, Benedict the eighth, Alexander the sixth, John the twentieth, and twenty-first, et cetera, who for the attaining of the popedom (as histories record) gave themselves to the Devil in the practice of witchcraft, that by the working of wonders, they might rise from one step of honor to another, until they had seated themselves in the chair of the papacy.[16] So great was their desire of eminency in the church that it caused them to dislike meaner conditions of life and never to cease aspiring, though they incurred thereby the hazard of good conscience and the loss of their souls.

The second degree of discontentment is in the mind and inward man, and that is curiosity, when a man resteth not satisfied with the measure of inward gifts received, as of knowledge, wit, understanding, memory, and such like, but aspires to search out such things as God would have kept secret and hence he is moved to attempt the cursed art of magic and witchcraft as a way to get further knowledge in matters secret and not revealed, that by working of wonders, he may purchase fame in the world and consequently reap more benefit by such unlawful courses than in likelihood he could have done by ordinary and lawful means.[17]

THE EARLY
COLONIES

Though witch trials continued to take place in England, our attention turns now to the first appearance of witchcraft in North America. While most witch trials occurred within the general boundaries of Puritan Massachusetts and Connecticut, isolated examples elsewhere pop up throughout the first few generations of English settlement. For the most part, early North American witchcraft incidents were narrow in scope, limited to one or two suspects. However, witch trials in North America proved to be more widespread than might have been previously thought. The prevalent and codified belief in the threat of witches took on a marked role in a wilderness of uncertain safety and within fragile communities. The need to identify who within the community did not belong manifested itself very quickly as part of the community-building project of colonization.

Another aspect worth noting is that witch trials in colonial North America tended to turn on questions of economics and family life. At the center of every pound of butter that would not churn or barrel of beer gone bad was the omnipresent question of scarcity. Many historians have pointed to the gender politics inherent in witch trials, which posed a greater threat to women than they did to men. But connected to the gendered form of the witch's body, which is reinforced by the oftentimes sexual content of the accusations levied against her, was the question of gendered labor. Witchcraft was perceived as harming families and household goods, the two primary engines under women's control for their economic security.

JOAN WRIGHT, CHESAPEAKE REGION, VIRGINIA 1626

Witchcraft was not a belief restricted to the English colonists in New England; belief in magic was interwoven in religious thought throughout the colonies, including New York and the Chesapeake. The first English settler accused of witchcraft to leave a record of herself, however scanty, was Goodwife Joan Wright in Virginia. Wright was tried but not convicted, following her suspected involvement with a difficult birth, for prophesying the death of several colonists (to be fair, not a difficult thing to do in colonial Virginia, given the high mortality rate), and for threatening that she would make a servant girl dance "stark naked." Wright might have been a kind of cunning woman, for she is not accused of dealings with the Devil, and she seemed to be consulted on matters of health and love.[1] However, the suggestion that she might have the power to cause a servant girl to dance naked points to the fear of female sexuality that appears frequently in early modern accounts of witches' gender.[2]

[A CASE OF WITCHCRAFT]

A Case of Witchcraft in Surry

Before a court held the 11th of September, 1626, appeared Lieutenant Giles Allington, a member of the London Company of Virginia[3] and a substantial citizen of the colony. By his testimony he accused Goodwife Joan Wright of witchcraft. She was the wife of Robert Wright, aged 44 in 1624–25, who came in the *Swan* in 1608. In 1625 he and his wife and two children both born in Virginia were living in Elizabeth City at Kicoughtan[4] but at the time of this trial had moved to Mr. Perry's plantation in Surry.

Giles Allington "sworn and examined saith that he had spoke to Goodwife Wright for to bring his wife to bed[5] but that the said Goodwife being left-handed, his wife desired him to get Mrs. Gray, which he did and said that the next day after his wife was delivered the said Goodwife Wright went away from his house very much discontented in regard the other midwife and brought his wife to bed. Shortly after this his wife's breast grew dangerously sore and it was a month or five weeks before she recovered, at which time this deponent himself fell sick and continued so for the space of three weeks. Further that his child after it was born fell sick and so continued for the space of a month and afterward fell into extreme pain for a space of five weeks and so departed."

Rebecca Gray sworn and examined "saith that Goodwife Wright did tell her, this deponent, that by a token that this deponent had in her forehead[6] she should bury her husband and further saith the Goodwife Wright did tell this deponent she told Mr. Felgate he would bury his wife, which came to pass, and further this deponent saith that Goodwife Wright did tell this deponent that she told Thomas Harris he should bury his first wife being then betrothed unto him, which came to pass, and further this deponent saith Goodwife Wright did tell her that a woman said to her, "I have a cross man for a husband," to whom Goodwife Wright replied, "be content for those shall shortly bury him" (which came to pass).

Thomas Jones (of whom we shall hear hereafter) was sworn and said that Sergeant Booth told him he had words with Goodwife Wright and after the said Sergeant Booth went forth with his piece to shoot and came to good game and very fair to shoot at but for a long time after he could never kill anything.

Robert Wright sworn and examined said he had been married to his wife sixteen years but knew nothing touching up "the crime she is accused of."

Mrs. Isabella Perry *** "saith that upon the losing of a log of lightwood out of the fort, Goodwife Wright railed upon a girl of Goodwife Yates for stealing the same, whereupon Goodwife Yates charged Goodwife Wright with witchcraft and said she had done many bad things at Kickotan, whereupon this examinant chided Goodwife Wright. *** and said why do thou not complain and clear thyself of same. Goodwife Wright replied, "God forgive them," and made light of it but that Goodwife Wright threatened Goodwife Yates's girl and told her if she did not bring the lightwoods again she would make her dance stark naked[7] and the next morning the lightwood was found in the fort.***

Alice Baylie sworn *** said she asked Goodwife Wright whether her husband should bury her or she bury him, to which Goodwife Wright answered, "I can tell you if I would but I am exclaimed against for such things and I'll tell no more."[8]

Goodwife Wright was found guilty by the court but was fined only 100 pounds of tobacco.

JANE JAMES, MARBLEHEAD, MASSACHUSETTS 1646

Jane James was repeatedly in court in Marblehead, though in slander cases as opposed to witchcraft trials, and so she serves as one example of the sometimes subtle ways in which witches whisper around the edges of the historical record. In her slander trials James was defending herself against rumors that she was a witch, a reputation which could be devastating in a tightly knit fishing community like Marblehead. Oftentimes a suspected witch would attempt to reclaim her tarnished reputation by going on the offensive, bringing those gossiping about her to court. However, to do so was a risky maneuver. If the defendants in a slander suit were found to be speaking the truth, rather than spreading rumors, the plaintiff could very quickly find herself on trial for witchcraft.[1]

Jane James illustrates both the central role of gossip and reputation in the small colonial community, and the fact that suspected witches were widespread, even if they did not always make it to the deadly end of the judicial process. This early account of Goody James shows her in a violent altercation with a neighbor over a shoulder of mutton; though brief, it provides a tantalizing portrait of behavior that was frowned upon in women, sometimes with dire consequences for their reputations.

THE CASE OF JANE JAMES

Salem, 10th month[2]
1646

Thomas Bo[torn] about 24 years testif[torn] that William [torn]
in the said deponent[torn] house, that the [torn] lying scandalous whores in M [torn] in any place in New England. W[? torn]
James said, Goodman Barber you [torn] whereupon the said William Barber said [torn] Jane, look at you for one of them, get you
out of doors you filthy old bawd or else I will cuttle your hide,
you old filthy baggage and took up a firebrand but did not throw
it at her. This deponent also testifieth that he saw William Barber carry away a shoulder of mutton that Jane James should have
had, giving her a push on the breast and said he could eat a shoulder of mutton as well as she. This is the sum of what I can say as
also witness my hand this 26th of 10th month, 1646.

 The mark of
 Thomas [his mark] Bowen

Elizabeth the wife of Thomas Bowen doth testify the same
thing, being also present at the same time. aprd [?] thereunto also
doth put to her hand this 26th of 10th month, 1646.

 The mark of
 Elizabeth [her mark] Bowen

MARGARET JONES, CHARLESTOWN, MASSACHUSETTS 1648

Margaret Jones was one of the first witches to be executed in Massachusetts; her husband, Thomas, was also suspected, though never brought to trial. John Winthrop's account suggests that she functioned as a cunning woman, which complicates the common picture of the witch as someone who was purely a deviant from social norms, or a scapegoat.[1] Cunning folk functioned in a shadowy moral universe in early modern English village life in that they filled a vital social role—that of offering occult services for a fee—while nevertheless being objects of fear. In fact, William Perkins was more concerned about cunning folk than about so-called hurting witches because the temptation that they presented to believers desperate for relief from supposed enchantment posed a threat to Christian faith.[2]

THE CASE OF MARGARET JONES[3]

At this court one Margaret Jones of Charles Towne was indicted and found guilty of witchcraft and hanged for it.[4] The evidence against her was: 1. That she was found to have such a malignant touch, as many persons (men and women and children) whom she stroked or touched (with any affection [illegible] displeasure or et cetera) were taken with deafness or vomiting or other violent pains or sickness. 2. She practicing physick, and her medicines being such things as (by her own confession) were harmless,[5] as aniseed, liquoris,[6] et cetera, yet had extraordinary violent effects. 3. She would use to tell such as would not make use of her physick, that they would never be healed,[7] and accordingly their diseases and hurts continued with relapses against the ordinary course and beyond the apprehension of all physicians and surgeons. 4. Some things which she foretold came to pass accordingly; other things she could tell of (as secret speeches, et cetera) which she had no ordinary means to come to the knowledge off.[8] 5. She had (upon search) an apparent teat in her secret parts, as fresh as if it had been newly sucked,[9] and after it had been searched, upon a second search, that was withered, and another began on the opposite side. 6. In the prison, in the clear daylight, there was seen in her arms (she sitting on the floor and her clothes up, et cetera) a little child, which ran from her into another room and the officer following it, it was vanished. The like child was seen in two other places, to which she had relation, and one maid that saw it fell sick upon it and was cured by the said Margaret, who used means[10] to be employed to that end. Her behavior at her trial was very intemperate, lying notoriously, and railing upon the jury and witnesses, et cetera and in the like distemper she died. The same day and hour she was executed there was a very great tempest at Connecticut, which blew down many trees, et cetera.

Margaret Jones also puts in an appearance in Reverend John Hale's 1697 account A Modest Enquiry into the Nature of Witchcraft, *published in Boston in 1702.[11] Hale was a minister in Beverly whose wife was accused during the Salem panic.* A Modest Enquiry *was his attempt to look at the nature of witchcraft in North America. He mistakenly cites Jones as the first person executed for witchcraft in New England; there is evidence that one Alice Young was executed in Windsor, Connecticut, in 1647, though very little record of her survives.[12]*

HALE'S ACCOUNT OF MARGARET JONES

Section 5. The first was a woman of Charlestown, anno 1647 or '48. She was suspected partly because that after some angry words passing between her and her neighbors, some mischief befell such neighbors in their creatures, or the like. Partly because some things supposed to be bewitched or have a charm upon them, being burned, she came to the fire and seemed concerned.[13]

The day of her execution, I went in company of some neighbors, who took great pains to bring her to confession and repentance. But she constantly professed herself innocent of that crime. Then one prayed her to consider if God did not bring this punishment upon her for some other crime and asked if she had not been guilty of stealing many years ago; she answered, she had stolen something, but it was long since and she had repented of it, and there was grace enough in Christ to pardon that long ago; but as for witchcraft she was wholly free from it, and so she said unto her death.

RALPH AND MARY HALL,
SETAUKET, NEW YORK[1]
1665

New York had vastly fewer witch trials than did New England due to the different religious structure in that region. New Netherland had some difficulty attracting Dutch settlers and as such the region in the seventeenth century was a more heterogeneous place than New England, peopled with Dutch, but also Huguenots and settlers from Scandinavia, to say nothing of African slaves. Control of the colony passed to England in 1664, thereby increasing immigration to the region from New England.[2] Could this subtle shift in the character of the inhabitants of New York account for the appearance of the first known witch trial the following year in New York? The nineteenth-century transcriber believes so, even going so far as to remark that Ralph and Mary Hall are fortunate to likely have been tried by a largely Dutch jury. If they had been tried on the same grounds in New England they would not have been let off so easily, as plenty of people were hanged as witches in New England for less.

INDICTMENT OF RALPH AND MARY HALL[3]

Witchcraft

The following is a correct copy of a bill of indictment preserved in the city of New York [and the proceedings thereon], against Ralph Hall and Mary, his wife, for witchcraft in the year 1665. This was the only trial for that offence in this colony. It is curious to read this relic of a barbarous age, and while we do so, we should not forget the lights of learning and civilization which have introduced a better order of things.

At a court of assizes held in New York, the 2nd day of October 1665, et cetera, the trial of Ralph Hall and Mary, his wife, upon suspicion of witchcraft. The names of the persons who served upon the grand jury are Thomas Baker, foreman of the jury, of Easthampton; Captain John Symonds of Hempstead; Mr. Helmet of Jamaica; Anthony Waters; Thomas Wardell of March Path Hill; Mr. Nichols of Stanford; Bethazar D. Haart, John Garland, Jacob Luster, Anthonio De Mill, Alexander Munro, Thomas Searle of New York.

The prisoner being brought to the bar by Allan Anthony, sheriff of New York, this following indictment was read, first against Ralph Hall and then against Mary, his wife, namely:

The constable and overseers of the town of Setalcott,[4] in the east riding of Yorkshire upon Long Island, do present for our sovereign lord the king that Ralph Hall of Setalcott aforesaid, upon the 25th day of December, being Christmas day last was twelve months, in the 15th year of the reign of our sovereign lord Charles 2nd by the grace of God king of England, Scotland, France and Ireland, defender of the faith, et cetera and several other days and times since that day, by some detestable and wicked arts, commonly called witchcraft and sorcery,[5] did (as is suspected) maliciously and feloniously practice and exercise at the said town of Setalcott in the east riding of Yorkshire, on Long Island aforesaid, on the person of George Wood, late of the same place, by which wicked and detestable arts the said George Wood (as is suspected) most dangerously and mortally sickened and languished, and not long after, by the aforesaid wicked and detestable arts, the said George Wood (as is likewise suspected) died.

Moreover, the constable and overseers of the said town do further present for our sovereign lord the king, that some while after the death of the said George Wood, the said Ralph Hall did, as is suspected, diverse times by the like wicked and detestable arts, commonly called witchcraft and sorcery, maliciously and feloniously practice and exercise at the said town of Setalcott, on the person of an infant child of Ann Rogers, widow of the aforesaid George Wood, deceased, by which wicked and detestable arts, the said infant child, as is suspected, most dangerously and mortally sickened and languished, and not long after, by the said

wicked and detestable arts (as is suspected) died. And so the said
constable and overseers do present that the said George Wood
and the said Infant child, by the ways and means aforesaid, most
wickedly and maliciously and feloniously were (as is suspected)
murdered by the said Ralph Hall at the times and places aforesaid, and against the laws of this government in such cases provided.

The like indictment was read against Mary, the wife of Ralph
Hall. Thereupon several depositions accusing the prisoners of
the fact for which they were indicted were read, but no witness
appeared to give testimony in court *vive voce*.[6] Then the clerk,
calling up Ralph Hall, bade him hold up his hand and read as
follows: "Ralph Hall thou standest here indicted for that having not the fear of God before thine eyes, thou didst upon the
25th day of December, being Christmas last was 12 months and
at several other times since (as is suspected) by some wicked and
detestable arts commonly called witchcraft and sorcery, maliciously and feloniously practice and exercise upon the bodies
of George Wood and an infant child of Ann Rogers, by which
said arts the said George Wood and the infant child (as is suspected) most dangerously and mortally fell sick and languished
unto death. Ralph Hall, what dost thou say for thyself—art thou
guilty, or not guilty?" Mary, the wife of Ralph Hall, was called
in like manner.[7] They both pleaded not guilty and threw themselves to be tried by God and the country. Whereupon the cause
was referred to the jury, who brought into court this following
verdict, namely:

We, having severally considered the case committed to our
charge against the prisoner at the bar, and having well weighed
the evidence, we find that there are some suspicions by the evidence of what the woman is charged with, but nothing of considerable of value to take away her life, but in reference to the man,
we find nothing considerable to charge him with.

The court thereupon gave this sentence. That the man should
be bound, body and goods, for his wife's appearance at the next
sessions, and so on from sessions to sessions as long as they stay
within this government. In the mean time to be of good behavior.
So they were returned to the sheriff's custody and upon entering
into a recognizance, according to the sentence of the court, they
were released.

It is worthy of remark that not a word was ever mentioned in this colony about the spectral evidence which was so much relied on the cases of witchcraft in New England. Cotton Mather in his *Magnalia*[8] states that the opinion of the Dutch and French ministers was asked in relation to the spectral accusation of the New England witch cases and that they made the following answer under their hands. "If we believe no venefick[9] witchcraft we must renounce the scripture of God and the consent of almost all the world; but that yet the apparition of a person afflicting another is very insufficient proof of a witch; nor is it inconsistent with the holy and righteous government of God over men to permit the affliction of the neighbors by devils in the shape of good men; and that a good name, obtained by a good life, should not be lost by mere spectral accusations."

This was the first and last prosecution for witchcraft in the government of New York, and although the Dutch are considered as superstitious, yet they invariably dismissed all complaint proffered for this alleged offence (see instances) and they punished all attempts to introduce superstition by publicly alarming the populace. (See punishment of fellow in New York for crying woe of Ephraim, et cetera.) It is worthy of remark that this solitary instance of a prosecution for witchcraft did not originate in that part of the colony settled by the sober burghers from the Naderlandt but among the emigrants from Connecticut and Massachusetts on the eastern part of Long Island, and it is fair to presume that if the majority of the jury had not been Dutchmen it would have gone hard with poor Ralph Hall and his wife. Many were executed in New England against whom the case was nothing like as strong as this.

EUNICE COLE, HAMPTON, MASSACHUSETTS, LATER NEW HAMPSHIRE 1647–1680

Eunice Cole battled suspicion of being a witch for most of her life. She was repeatedly tried for witchcraft and ultimately imprisoned, though not put to death. Cole spent a good portion of her life in jail in Boston. Her repeated appearances in the Essex County court records paint a portrait of a quarrelsome woman whose life took a precipitous turn for the worse following her husband's death. Possibly the most notorious moment in Cole's many decades of suspicion is the 1673 escapade in which she attempted to entice a young girl, nine-year-old Ann Smith, into living with her. On many different occasions the relationship between witchcraft and children draws special attention. Often infants and children are the supposed victims of interference by witches or the objects of their covetous envy.[1] Eunice Cole demonstrates the delicate relationship between class status, economic security, and reputation for women in this region during the first several decades of settlement, in which she served as both a foil and a potential cautionary tale to the other women in her community.

Complaint Against Eunice Cole[2]

Seventh month, 1647

Presentments made by the grand jury at the court holden at Ipswich upon 28th day of 7th month, 1647.

[· · ·]

We do present Eunice Cole, the wife of William Cole of Hampton, for crying Murder! Murder! when as the constable did go to serve the execution (upon that which he had formerly differed on) witnesseth: William Fuller, William English, and Jack Perkins of Hampton affirm it on their oath.

We do present William Cole of Hampton for offering to rescue goods out of the constable's hands being legally proceeded against for the same as also [illegible] himself and wife for the biting the constable by his hands at the same time. Witness:—William Fuller, William English, and Jack Perkins of Hampton affirm it on their oaths. William English affirmeth he saw them pull the constable down and pull the swines from him.

We do present the wife of William Cole of Hampton for saying that there was thieves there in the town and that William Fuller who is the constable was as bad as any of them. Witness: Wife [fuller?] csh: Jack Perkins of Hampton affirms on oath she said I do not know but he may be as bad as any of them.

We do present the wife of William Cole of Hampton for saying there was some persons in the town of Hampton which did forswear themselves and so did William Fuller forswear himself against his witness. William English and Jack Perkins of Hampton, William Fuller affirmeth this presentment on his oath.

Deposition of Goody Maston[3]

The deposition of Goody Maston and Goodwife Palmer, who, being sworn, saith that Goodwife Cole said that she was sure there was a witch in the town and she knew where he dwelt and who they are and that thirteen years ago she knew one bewitched as Goodwife Maston's child was and she said she was sure that party was bewitched for it told her so and it was changed from a man to an ape as Goody Maston's child was and she had prayed this thirteen years that God would discover that witch and further that deponent saith not.

Taken upon oath before the commissioners of Hampton
The 8th of the 2nd month, 1656 William Fuller Henry Dow
Vera copia per me[4] Thomas Bradbury
Sworn in court rec 4 September, 1656, per Edward Rawson, secretary

Deposition of Thomas Philbrick

The deposition of Thomas Philbrick. This deponent saith that Goodwife Cole said that if this deponent's calves if they did eat any of his grass she wished it might poison them or choke them and one of them I never see it more and the other calf came home and died about a week after.

   Taken upon oath before me, Thomas Wiggin
   Vera copia per me, Thomas Bradbury rec
   Sworn in court 4 September, 1656, Edward Rawson, secretary

The Deposition of Thomas Mouton's Wife, Sobriety,[5] and Goodwife Sleeper

These deponents testifieth that were being talking about Goodwife Cole and Goodwife Marston's child and on the sudden we heard something scrape against the boards of the window and we went out and looked about and could see nothing and then we went in again and began to talk the same also again concerning she and Goodwife Marston's child and then we heard the scraping again and then we went out again and looked about and could see nothing, and the scraping was so loud that if a dog or a cat had done it we should have seen the marks in the boards and we could see none. The house where we were was Thomas Sleeper's house and further these deponents saith not. Taken upon oath [torn] the commissioners of Hampton the 10th 2nd month, 1656.

   Vera copia per Thomas Bradbury received William Fuller Henry Dow
   Sworn in court 4 September, 1656, Edward (smeared) Rawson, secretary

Deposition of Mary Coleman

The deposition of Mary Coleman, the wife of Thomas Coleman

This deponent witnesseth that Goody Cole came to her house and said that her husband had made a great complaint against this deponent to Nathaniel Boulton of some words that were spoke betwixt this deponent and her husband in their own house in private and Goody Cole did repeat the words[6] to this deponent that she and her husband spake together which words of discontent but those words were never spoken to any person neither by this deponent nor her husband as he saith and to this they will take their oaths of. Thomas Coleman also affirms that he never spake the words to any person.

Sworn in court, Thomas Bradbury

Vera copia per me, Thomas Bradbury received

Sworn in court 4 September, 1656, Edward Rawson, secretary

Deposition of Richard Ormsbey[7]

The deposition of Richard Ormsbey, constable of Salisbury That being about to strip Eunice Cole to be whipped (by the judgment of the court at Salisbury) looking upon her breasts under one of her breasts (I think her left breast) I saw a blue thing like unto a teat hanging downward about three quarters of an inch long not very thick and having a great suspicion in my mind about it (she being suspected for a witch), desired the court to send some women to look of it and presently hereupon she pulled or scratched it off in a violent manner, and some blood with other moistness did appear clearly to my apprehension and she said it was a sore. Jon Goddard doth testify that he saw her with her hand violently scratch it away. Sworn in the court at Sudbury 12th 2nd month, 1656, Thomas Bradbury.

Vera copia per me, Thomas Bradbury

Sworn in court 4 September, 1656, and Abraham Perkins and Jon Redman[8] affirmed I stood by saw the constable rip her shift down and saw the place raw and fresh blood where Goody Cole[9]

The court presently stepping to her saw a place raw with some fresh blood but no appearance of any old sore, Thomas Bradbury received in the name of the court.

Sworn in court 4 September, 1656, I, Richard Ormsbey, Edward Rawson, secretary, also Abraham Perkins and Jon Redman affirmed on oath that they stood by (torn) her shift and saw the place raw and where she had tore of her teat and fresh blood came from it and saw her (illegible) her hand to tear off that was torn off.

The Deposition of Abraham Drake

This deponent saith about this time twelve month my neighbor Coles lost a cow and when we had found it I and others brought the cow home to his house and he and she desired me to flea[10] this cow, and presently after she charged me with killing her cow and said they should know he had killed the cow for the just hand of God was upon my cattle and forthwith I lost two cattle and the latter end of summer I lost one cow[11] more. Sworn in court, Thomas Bradbury received.

Sworn in court 4, September, 1656
Edward Rawson, secretary[12]

Deposition of Thomas Coleman and Abraham Drake[13]

The deposition of Thomas Coleman and Abraham Drake
These deponents saith about a year and a half ago, they being at Robert Drake's house at a meeting with the selectmen, Eunice Cole came into the said house and demanded help of the selectmen for wood or other things and the selectmen told her she had an estate of her own, and needed no help of town, whereupon Eunice answered they could help Goodman Robert, being a lusty[14] man and she could have none, but Eunice said all could not or should not do and about two or three days after this said Robert left a cow and a sheep very strangely and one of the men then present told Eunice Cole she should look at a hand of God in it, for withdrawing the people's hearts from helping of her.[15] Eunice Cole answered, no, twas the Devil did this. Deposed in court, 5 September, 1656, Edward Rawson, secretary. Thomas Coleman and John Redman deposed to the evidence and particularly to the words "should not do," 5th September, 1656 Edward Rawson, secretary.

Deposition of Ann Higgins[16]

The Deposition of Ann Higgins, aged about 14 years
This deponent testifieth that as she and this other girl were a coming by the place where Goody Cole lives, she came out of her house and asked this Ann Smith to live with her, and she said that there was a gentleman within would give her some plumes[17] and the girl not being willing to go with her, she laid hold on her

to pull her to her and then this deponent said that she should go about her business for she had nothing to do with her.[18] And Goody Cole said that she would ask her mother if she would let her live with her, and further this deponent saith not. Given the 12th 8th month, 1672.

Before me
Samuel Dalton Com

Deposition of Sarah Clifford[19]

The Deposition of Sarah Clifford, aged about 30 years
This deponent testifieth that she heard Ann Smith cry and she going out found this Ann in the orchard with her mouth bloody and blood on the paths, and this deponent asked her several questions and asked her how she came so and Ann answered she knew not how and after she came into the house those that were with her asked her whether she knew any body and by what they did perceive she knew none there and after this deponent took her in her arms and carried her into another house, and then she child told her that there came an old woman into the garden with a blue coat and a blue cap and a blue apron and a white neck cloth and took this girl as she told us up by the hand and carried her into the orchard and threw her under a pearmain[20] tree, and she was asked to live with this old woman and she said if she would live with her she would give her a baby and some plumes,[21] and the girl told her that she would not, and then this old woman said that she would kill her if she could, and then the old woman took up a stone and stroke her on the head, and when she had so done she turned into a little dog and ran upon this pearmain tree, and so then she was like an eagle, and further this deponent saith that this girl as we thought very ill on the last sixth day at night, and we asked her what she ailed and the girl complained of cats and she said that she was pricked with pins. Sworn the 12th day 8th month, 1672, before me Samuel Dutton Comiss.

Deposition of Ann Smith[22]

The Deposition of Ann Smith, about the age of 9 years
This deponent testifieth that when she went in the cabbage yard that there came a woman to her in a blue coat and blue cape and

blue apron and a white neck cloth, and she woman took her by the hand and carried her into the orchard under the pearmain tree, and there she took up a stone and knocked her on the head, then she turned into a little dog and ran upon the tree, then she flew away like an eagle, and further this deponent saith that if she came again she would kill her, and at another time since that, she sitting in the corner that there came a thing like a gray cat and spake to her and said to her that if she would come to her on the verily[23] day she would give her fine things and further this deponent saith not. Ann Smith affirmed to this above written the 12th day, 8th month (illegible), 1672, before me Samuel Dalton C.

Court Record, Salisbury[24]

At the county court held at Salisbury 29th of April, 1673 Second Sessions

The court upon the hearing of the evidence against Eunice Cole now presented, and consideration of former things against her, do judge that she shall be committed to Boston Jail there to be kept in order to her further trial. And the constable of Hampton is ordered by this court to carry down Eunice Cole by the first opportunity to Boston Jail to be secured according to the court's order.

This is a true copy as attested

Thomas Bradbury, received

The presents of the grand jury of Norfolk at Hampton 1672, October the 9th

We present Eunice Cole, widow, for enticing Ann Smith to come to live with her, for Jon Clifford senior who hath the charge of her by her father. Witness: Jon Clifford senior and Ann Huggins and Ann Smith. *Vera copia* per me, Thomas Bradbury received.[25]

MARY PHILIPS, CAMBRIDGE, MASSACHUSETTS 1659

The case of Mary Philips demonstrates aspects of both witchcraft in seventeenth-century New England and of the early practice of witchcraft scholarship. Many early accounts of witchcraft, particularly those from outside of the unusually well-documented Essex County in Massachusetts, survive not in their original state but as transcriptions copied down by nineteenth- and early twentieth-century witchcraft scholars. George Kittredge, who would go on to pen one of the best-known accounts of witchcraft at Salem, kept a notebook of witchcraft records that he copied down while an undergraduate. What follows illustrates the suspicions attached to Quakers in the predominantly Puritan realm of New England, but it derives from a source that Kittredge described only as a "Quaint Old Pamphlet of 1659," and so is difficult to otherwise support. Kittredge's early scholarship, while respectful, nevertheless treats witch belief as a bizarre "curio," a remnant of medieval superstition that has nothing to do with reality.

Kittredge's Notes on Mary Philips[1]

Strange and terrible news from Cambridge, being a true relation and trial of some Quakers who bewitched Mary Philips out of the bed, from her husband, and having transformed her into a mare, rode her from Dinton[2] toward Cambridge, with the manner how she became visible again, in her own likeness and shape, with all her sides rent and torn, as if she had been spur-galled.[3]

JOHN GODFREY,
HAVERHILL,
MASSACHUSETTS
1659–1665

John Godfrey's presence in the Essex County court records extends well beyond these readings, beginning in the 1640s and extending all the way to his death in 1675.[1] While early New Englanders were notable for their litigiousness, Godfrey presents a special case, not only for his repeated appearances, but also for the substance of his various legal troubles. Whereas men appeared as accused witches from time to time, they almost universally were affiliated with—most often were married to—women who themselves had been accused. John Godfrey emerges as a unique character within the history of North American witchcraft for the simple reason that he was male, with a witchy reputation of his own, and no wife.

Employed sporadically for much of his life as a herdsman who also was unusually mobile, suggesting rootlessness and economic difficulty, Godfrey seemed to enjoy being a provocateur. He was known to speak often of the power of witches or to allude to his own association with the Devil. Like Eunice Cole and other New Englanders with long-standing poor reputations, Godfrey dodged conviction for much of his adult life. He was tried and acquitted three different times.

Another unusual aspect of the suspicion surrounding Godfrey is that after his 1659 trial, he rejoined the same community, with very little change in his circumstances.[2]

However, Godfrey's quarrelsome nature and complex financial entanglements with his neighbors would result in his subsequent trial for witchcraft in 1665–1666, a trial during which he was acquitted on a technicality, though the court left little doubt as to their private opinions on his guilt.

Court List of Witnesses Against Godfrey[3]

To the honored court to be holden at Ipswich this twelfth month, 1658 or 1659

Whereas diverse of esteem with us and as we hear in other places also have for some times have suffered losses in their estates and some affliction on their bodies also, which as they suppose doth not arise from any natural cause or any neglect in themselves but rather from some ill-disposed person, that upon differences had betwixt themselves and one John Godfrey, resident at Andover or elsewhere at his pleasure we whose names are underwritten do make bold to sue by way of request to this honored court that you in your wisdom will be pleased if you see cause for it to call him in question and to hear at present or at some after sessions what may be said in this respect.

James Davis, senior, in the behalf of his son Ephraim Davis
John Heseltine and Jane, his wife
Abraham Whittaker for his ox and other things
Ephraim Davis in the behalf of himself
Some things we hear of and it may be they may be of consequence
Benjamin Sweet in the case of his child
Isabell Holdred hearing a voice and being afflicted in her body
Job Tyler of Andover for a bird coming to suck his wife
Charles Browne's son for what he did see, although we say no more at present
Widow Ayres's daughter and Goodman Procter's daughter for a pail with something in it

Testimony Against Godfrey[4]

Thomas Hayne testifieth that being with Goodwife Holdridge she told me that she saw a great horse and showed me where it stood: I then took a stick and stroke on the place but felt nothing and I heard the door shake and goodwife said it was gone out at the door. Immediately after she was taken with extremity of fear and pain so that she presently fell into a sweat and I thought she would swoon away. She trembled and shook like a leaf.

    Thomas Hayne

Nathan Gould being with Goodwife Holdred ong [scored out] night there appeared a great snake as she said with open mouth and she being weak, hardly able to go alone, yet then ran and laid hold of Nathan Gould by the head and could not speak for the space of half an hour.

    Nathan Gould

Deposition of Isabel Holdred[5]

The deposition of Isabel Holdred

Who testifieth that John Godfrey came to the house [where] Henry Blasda[torn] her husband and herself were and demanded a debt of her husband and said a warrant was out and Goodman Lord was suddenly to come. John Godfrey [torn]ed if we would not pay him. The deponent answered yes, tonight [torn]morrow if we had it. John Godfrey said of must begin and must [torn] man Lord the deponent answered [illegible][foregoing in brackets scored out] for I believe we shall not [torn] we are in thy debt. John Godfrey answered that's a bitter word said. I must begin and must send Goodman Lord. The deponent answ[torn] when thou wilt. I fear thee not nor all the devils in hell, and further [torn] deponent testifieth that two days after this she was taken with those strange fits with which she was tormented a fortnight together night and day and several apparitions appeared to the deponent in the night: the first night a humble bee,[6] the next night a bear appeared, which ground the teeth and shook the claw. Thou sayest thou art not afraid. Then thinkest Harry Blasdell's house will save thee? The deponent answered, I hope the Lord Jesus Christ will save me. The apparition then spake. Thou sayest thou art not afraid of all the devils in hell but I will have thy heart blood within a few hours. The next was the apparition of a great snake at which the deponent was exceedingly affrighted and skipped to Nathan Gold, who was in the opposite chimney corner and caught hold of the hair of his head and her speech was taken away for the space of half an hour. The next night appeared a great horse and Thomas Hayne being there, the deponent told him of it and showed him where. The said Thomas Hayne took a stick and struck at the place where apparition was and his stroke glanced by the side of it and it went [torn] the table and he went to strike again. Then the apparition fled to the [torn] and made it shake and went away and about a week after the deponent [torn] son were at the door of Nathan Gold and heard a rushing in the [torn] The deponent said to her son, yonder is a beast. He answered, 'tis one of Goodman Cobby's black oxen and it came toward them and came within [torn] yard of them. The deponent, her heart began to ache for it seemed to have great eyes and spake to the boy, lets go in. But suddenly the oxen beat her against the wall and struck her down and she was much hurt by it, not being able to rise up but some other carried me into the house, all my face being bloody being much bruised.

The boy was much affrighted a long time after and for the space of two hours was in a sweat that one might have washed hands on his hair, [torn]their the deponent affirmeth that she hath been often troubled with a black cat sometimes appearing in the house and sometimes in the night [torn] bed and lay on her and sometimes stroking her face [torn] the cat [torn] hrice as big as an ordinary cat.

Deposition of Charles Browne and Wife[7]

The deposition of Charles Browne and his wife

This deponent saith about 6 or 7 years since in the meeting house of Towley, being in the gallery in the first seat, there was one in the second seat (whom he doth to his best remembrance think and verily believe it was John Godfrey). This deponent did see him yawning open his mouth and while he did yawn this deponent did see a small teat under his tongue[8] and further this deponent saith that John Godfrey was at this deponent's house about 3 years since speaking about the power of witches. He the said Godfrey spoke that if witches were not kindly entertained the Devil will appear unto them and ask them if they were grieved or vexed with anybody and ask them what he should do for them and if they would not give them beer or victuals, they might let all the beer run out of the cellar and if they looked steadfastly upon any creature it would die and it were hard to some witches to take away life either of man or beast yet when they once begin it, then it is easy to them.

Testimony of William Osgood[9]

William Osgood testifieth that in the year 1640[10] in the month
of August, he being then building a barn for Mr. Spencer, John
Godfrey being then Mr. Spencer's herdsman, he on an evening came to the frame where diverse men were at work and
said that he had gotten a new master against the time he had
done keeping cows. The said William Osgood asked him who it
was. He answered he knew not. He again asked him where he
dwelt. He answered he knew not. He asked him what his name
was. He answered he knew not. He then said to him, how then
wilt thou go to him when thy time is out? He said, the man will
come and fetch me. The W[illiam]: I asked him hast thou made an
absolute bargain. He answered that a covenant was made. He had
set his hand to it. He then asked of him whether he had not a coun-
ter covenant. Godfrey answered no. William Osgood said what a
mad fellow art thou to make a covenant in this manner. He said
he's an honest man. How knowest thou said William Osgood.
John Godfrey answered, he looks like one. William Osgood then
answered, I am persuaded thou hast made a covenant with the
Devil. the then skipped about and said I ptesse, I ptesse.[11]

1663–1664

Deposition of John Remington[12]

The deposition of John Remington and Edw[torn]
These deponents being at the last court held at Ip[torn].[13] Jonathan Singletary being there in the court [torn] that John Godfrey
came to him in the [torn] when the prison door was locked [torn]
Jonathan, and said now I can speak [torn] pay the executions you
are in prison, for you may soon [torn] forth, and further Jonathan
said before Godfrey came thus unto him and spake to him,[14] he
heard a noise and the prison shake and the locks and doors chat-
tering as if they did open and shut at his coming in and also that
he see Godfrey's face as plain in the prison as he did in the court.
Taken upon the oaths of John Remington and Edward Yeomans,
20th day, 4th month, 1663, before me, Simon Bradstreet. Copy
made by Hilliard Vere, cleric.

Deposition of Jonathan Singletary[15]

14th day, 12th month, 1662

The deposition of Jonathan Singletary, aged about 23, who testifieth that I, being in the prison at Ipswich this night last past between nine and ten of the clock at night after the bell had rung, I, being set in a corner of the prison, upon a sudden I heard a great noise as if many cats had been climbing up the prison walls and skipping in the house at the windows and jumping about the chamber. And a noise as boards' ends or stools had been thrown about and men walking in the chambers and a crackling and shaking as if the house would have fallen upon me. I, seeing this and considering what I knew by a young man that kept at my house last Indian harvest, and upon some difference with John Godfrey, he was presently several nights in a strange manner. Troubled and complaining as he did and upon consideration of this and other things that I knew by him I was at present something affrighted that considering what I had lately heard made out by Mr. Mitchell at Cambridge that there is more good in God than there is evil in sin and that although God is the greatest good and sin the greatest evil that the first being of evil cannot wear the scales or over power the first being of good. So considering that the author of good was of greater power than the author of evil. God was pleased of his goodness to keep me from being out of measure frighted so. This noise above said held as I suppose about a quarter of an hour and then ceased and presently I heard the bolt of the door shoot or go back as perfidy to my thinking as I did the next morning when the keeper came to unlock it and I could not see the door open but I saw John Godfrey stand within the door and said, Jonathan, Jonathan. So I, looking on him, said, what have you to do with me? He said, I come to see you. Are you weary of your place? That I answered, I take no delight in being here but I will be out as soon. As I can, he said. If you will pay me in corn, you shall come out.[16] I answered no. If that had been my intent, I would have paid the marshal and never have come hither. He, knocking of his fist at me in a kind of a threatening way, said he would make me weary of my part and so went away I know not how nor which way and as I was walking about in the prison I tripped upon a stone with my heel and took it up in my hand, thinking that if he came again I would trick at him. So as I was walking about he called at the window. Jonathan, said he.

If you will pay me corn I will give you two Thursday and we will come to an agreement. I answered him, saying, why do you come dissembling and playing the Devil's part here? Your nature is nothing but envy and malice which you will vent though to your own loss and you seek peace with no man. I do not dissemble, said he I will give you my hand upon it. I am in earnest. So he put his hand in at the window and I took hold of it with my left hand and pulled him to me and with the stone in my right hand I thought I struck him and went to recover my hand to strike again and his hand was gone and I would have struck but there was nothing to strike and how he went away I know not for I could neither tell when his hand went out of mine nor see which way he went.

1665

Deposition of John Remington

Fourteenth paper:
The Deposition of John Remington
This deponent testifieth that I heard John Godfrey say to my father that if he drived the cattle up the woods to winter, then my father should say and have cause to repent that he did drive them up and these words he said in a great rage and passion and of [lost] this. My father and I did drive up the cattle and I for the most part did tend them and about the middle of December last as I was a coming home from the cattle about a mile from them, then the horse I rid on begun to start and snort and the dog that was with me begun to whine and cry and it still. I made a shift to sit on the horse still for a matter of a quarter of a mile and then I smelt a sweet smell like seder[17] and presently I looked up into the swamp and I see a crow come toward me flying and perched upon a tree against me and she look at me and the horse and dog and it had a very great and quick eye and it had a very great bill and then the said crow flew off that tree to another after me. Then I begun to mistrust and think it was no crow and thought if it was not a crow, it could not hurt my soul though it hurt my body[18] and horse and as I was a thinking thus to myself the horse I was upon fell down upon one side in pain grown upon my leg and as soon as I [lost] the horse was fallen then the crow came and flew round

me several times as if she would light upon me but she [should] [scored out] did not touch me. Then the horse rise and went about four rod[19] and then stood still and I lay on the ground still and was not able to follow him for the present. Then when I came a little better to myself I made a shift to cripe[20] on my hands and knees. The horse and the crow scre[lost]d and made a noise like a cat and the hollowing of a man. Then I got upon the horse and went on then. The crow appeared to me sometimes a great crow and sometimes like a little bird and so continued with me about a mile and a half farther and she flew upon the dog and beat him to the last all this while. After I fell with the horse I was taken very sick and thought I should have died til such time the crow left me and then the dog mad on me and rejoiced very much after the crow left us. And then the second day following I, being at home, John Godfrey came to my father's house in a great rage and asked of me how I did and I told him pretty well only I was lame with the horse falling on me two days before. Then said Godfrey, every cockating[21] boy must ride. I unhorsed one boy t'other day. I will unhorse thee shortly too if thee rides my horse. Then said I, I am not able to carry vittles[22] upon my back. Then said Godfrey, 'tis a sorry horse cannot carry his own provender. Then said Godfrey to me, John, if thee had been a man as thee was a boy thee hadt died on the spot where thee got the fall. Then said my mother to Godfrey, how can thee tell that? There is none but God can tell that and except thee be more than an ordinary man[23] thee cannot tell that. Then Godfrey bade my mother hold her tongue. He knew what he said better than she and said, I say again had he been a man as he was a boy he had died on the spot where he fell.

Godfrey saith that he knows not that he said if he had been a man as he was a boy he had died that he had knowledge of [lost] the boy.

    E R S

This was dd [struck out] in on his oath in this court 7 March, 16 [lost] S.

[· · ·]

Court Record of Accusation

At a Court of Assistants Held at Boston, 6th March, 1665 John Godfrey being bound over to this court by the county court in January last in Boston on the complaint and accusation of Job

Tyler and John Remington on suspicion of witchcraft, the said Job Tyler and John Remington being also bound over to prosecute against the said John Godfrey, summons for witnesses being granted out and many appeared. Edward Theomans, Robert Swan, Mathias Butten, William Symons, and John Remington deposed in court that whatever evidence either of them shall give into the grand jury in relation to John Godfrey shall be the truth, whole truth, and nothing but the truth, and diverse others with them being sworn in court before and against the prisoner, which are on file. John Godfrey being brought to the bar, it was declared that the grand jury had found him guilty and putting him on trial for his life. The jury was impaneled. The said John Godfrey holding up his hand at the bar, he was indicted by the name of John Godfrey of Newbery for, not having the fear of God before your eyes, did or have consulted with a familiar spirit, and being instigated by the Devil have done much hurt and mischief by several acts of witchcraft to the bodies and goods of several persons as by several evidences may appear contrary to the peace of our sovereign lord, the king, his crown and dignity, and the wholesome laws of this jurisdiction. To which he pleaded not guilty and referred himself for his trial to God and the country. The several evidences produced against the prisoner being read, committed to the jury and remain on file with the records of this court. The jury brought in their verdict, that is, we find him not to have the fear of God in his heart. He have made himself to us being suspiciously guilty of witchcraft but not legally guilty, according to law and evidence we have received. This verdict was accepted and party discharged.

It is ordered that the treasurer of the country discharge the charge of the witnesses in the case of John Godfrey to value of six days' allowance per each witness and make it up to that value. Only the two prosecutors, Job Tyler and Jon Remington, shall be allowed for eleven days apiece two shillings per each day apiece and that the said John Godfrey discharge the costs of the trial to the treasurer of the country and stand committed till he perform this order and then to be discharged. That this is a true copy taken out of the court of assistants' records. Attests Edward Rawson, secretary.

REBECCA AND NATHANIEL GREENSMITH, HARTFORD, CONNECTICUT 1662

Salem was not the first widespread witchcraft panic in New England; an outbreak also occurred in Hartford, Connecticut, beginning in 1662, and stemmed in large part from disagreements over an inheritance. In Hartford, at least eight individuals were accused, and three, including Rebecca and Nathaniel Greensmith, were put to death. Rebecca was unusual in that she confessed to a number of witchcraft-related crimes, including having "familiarity with the Devil," and described attending witches' sabbaths in the woods alongside other accused Hartford townsfolk. Another intriguing aspect of the Hartford outbreak is its apparent reliance on the swimming test, in which suspected witches were bound and flung into water to test their guilt. It is probable that the two people subjected to the swimming test were the Greensmiths, though that has not been completely proven.[1]

John Whiting's Letter to Reverend Increase Mather[2]

These for the Reverend Mr. Increase Mather, teacher of a church in Boston.

An account of a remarkable passage of divine providence that happened in Hartford in the year of our Lord 1662.

The subject was Ann Cole (the daughter of John Cole, a godly man among us then, next neighbor to the man and woman that afterward suffered for witchcraft), who had for some time been afflicted and in some fears about her spiritual estate. Two of her brethren also were very lame, one of them so continuing to this day, his knee-joint of one leg having no motion, but otherwise well for many years. She hath been and is a person esteemed pious, behaving herself with a pleasant mixture of humility and faith under her heavy sufferings, professing (as she did sundry times) that she knew nothing of those things that were spoken by her, but that her tongue was improved to express what was never in her mind, which was matter of great affliction to her. Since the abatement of her sorrows she is joined to the church and therein has been a humble walker for many years. And since also married to a good man, hath born him several children, and in her constant way approved herself truly godly to the charity of all observers.

The matter is, that anno 1662 this Ann Cole (living in her father's family) was taken with strange fits, wherein she (or rather the Devil, as 'tis judged, making use of her lips) held a discourse for a considerable time. The general purport of it was to this purpose, that a company of familiars of the evil one (who were named in the discourse that passed from her) were contriving how to carry on their mischievous designs against some and especially against her, mentioning sundry ways they would take to that end, as that they would afflict her body, spoil her name, hinder her marriage, et cetera, wherein the general answer made among them was, she runs to her rock. This method having been continued some hours; the conclusion was, let us confound her language so she may tell no more tales. And then after some time of unintelligible muttering the discourse passed into a Dutch tone (a family of Dutch then living in the town) and therein an account was given of some afflictions that had befallen diverse, among the rest a young woman (next neighbor to that Dutch family) that could speak but very little (laboring of that infirmity from her youth), had met with great sorrow, as pinchings of her arms in the dark, et cetera, whereof she had before informed her brother (one of the ministers in Hartford). In that Dutch-toned discourse there were plain intimations given by whom and for what cause such a course had been taken with her. Judicious Mr. Stone[3] (who is now with God) being by, when this latter discourse passed, declared it in his thoughts impossible that one not familiarly acquainted with the Dutch (which Ann Cole had not

at all been) should so exactly imitate the Dutch tone in the pro-
nunciation of English. Sundry times such kind of discourse was
uttered by her, which was very awful and amazing to the hearers.
Mr. Samuel Hooker[4] was present the first time, and Mr. Joseph
Haynes,[5] who wrote what was said, so did the relator also, when
he came into the house sometime after the discourse began—
extremely violent bodily motions she many times had, even to the
hazard of her life in the apprehensions of those that saw them.
And very often great disturbance was given in the public worship of God by her and two other women who had also strange
fits. Once in special on a day of prayer kept on that account, the
motion and noise of the afflicted was so terrible that a godly person fainted under the appearance of it.

The consequent was that one of the persons presented as active
in the aforementioned discourse (a lewd, ignorant, considerably
aged woman)[6] being a prisoner upon suspicion of witchcraft, the
court sent for Mr. Haynes and myself to read what we had written;
which, when Mr. Haynes had done (the prisoner being present),
she forthwith and freely confessed those things to be true, that she
(and other persons named in the discourse) had familiarity with
the Devil. Being asked whether she had made an express covenant
with him, she answered she had not, only as she promised to go
with him when he called (which she had accordingly done sundry
times). But that the Devil told her that at Christmas they would
have a merry meeting, and then the covenant should be drawn and
subscribed. Thereupon the forementioned Mr. Stone (being then in
court) with much weight and earnestness laid forth the exceeding
heinousness and hazard of that dreadful sin, and therewith sol-
emnly took notice (upon the occasion given) of the Devil's loving
Christmas.[7]

A person at the same time present being desired, the next day
more particularly to inquire of her about her guilt, it was accordingly done, to whom she acknowledged that though when Mr.
Haynes began to read, she could have torn him in pieces, and
was as much resolved as might be to deny her guilt (as she had
done before), that after he had read awhile, she was as if her flesh
had been pulled from her bones (such was her expression) and so
could not deny any longer. She also declared that the Devil first
appeared to her in the form of a deer or fawn, skipping about
her, wherewith she was not much affrighted, but by degrees he

contrived to talk with her; and that their meetings were frequently at such a place (near her own house) that some of the company came in one shape, and some in another, and one in particular in the shape of a crow came flying to them.

Amongst other things she owned that the Devil had frequent use of her body with much seeming (but indeed horrible, hellish) delight to her.

This with the concurrent evidence, brought the woman and her husband to their death as the Devil's familiars, and most of the other persons mentioned in the discourse made their escape into another part of the country.

After this execution of some and escape of others, the good woman had abatement of her sorrows, which hath continued sundry years, and she that remains maintaining her integrity, walking therein with much humble comfort after her so sore and amazing affliction. The works of the Lord are great sought out of all them that have pleasure therein.

Reverend and dear sir, I had thought of sending the precedent account before now but I could not (nor that can) find my papers wherein I wrote what came from Ann Cole in her fits. However, I have gathered up the main sum and now send it. If you think fit to insert the whole or anything of it, not varying the substance, it is left with you.

There are some other remarkables I have some acquaintance with, wherein I have moved others that know them more fully to give an information: The Lord be with you, succeeding at your holy labors to his honor and the good of souls: Forget not yours sincerely in our dear Savior, John Whiting. Hartford, December 4, 1682.

Mather's Description of the Swim Test

There were some that had a mind to try whether the stories of witches not being able to sink under water were true; and accordingly a man and woman mentioned in Ann Cole's Dutch-tone discourse had their hands and feet tied, and so were cast into the water, and they both apparently swam after the manner of a buoy, part under, part above the water. A by-stander imagining that any person bound in that posture would be so born up, offered himself for trial, but being in the like matter gently laid on the water, he immediately sunk right down. This was no legal evidence against the suspected persons, nor were they proceeded against on any such account. However, doubting that a halter would choke them though the water would not, they very fairly took their flight, not having been seen in that part of the world since. Whether this experiment were lawful, or rather superstitious and magical, we shall enquire afterward.[8]

A TRYAL OF WITCHES, BURY ST. EDMUNDS, ENGLAND 1662

Bury St. Edmunds in England was the site of several witch trials in the last half of the seventeenth century. For an understanding of witch trials in North America, the Bury St. Edmunds cases serve two crucial functions. First, these trials created the template for English witch trials after the passage of King James I's Witchcraft Act of 1604, which reinforced the felonious—and more important, civil rather than ecclesiastical—nature of the invocation of evil spirits, and which replaced life imprisonment with death as the penalty, even when the ostensible magic did not itself result in a victim's death. Some historians have pointed to the 1604 statute as an example of English attitudes toward witchcraft assuming a more Continental flavor, in that they sought to punish all forms of magical intent without requiring a compact with the Devil for proof. They also reaffirm witchcraft as a legal problem, rather than a purely religious matter of heresy.[1]

The trials at Bury St. Edmunds, however, serve an extra purpose in that they directly inform the prosecution of the largest North American witch trial, held at Salem in 1692. The following publication, A Tryal of Witches, is referenced in both Cotton Mather's writings on witchcraft at Salem in Wonders of the Invisible World *(1693) and Reverend John Hale's account* A Modest Enquiry into the Nature of Witchcraft *(1702). Hale described the Salem judges turning to A Tryal of Witches for guidance on how to treat so-called spectral evidence. The structures of the Bury St. Edmunds and Salem trials*

*are remarkably similar, despite their being separated by
an ocean and a generation: in both cases, a small group
of middle-aged women is accused of bewitching a cadre
of mostly adolescent girls. Though the accused witches
had little in common, even coming from different class
backgrounds, they were all tried, found guilty, and
hanged. The admission of spectral evidence, or evidence
gleaned in a dream or vision, as legal evidence at Bury
St. Edmunds determined the conduct of witch trials in
North America thereafter.*[2]

A TRYAL OF WITCHES

At the assizes[3] and general jail delivery, held at Bury St. Edmonds for
the County of Suffolk, the tenth day of March, in the sixteenth year
of the reign of our sovereign lord, King Charles II, before Matthew
Hale, knight, lord chief baron of His Majesty's Court of Exche-
quer, Rose Cullender and Amy Duny, widows, both of Lethistoff,
in the county aforesaid, were severally indicted for bewitching
Elizabeth and Ann Durent, Jane Booking, Susan Chandler, William Durent, Elizabeth and Deborah Pacy. And the said Cullender
and Duny, being arraigned upon the said indictments, pleaded not
guilty. And afterward, upon a long evidence, were found guilty
and thereupon had judgment to die for the same.

The evidence whereupon these persons were convicted of witchcraft stands upon diverse particular circumstances.

1. Three of the parties above-named, namely, Ann Durent,
Susan Chandler, and Elizabeth Pacy, were brought to Bury to the
assizes and were in a reasonable good condition. But that morning they came into the hall to give instructions for the drawing
of their bills of indictments, the three persons fell into strange
and violent fits, screeching out in a most sad manner, so that they
could not in any wise give any instructions in the court who were
the cause of their distemper. And although they did after some
certain space recover out of their fits, that they were every one of
them struck dumb, so that none of them could speak neither at
that time nor during the assizes until the conviction of the supposed witches.

As concerning William Durent, being an infant, his mother,

Dorothy Durent, sworn and examined, deposed in open court that about the tenth of March, *Nono Caroli Secundi*,[4] she, having a special occasion to go from home, and having none in her house to take care of her said child (it then sucking) desired Amy Duny, her neighbor, to look to her child during her absence, for which she promised her to give her a penny. But the said Dorothy Durent desired the said Amy not to suckle her child and laid a great charge upon her not to do it. Upon which it was asked by the court, why she did give that direction, she being an old woman and not capable of giving suck? It was answered by the said Dorothy Durent that she very well knew that she did not give suck,[5] but that for some years before, she had gone under the reputation of a witch, which was one cause made her give her the caution. Another was that it was customary with old women that if they did look after a sucking child, and nothing would please it but the breast, they did use to please the child to give it the breast, and it did please the child, but it sucked nothing but wind, which did the child hurt. Nevertheless, after the departure of this deponent, the said Amy did suckle the child. And after the return of the said Dorothy, the said Amy did acquaint her that she had given suck to the child, contrary to her command. Whereupon, the deponent was very angry with the said Amy for the same, at which the said Amy was much discontented, and used many high expressions and threatening speeches toward her, telling her that she had as good to have done otherwise than to have found fault with her and so departed out of her house. And that very night her son fell into strange fits of swounding,[6] and was held in such terrible manner, that she was much affrighted therewith, and so continued for diverse weeks. And the said examinant further said that she being exceedingly troubled at her child's distemper, did go to a certain person named Doctor Jacob, who lived at Yarmouth, who had the reputation in the country to help children that were bewitched,[7] who advised her to hang up the child's blanket in the chimney corner all day, and at night when she put the child to bed, to put it into the said blanket, and if she found anything in it, she should not be afraid, but to throw it into the fire. And this deponent did according to his direction, and at night when she took down the blanket with an intent to put her child therein, there fell out of the same a great toad, which ran up and down the hearth, and she having a young youth only with her in the house, desired him to catch the toad, and throw it into the fire, which the youth did accordingly, and held it there with the tongs, and as soon as it was in the fire it made a great and horrible noise, and after a space there was a flashing in the fire like gunpowder, making a noise like the discharge of a pistol, and thereupon the toad was no more seen nor heard. It was asked by the court, if that after the noise and flashing, there was not the substance of the toad to be seen to consume in the fire? And it was answered by the said Dorothy Durent that after the flashing and noise, there was no more seen than if there had been none there. The next day there came a young woman, a kinswoman of the said Amy and a neighbor of this deponent, and told this deponent, that her aunt (meaning the said Amy) was in a most lamentable condition, having her face all scorched with fire,[8] and that she was sitting alone in her house in her smock without any fire. And thereupon this deponent went into the house of the said Amy Duny to see her, and found her in the same condition as was related to her; for her face, her legs, and thighs, which this deponent saw, seemed very much scorched and burnt with fire, at which this deponent seemed much to wonder. And asked the said Amy how she came into that sad condition? And the said Amy replied, she might thank her for it, for that she this deponent was the cause thereof, but that she should live to see some of her children dead, and she upon crutches. And this deponent further saith, that after the burning of the said toad, her child recovered, and was well again, and was living at the time of the assizes.

And this deponent further saith that about the 6th of March, 11 Charles 2, her daughter Elizabeth Durent, being about the age of ten years, was taken in like manner as her first child was, and in her fits complained much of Amy Duny, and said that she did appear to her and afflict her in such manner as the former. And she, this deponent, going to the apothecaries for something for her said child, when she did return to her own house, she found the said Amy Duny there and asked her what she did do there? And her answer was that she came to see her child and to give it some water. But she, this deponent, was very angry with her and thrust her forth of her doors, and when she was out of doors, she said, You need not be so angry, for your child will not live long. And this was on a Saturday and the child died on the Monday following.[9] The cause of whose death this deponent verily believeth was occasioned by the witchcraft of the said Amy Duny. For that the said Amy hath been long reputed to be a witch, and a person of very evil behavior, whose kindred and relations have been many of them accused for witchcraft, and some of them have been condemned.

The said deponent further saith that not long after the death of her daughter Elizabeth Durent, she, this deponent, was taken with a lameness in both her legs, from the knees downward, that she was fain to go upon crutches, and that she had no other use of them but only to bear a little upon them till she did remove her crutches, and so continued till the time of the assizes, that the witch came to be tried, and was there upon her crutches. The court asked her that at the time she was taken with this lameness, if it were with her according to the custom of women.[10] Her answer was that it was so, and that she never had any stoppages of those things, but when she was with child.

This is the substance of her evidence to this indictment.

There was one thing very remarkable, that after she had gone upon crutches for upward of three years, and went upon them at the time of the assizes in the court when she gave her evidence, and upon the juries bringing in their verdict, by which the said Amy Duny was found guilty, to the great admiration of all persons, the said Dorothy Durent was restored to the use of her limbs, and went home without making use of her crutches.

2. As concerning Elizabeth and Deborah Pacy, the first of the age of eleven years, the other of the age of nine years or thereabouts, as to the elder, she was brought into the court at the time of the instructions given to draw up the indictments, and afterward at the time of trial of the said prisoners, but could not speak one word all the time, and for the most part she remained as one wholly senseless as one in a deep sleep and could move no part of her body, and all the motion of life that appeared in her was that as she lay upon cushions in the court upon her back, her stomach and belly by the drawing of her breath would arise to a great height. And after the said Elizabeth had lain a long time on the table in the court, she came a little to herself and sat up but could neither see nor speak but was sensible of what was said to her. And after a while she laid her head on the bar of the court with a cushion under it and her hand and her apron upon that, and there she lay a good space of time. And by the direction of the judge, Amy Duny was privately brought to Elizabeth Pacy, and

she touched her hand;[11] whereupon the child without so much as seeing her, for her eyes were closed all the while, suddenly leaped up, and catched Amy Duny by the hand, and afterward by the face; and with her nails scratched her till blood came, and would by no means leave her till she was taken from her, and afterward the child would still be pressing toward her and making signs of anger conceived against her.

Deborah, the younger daughter, was held in such extreme manner that her parents wholly despaired of her life, and therefore could not bring her to the assizes.

The evidence which was given concerning these two children was to this effect.

Samuel Pacy, a merchant of Lethistoff aforesaid (a man who carried himself with much soberness during the trial, from whom proceeded no words either of passion or malice, though his children were so greatly afflicted), sworn and examined, deposeth that his younger daughter, Deborah, upon Thursday the tenth of October last, was suddenly taken with a lameness in her legs so that she could not stand, neither had she any strength in her limbs to support her, and so she continued until the seventeenth day of the same month, which day being fair and sunshiny, the Child desired to be carried on the east part of the house, to be set upon the bank which looketh upon the sea, and whilst she was sitting there, Amy Duny came to this deponent's house to buy some herrings, but being denied she went away discontented, and presently returned again and was denied, and likewise the third time and was denied as at first, and at her last going away, she went away grumbling,[12] but what she said was not perfectly understood. But at the very same instant of time, the said child was taken with most violent fits, feeling most extreme pain in her stomach, like the pricking of pins, and shrieking out in a most dreadful manner, like unto a whelp,[13] and not like unto a sensible creature. And in this extremity the child continued to the great grief of the parents until the thirtieth of the same month. During this time this deponent sent for one Dr. Feavor, a doctor of physick,[14] to take his advice concerning his child's distemper. The doctor being come, he saw the child in those fits but could not conjecture (as he then told this deponent, and afterward affirmed in open court at this trial) what might be the cause of the child's affliction. And this deponent further saith that by reason of the circumstances aforesaid, and in regard Amy Duny is a woman of an ill fame, and commonly reported to be a witch and a sorceress, and for that the said child in her fits would cry out of Amy Duny as the cause of her malady, and that she did affright her with apparitions of her person (as the child in the intervals of her fits related) he, this deponent, did suspect the said Amy Duny for a witch, and charged her with the injury and wrong to his child, and caused her to be set in the stocks on the twenty-eighth of the same October, and during the time of her continuance there, one Alice Letteridge and Jane Buxton demanding of her (as they also affirmed in court upon their oaths) what should be the reason of Mr. Pacy's child's distemper, telling her that she was suspected to be the cause thereof; she replied, Mr. Pacy keeps a great stir about his child, but let him stay until he hath done as much by his children as I have done by mine. And being further examined, what she had done to her children, she answered that she had been fain to open her child's mouth with a tap to give it victuals.

And the said deponent further deposeth that within two days after speaking of the said words, being the thirtieth of October, the eldest daughter, Elizabeth, fell into extreme fits, insomuch that they could not open her mouth to give her breath to preserve her life without the help of a tap which they were enforced to use, and the younger child was in the like manner afflicted, so that they used the same also for her relief.

And further the said children being grievously afflicted would severally complain in their extremity, and also in the intervals, that Amy Duny (together with one other woman whose person and clothes they described) did thus afflict them, their apparitions appearing before them to their great terror and affrightment. And sometimes they would cry out, saying, There stands Amy Duny, and there Rose Cullender, the other person troubling them.[15]

Their fits were various. Sometimes they would be lame on one side of their bodies, sometimes on the other. Sometimes a soreness over their whole bodies, so as they could endure none to touch them. At other times they would be restored to the perfect use of their limbs and deprived of their hearing, at other times of their sight, at other times of their speech sometimes by the space of one day, sometimes for two. And once they were wholly deprived of their speech for eight days together, and then restored to their speech again. At other times they would fall into swoundings, and upon the recovery to their speech they would cough extremely and bring up much phlegm, and with the same crooked pins, and one time a two-penny nail with a very broad head, which pins (amounting to forty or more), together with the two-penny nail were produced in court, with the affirmation of the said deponent that he was present when the said nail was vomited up,[16] and also most of the pins. Commonly at the end of every fit they would cast up a pin, and sometimes they would have four or five fits in one day.

In this manner the said children continued with this deponent for the space of two months, during which time in their intervals this deponent would cause them to read some chapters in the New Testament. Whereupon this deponent several times observed that they would read till they came to the name of Lord or Jesus or Christ; and then before they could pronounce either of the said words, they would suddenly fall into their fits. But when they came to the name of Satan, or Devil, they would clap their fingers upon the book, crying out, This bites, but makes me speak right well.

At such time as they be recovered out of their fits (occasioned as this deponent conceives upon their naming of Lord or Jesus or Christ), this deponent hath demanded of them, what is the cause they cannot pronounce those words. They reply and say that Amy Duny saith I must not use that name.

And further, the said children after their fits were past would tell how that Amy Duny and Rose Cullender would appear before them, holding their fists at them, threatening that if they related either what they saw or heard that they would torment them ten times more than ever they did before.

In their fits they would cry out, There stands Amy Duny, or Rose Cullender, and sometimes in one place and sometimes in another, running with great violence to the place where they fancied them to stand, striking at them as if they were present. They would appear to them sometimes spinning and sometimes reeling, or in other postures, deriding or threatening them.[17]

KATHERINE HARRISON, WEYERSFIELD, CONNECTICUT, AND WESTCHESTER, NEW YORK 1669

Katherine Harrison combines elements of both typical and atypical witch cases in North America. She was unusual in that her trial occurred outside of Massachusetts. However, in other respects Katherine Harrison typified the accused witch of the time. Her encounters in her community were marked by conflict, including litigious relationships with her neighbors.[1] In the testimony below, Katherine Harrison speaks in her own defense, offering a point by point rebuttal of all the various complaints lodged against her. She even describes her neighbors' vandalizing her property and livestock in revenge for her reputed witchery. Harrison had also been made vulnerable by the death of her husband, which left her to work her land and raise her children alone. Perhaps because the heritage of witch trials is thinner in Connecticut than Massachusetts, though found guilty, Katherine Harrison was spared execution provided she left Weyersfield, never to return.

Testimonies Against Katherine Harrison[2]

These objections I humbly present against these testimonies following.

To Joan Francis's testimony, Goodwife Harrison denies it and saith that her child by her own acknowledgment died of a pleurisy[3] and that she is prejudiced with her by reason of her denying to let her have goods of her.[4] To Mrs. Wickham's testimony she saith that her testimony is false and that her, the said Wickham's, putting of a child to nurse to her, since the time she saw the apparition she mentions in her testimony will evidence that she did not see any such apparition as should make her have suspicion that I was guilty of witchcraft. To Goodwife Johnson's testimony, she saith that she is greatly prejudiced with her, the said Harrison, and that she and her husband were good friends and help to them, and besides, she saith her testimony doth not carry the face of truth with it, especially in that particular that when she covered her face with the sheet she saw them better. To Goodwife Garret's testimony, I desire the peremptory expressions used in that testimony may be considered and compared with the said Garret's acknowledgment before the governor and Captain Talcott and then she hopes that there will appear no weight nor much verity in that testimony. To Sarah Deming's testimony, I acknowledge that I had discourse with her about the salt seller mentioned (but never threatened her), but as to the apparitions she mentions I know not what they mean, and the woman being since departed, I shall spare speaking what otherwise I would. To her second testimony, I do not know that it concerns me and therefore leave it.

To Michael Griswold and his wife's testimony, this I must say, that their earnest prosecution of me at court and receiving more than twenty pounds of my estate for a slander, when I tendered to make as public satisfaction as the rule required or they could desire, to me evidenceth great prejudice, and that loving[5] commerce that was between them and us after the death of the child and their inviting my husband myself and children to the child's burial may evidence to all that hear it that they then had no such thoughts of me, as now they have but upon what account, I know not and I do not know of any truth that is in their tests.[6]

To Mary Haile's testimony, I say there is no truth in it so far as I am mentioned in it, and I desire it may be considered how any person can affirm (that by a small firelight) they can clearly and distinctly know my head on a dog.[7] I know not the meaning of those things. Besides, I cannot but look at it as an accusation against me and I do not know that I ever was in that house but once and that was when I went to demand a debt due to me from Mrs. Dolman.

To Brace's testimony I must say it is false and that it was neither taken before my face and so not legal. In such a case as mine, and whereas he saith he saw a calf's head on the cart, I conclude it a lie. Possible he might see or hear of a pig's head on the cart, for we brought a pig out of the meadow upon a cart load of corn or hay about that time.

To Elizabeth Smith's testimony, I know nothing of truth in what she speaks of me. Besides, if it be considered what Mr. Mygatt testified in court, namely, that the reason why my master could not keep me was by reason of some disagreement between me and the widow that was then Captain Cullick's servant, and upon that account, I went from him. Besides, Captain Cullick's coming to visit me at Weyersfield doth speak that he did not so judge of me as she speaks.

The same answer may serve for Thomas Whaple's testimony with this addition that the latter part of his testimony referring to Goody Greensmith, I know nothing of it.

To William Warren's testimony, I must say I know nothing of it, only I desire it may be considered whither William Warren's memory may not fail him in seventeen years, he being so young a lad then.[8]

To Mr. Treat's testimony, she saith that it is a real mistake and she is abused thereby, for it was not that day that Catlin came for me but the next day. That day that Mr. Treat was with me, my daughter was with me, but when Catlin came for me I was alone.

To Phillip Goff's testimony, I know nothing of it, only indeed there was a falling out between us by reason of some slanders he had reported or raised of me and my husband about a horse.

To Richard Mountain and his daughter's testimony, I can say I know nothing of truth in it, besides they were not taken before me, and I have to object against them, if they were present.

POSSESSION OF ELIZABETH KNAPP, GROTON, MASSACHUSETTS 1671–1672

Elizabeth Knapp was a teenage servant in the house-hold of Reverend Samuel Willard. In October 1671 she abruptly began to experience extreme physical fits, which soon blossomed into a full-on demonic posses-sion. Knapp's possession anticipates the later Salem panic in several respects, most notably in that the strange behaviors manifested in an adolescent female servant in a respected Puritan religious leader's household. Wil-lard approached Knapp's possession with scientific interest, writing a detailed account of her experiences. Willard described the possession in lengthy letters to Cotton Mather, who would go on to publish the episode as part of his Magnalia Christi Americana *(1702). An account of Knapp's possession also appeared in Increase Mather's* An Essay for the Recording of Illustrious Provi-dences *(1684).*

Explanations for Knapp's behavior differ, particularly as her case does not result in accusations of witchcraft against other women in her community. In effect, she is a bewitched victim without a witch. However, like the adolescent girls in Salem a generation later, Knapp lived in a rigidly hierarchical society divided along strict lines of class and gender. With the onset of her symp-toms, Knapp enjoyed a newfound ease from her labors, together with the rapt attention and sympathy of every-one in her surrounding community. Even without resorting to psychoanalytic arguments about the specific

pathology of Knapp's frame of mind or personality, a
case can be made for the religious expression of extreme
distress that could not be legitimately expressed in any
other avenue, particularly concerning her general dis-
content with her labor and the state of her life.[1]

As a well-known and infamous case, the Knapp pos-
session influenced how the Salem girls were understood
a generation later. Her possession did not become a legal
problem because there were no accusations made of
witchcraft. In the case of her possession the Devil did
not act through a witch.[2]

Willard's Account of Knapp's Possession

A brief account of a strange and unusual providence
of God befallen to Elizabeth Knapp of Groton by me,
Samuel Willard.

This poor and miserable object, about a fortnight before she was
taken, we observed to carry herself in a strange and unwonted
manner. Sometimes she would give sudden shrieks, and if we
enquired a reason, would always put it off with some excuse and
then would burst forth into immoderate and extravagant laugh-
ter, in such wise as sometimes she fell onto the ground with it. I
myself observed oftentimes a strange change in her countenance
but could not suspect the true reason but conceived she might
be ill and therefore diverse times enquired how she did, and she
always answered well, which made me wonder. But the tragedy
began to unfold itself upon Monday, October 30, 1671, after this
manner (as I received by credible information, being that day
myself gone from home).

In the evening, a little before she went to bed, sitting by the
fire, she cried out, "Oh, my legs!" and clapped her hand on them
immediately. "Oh, my breast!" and removed her hands thither.
And forthwith, "Oh, I am strangled," and put her hands on her
throat. Those that observed her could not see what to make of
it, whether she was in earnest or dissembled and in this manner they left her (excepting the person that lay with her)[3] complaining of her breath being stopped. The next day she was in a
strange frame (as was observed by diverse), sometimes weeping,

sometimes laughing, and many foolish and apish gestures. In the evening, going into the cellar, she shrieked suddenly, and being enquired of the cause, she answered, that she saw two persons in the cellar, whereupon some went down with her to search but found none, she also looking with them. At last she turned her head and looking one way steadfastly, used the expression "What cheer, old man?" Which, they that were with her took for a fancy, and so ceased. Afterward (the same evening), the rest of the family being in bed, she was (as one lying in the room saw, and she herself also afterward related) suddenly thrown down into the midst of the floor with violence and taken with a violent fit, whereupon the whole family was raised, and with much ado was she kept out of the fire from destroying herself after which time she was followed with fits from thence till the Sabbath day, in which she was violent in bodily motions, leapings, strainings, and strange agitations, scarce to be held in bounds by the strength of 3 or 4. Violent also in roarings and screamings, representing a dark resemblance of hellish torments and frequently using in these fits diverse words, sometimes crying out, "Money, money"; sometimes "Sin and misery" with other words.

On Wednesday, being in the time of intermission questioned about the case she was in, with reference to the cause or occasion of it, she seemed to impeach one of the neighbors, a person (I doubt not) of sincere uprightness before God, as though either she or the Devil in her likeness and habit, particularly her riding hood,[4] had come down the chimney, stricken her that night she was first taken violently, which was the occasion of her being cast into the floor. Whereupon those about her sent to request the person to come to her, who coming unwittingly, was at the first assaulted by her strangely, for though her eyes were (as it were) sealed up (as they were always, or for the most part, in those fits, and so continue in them all to this day), she that knew her very touch from any other, though no voice were uttered, and discovered it evidently by her gestures, so powerful were Satan's suggestions in her, that afterward God was pleased to vindicate the case and justify the innocent, even to remove jealousies from the spirits of the party concerned and satisfaction of the bystanders. For after she had gone to prayer with her, she confessed that she believed Satan had deluded her and hath never since complained of any such apparition or disturbance from the person. These fits continuing (though with intermission), diverse (when they had opportunity) pressed upon her to declare what might be the true and real occasion of these amazing fits. She used many tergiversations[5] and excuses, pretending she would to this and that young person, who coming, she put it off to another, till at the last, on Thursday night, she brake forth into a large confession in the presence of many, the substance whereof amounted to this much.

That the Devil had oftentimes appeared to her, presenting the treaty of a covenant, and preferring largely to her, namely, such things as suited her youthful fancy, money, silks, fine clothes, ease from labor, to show her the whole world,[6] et cetera. That it had been then 3 years since his first appearance, occasioned by her discontent. That at first his apparitions had been more rare but lately more frequent. That those few weeks that she had dwelt with us almost constant. That she seldom went out of one room into another, but he appeared to her, urging of her. And that he had presented her a book written with blood of covenants made by others with him and told her such and such (of some whereof we hope better things) had a name there. That he urged upon her constant temptations to murder her parents, her neighbors, our children, especially the youngest, tempting her to throw it into the fire, on the hearth, into the oven, and that once he put a bill hook into her hand to murder myself, persuading her I was asleep, but coming about it, she met me on the stairs at which she was affrighted. The time I remember well and observed a strange frame in her countenance and saw she endeavored to hide something, but I knew not what, neither did I at all suspect any such matter, and that often he persuaded her to make away with herself and once she was going to drown herself in the well, for, looking into it, she saw such sights as allured her,[7] and was gotten within the curb and was by God's providence prevented. Many other like things she related, too tedious to recollect. But being pressed to declare whether she had not consented to a covenant with the Devil, she with solemn assertions denied it. She asserted that she had never so much as consented to discourse with him, nor had ever but once before that night used the expression "What cheer, old man?" And this argument she used, that the providence of God had ordered it so, that all his apparitions had been frightful to her. That this she acknowledged, which seemed contradictory, namely, that when she came to our house to school, before such time as she dwelt with us, she delayed her going home in the evening till it was dark (which we observed), upon his persuasion to have his company home, and that she could not, when he appeared, but go to him. One evident testimony whereof we can say something to, namely, the night before the Thanksgiving, October 19, she was with another maid that boarded in the house, where both of them saw the appearance of a man's head and shoulders, with a great white neck cloth, looking in at the window, at which they came up affrighted both into the chamber where the rest of us were. They declaring the case, one of us went down to see who it might be, but she ran immediately out of the door before him, which she hath since confessed was the Devil coming to her. She also acknowledged the reason of her former sudden shriekings was from a sudden apparition, and that the Devil put these excuses into her mouth and bid her so to say and hurried her into those violent (but she saith feigned and forced) laughters. She then also complained against herself of many sins, disobedience to parents, neglect of attendance upon ordinances, attempts to murder herself and others. But this particular of a covenant she utterly disclaimed, which relation seemed fair, especially in that it was attended with bitter tears, self-condemnations, good counsels given to all about her, especially the youth then present, and an earnest desire of prayers. She sent to Lancaster for Mr. Rowlandson, who came and prayed with her and gave her serious counsels. But she was still followed, all this notwithstanding, with these fits. And in this state (coming home on Friday) I found her; but could get nothing from her. Whenever I came in her presence she fell into those fits. Concerning which fits, I find this noteworthy: she knew and understood what was spoken to her but could not answer nor use any other words but the forementioned money, et cetera as long as the fit continued. For when she came out of it, she could give a relation of all that had been spoken to her. She was demanded a reason why she used those words in her fits and signified that the Devil presented her with such things to tempt her, and with sin and misery to terrify her. She also declared that she had seen the devils in their hellish shapes, and more devils than anyone there ever saw men in the world. Many of these things I heard her declare on Saturday at night.

On the Sabbath the physician came, who judged a main point

of her distemper to be natural, arising from the foulness of her stomach and corruptness of her blood, occasioning fumes in her brain and strange fancies. Whereupon (in order to further trial and administration), she was removed home, and the succeeding week she took physick and was not in such violence handled in her fits as before, but enjoyed an intermission and gave some hopes of recovery, in which intermission she was altogether senseless (as to our discovery) of her state, held under security and hardness of heart, professing she had no trouble upon her spirits, she cried Satan had left her. A solemn day was kept with her,[8] that it had then (as I apprehend) little efficacy upon her. She that day again expressed hopes that the Devil had left her, but there was little ground to think so because she remained under such extreme senselessness of her own estate. And thus she continued being exercised with some moderate fits, in which she used none of the former expressions but sometimes fainted away, sometimes used some strugglings, that not with extremity, till the Wednesday following, which day was spent in prayer with her. When her fits something more increased, and her tongue was for many hours together drawn into a semicircle up to the roof of her mouth, and not to be removed, for some tried with the fingers to do it, from thence till the Sabbath seven nights following, she continued alike, only she added to former confessions of her twice consenting to travel with the Devil in her company between Groton and Lancaster, who accompanied her in form of a black dog with eyes in his back, sometimes stopping her horse, sometimes leaping up behind, and keeping her (when she came home with company) 40 rod at least behind, leading her out of the way into a swamp, et cetera. But still no conference would she own, but urged that the Devil's quarrel with her was because she would not seal a covenant with him, and that this was the ground of her first being taken. Besides this nothing observable came from her, only one morning she said, God is a father, the next morning, God is my father, which words (it is to be feared) were words of presumption put into her mouth by the adversary.[9]

I, suspecting the truth of her former story, pressed whether she never verbally promised to covenant with him, which she stoutly denied. Only acknowledged that she had had some thoughts so to do. But on the forenamed November 26 she was again with violence and extremity seized by her fits, in such wise that 6 persons could hardly hold her, but she leaped and skipped about the house perforce roaring and yelling extremely and fetching deadly sighs, as if her heartstrings would have broken and looking with a frightful aspect to the amazement and astonishment of all the beholders, of which I was an eyewitness. The physician being then again with her consented that the distemper was diabolical, refused further to administer, advised to extraordinary fasting, whereupon some of God's ministers were sent for. She meanwhile continued extremely tormented night and day, till Tuesday about noon, having this added on Monday and Tuesday morning that she barked like a dog and bleated like a calf, in which her organs were visibly made use of. Yea (as was carefully observed), on Monday night and Tuesday morning, whenever any came near the house, though they within heard nothing at all, that would she bark till they were come into the house. On Tuesday, about 12 of the clock, she came out of the fit, which had held her from Sabbath day about the same time, at least 48 hours, with little or no intermission, and then her speech was restored to her, and she expressed a great seeming sense of her state. Many bitter tears, sighings, sobbings, complainings she uttered, bewailing of many sins fore mentioned, begging prayers, and in the hour of prayer expressing much affection. I then pressed if there were anything behind in reference to the dealings between her and Satan, when she again professed that she had related all and declared that in those fits the Devil had assaulted her many ways, that he came down the chimney, and she essayed to escape him, but was seized upon by him, that he sat upon her breast and used many arguments with her and that he urged her at one time with persuasions and promises of ease and great matters, told her that she had done enough in what she had already confessed, she might henceforth serve him more securely. Anon told her her time was past and there was no hope unless she would serve him. And it was observed in the time of her extremity, once when a little moment's respite was granted her of speech, she advised us to make our peace with God, and use our time better then she had done. The party advised her also to bethink herself of making her peace. She replied, "It is too late for me." The next day was solemnized, when we had the presence of Mr. Bulkley, Mr. Rowlandson, and Mr. Estabrooke, whither coming. We found her returned to a sottish and stupid kind of frame. Much was pressed upon her, but no affection at all discovered, though she was little or nothing exercised with any fits, and her speech also continued. Though a day or two after she was melancholy and being enquired of a reason, she complained that she was grieved that so much pains were taken with her and did her no good, but this held her not long. And thus she remained till Monday, when to some neighbors there present, she related something more of the converse with the Devil, namely, that it had been 5 years or thereabouts since she first saw him, and declared methodically the sundry apparitions from time to time, till she was thus dreadfully assaulted, in which, the principal was that after many assaults, she had resolved to seal a covenant with Satan, thinking she had better do it, than be thus followed by him, that once, when she lived at Lancaster, he presented himself and desired of her blood, and she would have done it, but wanted a knife. In the parley[10] she was prevented by the providence of God interposing my father. A 2nd time in the house he met her and presented her a knife, and as she was going about it, my father stepped in again and prevented, that when she sought and enquired for the knife, it was not to be found, and that afterward she saw it sticking in the top of the barn, and some other like passages. She again owned an observable passage which she also had confessed in her first declaration, but is not there inserted, namely, that the Devil had often proffered her his service, but she accepted not, and once in ptic[?] to bring her in chips for the fire. She refused but when she came in she saw them lie by the fireside and was afraid, and this I remark, I sitting by the fire spake to her to lay them on, and she turned away in an unwonted manner. She then also declared against herself her unprofitable life she had led, and how justly God had thus permitted Satan to handle her, telling them they little knew what a sad case she was in. I after asked her concerning these passages, and she owned the truth of them and declared that now she hoped the Devil had left her, but being pressed whether there were not a covenant, she earnestly professed that by God's goodness she had been prevented from doing that, which she of herself had been ready enough to assent to and she thanked God there was no such thing.

The same day she was again taken with a new kind of unwonted fit in which after she had been awhile exercised with violence. She got her a stick and went up and down, thrusting and pushing here and there,[11] and anon looking out at a window, and cried out of a witch appearing in a strange manner in form of a dog downward with a woman's head, and declared the person, other whiles that she appeared in her whole likeness, and described her shape and habit, signified that she went up the chimney and went her way. What impression we read in the clay of the chimney, in similitude of a dog's paw, by the operation of Satan and in the form of a dog's going in the same place she told of, I shall not conclude, though something there was, as I myself saw in the chimney in the same place where she declared the foot was set to go up.

In this manner was she handled that night and the 2 next days, using strange gestures, complaining by signs when she could not speak, explaining that she was sometimes in the chamber, sometimes in the chimney, and anon assaults her, sometimes scratching her breast, beating her sides, strangling her throat, and she did oftentimes seemed to our apprehension as if she would forthwith be strangled. She declared that if the party were apprehended she should forthwith be well, but never till then. Whereupon her father went and procured the coming of the woman impeached by her, who came down to her on Thursday night, where (being desired to be present) I observed that she was violently handled and lamentably tormented by the adversary, and uttered unusual shrieks at the instant of the person's coming in, though her eyes were fast closed. But having experience of such former actings, we made nothing of it, but waited the issue. God therefore was sought to, to signify something whereby the innocent might be acquitted or the guilty discovered,[12] and he answered our prayers, for by 2 evident and clear mistakes she was cleared, and then all prejudices ceased, and she never more to this day hath impeached her of any apparition. In the fore mentioned allegation of the person, she also signified that sometimes the Devil also in the likeness of a little boy appeared together with the person. Friday was a sad day with her, for she was sorely handled with fits, which some perceiving, pressed that there was something that behind not discovered by her, and she, after a violent fit, holding her between 2 and 3 hours did first to one and afterward to many acknowledge that she had given of her blood to the Devil and made a covenant with him, whereupon I was sent for to her, and understanding how things had passed, I found that there was no room for privacy, in another already made by her so public. I therefore examined her concerning the matter and found her not so forward to confess as she had been to others, that this much I gathered from her confession.

That after she came to dwell with us, one day as she was alone in a lower room, all the rest of us being in the chamber, she looked out at the window and saw the Devil in the habit of an old man coming over a great meadow lying near the house, and suspecting his design, she had thoughts to have gone away, that at length resolved to tarry it out and hear what he had to say to her. When he came he demanded of her some of her blood, which she forthwith consented to, and with a knife cut her finger. He caught the blood in his hand and then told her she must write her name in his book. She answered she could not write, but he told her he would direct her hand and then took a little sharpened stick and dipped in the blood and put it into her hand and guided it, and she wrote her name with his help. What was the matter she set her hand to, I could not learn from her; but thus much she confessed, that the term of time agreed upon with him was for 7 years. One year she was to be faithful in his service, and then the other six he would serve her and make her a witch. She also related that the ground of contest between her and the Devil, which was the occasion of this sad providence, was this: that after her covenant made, the Devil showed her hell and the damned and told her if she were not faithful to him, she should go thither and be tormented there. She desired of him to show her heaven, but he told her that heaven was an ugly place and that none went thither but a company of base rogues whom he hated. But if she would obey him, it should be well with her. But afterward she considered with herself that the term of her covenant was but short and would soon be at an end and she doubted (for all the Devil's promises) she must at last come to the place he had shown her. And withal, feared if she were a witch, she should be discovered and brought to a shameful end, which was many times a trouble on her spirits. This the Devil perceiving, urged upon her to give him more of her blood and set her hand again to his book, which she refused to do, but partly through promises, partly by threatenings, he brought her at last to a promise that she would sometime do it. After which he left not incessantly to urge her to the performance of it. Once he met her on the stairs and often elsewhere, pressing her with vehemence, but she still put it off, till the first night she was taken when the Devil came to her and told her he would not tarry any longer. She told him she would not do it. He answered she had done it already and what further damage would it be to do it again, for she was his sure enough. She rejoined she had done it already and if she were his sure enough, what need he to desire any more of her. Whereupon he struck her the first night, again more violently the 2nd as is above expressed.

This is the sum of the relation I then had from her, which at that time seemed to be methodical. These things she uttered with great affection, overflowing of tears, and seeming bitterness. I asked of the reason of her weeping and bitterness. She complained of her sins and some in particular, profanation of the Sabbath, et cetera, but nothing of this sin of renouncing the government of God and giving herself up to the Devil. I therefore (as God helped) applied it to her and asked her whether she desired not prayers with and for her. She assented with earnestness and in prayer seemed to bewail the sin as God helped, then in the aggravation of it and afterward declared a desire to rely on the power and mercy of God in Christ. She then also declared that the Devil had deceived her concerning those persons impeached by her, that he had in their likeness or resemblance tormented her, persuading her that it was they, that they bore her a spleen, but he loved her and would free her from them and pressed on her to endeavor to bring them forth to the censure of the law.

In this case I left her but (not being satisfied in some things) I promised to visit her again the next day, which accordingly I did, but coming to her, I found her (though her speech still remained) in a case sad enough, her tears dried up and senses stupefied, and (as was observed) when I could get nothing from her and therefore applied myself in counsel to her, she regarded it not, but fixed her eye steadfastly upon a place, as she was wont when the Devil presented himself to her, which was a grief to her parents, and brought me to a stand. In the condition I left her.

The next day, being the Sabbath, whether upon any hint given her or any advantage Satan took by it upon her, she sent for me in haste at noon. Coming to her, she immediately with tears told me that she had belied the Devil in saying she had given him of her blood, et cetera. Professed that the most of the apparitions she had spoken of were but fancies, as images represented in a dream, earnestly entreated me to believe her, called God to witness to her assertion. I told her I would willingly hope the best and believe what I had any good grounds to apprehend. If therefore she would tell a more methodical relation than the former, it would be well, but if otherwise, she must be content that everyone should censure according to their apprehension. She promised so to do and expressed a desire that all that would might hear her, that as they had heard so many lies and untruths, they might now hear the truth, and engaged that in the evening she would do it. I then repaired to her, and diverse more then went. She then declared this much, that the Devil had sometimes appeared to her, that the occasion of it was her discontent, that her condition displeased her, her labor was burdensome to her, she was neither content to be at home nor abroad and had oftentimes strong persuasions to practice in witchcraft, had often wished the Devil would come to her at such and such times and resolved that if he would, she would give herself up to him soul and body. But (though he had oft times appeared to her) at such times he had not discovered himself, and therefore she had been preserved from such a thing. I declared a suspicion of the truth of the relation and gave her some reasons. But by reason of the company did not say much, neither could anything further be gotten from her. But the next day I went to her and opened my mind to her alone and left it with her declared (among other things) that she had used preposterous courses and therefore it was no marvel that she had been led into such contradictions and tendered her all the help I could, if she would make use of me and more privately relate any weighty and serious case of conscience to me. She promised me she would if she knew anything but said that then she knew nothing at all but stood to the story she had told the foregoing evening. And indeed what to make of these things I at present know not, but am waiting till God (if he see meet) wind up the story and make a more clear discovery.

It was not many days ere she was hurried again into violent fits after a different manner, being taken again speechless and using all endeavors to make away with herself and do mischief unto others, striking those that held her, spitting in their faces. And if at any time she had done any harm or frightened them, she would laugh immediately, which fits held her sometimes longer, sometimes shorter. Few occasions she had of speech, but when she could speak, she complained of a hard heart, counseled some to beware of sin, for that had brought her to this, bewailed that so many prayers had been put up for her and she still so hard hearted, and no more good wrought upon her. But being asked whether she were willing to repent, shaked her head and said nothing. Thus she continued till the next Sabbath in the afternoon, on which day in the morning, being something better than at other times, she had but little company tarried with her in the afternoon, when the Devil began to make more full discovery of himself.

It had been a question before whether she might properly be called a demoniac, or person possessed of the Devil, but it was then put out of question. He began (as the persons with her testify) by drawing her tongue out of her mouth most frightfully to an extraordinary length and greatness, and many amazing postures of her body, and then by speaking vocally in her, whereupon her father and another neighbor were called from the meeting, on whom (as soon as they came in) he railed, calling them rogues, charging them for folly in going to hear a black rogue who told them nothing but a parcel of lies and deceived them, and many like expressions. After exercise I was called, but understood not the occasion till I came and heard the same voice, a grim, low, that audible voice it was. The first salutation I had was, "Oh! You are a great rogue." I was at the first something daunted and amazed and many reluctances I had upon my spirits, which brought me to a silence and amazement in my spirits, till at last God heard my groans and gave me both refreshment in Christ and courage. I then called for a light to see whether it might not appear a counterfeit and observed not any of her organs to move. The voice was hollow, as if it issued out of her throat. He then again called me great black rogue. I challenged him to make it appear, but all the answer was, you tell the people a company of lies. I reflected on myself and could not but magnify the goodness of God not to suffer Satan to bespatter the names of his people with those sins which he himself hath pardoned in the blood of Christ.

I answered, "Satan, thou art a liar and a deceiver, and God will vindicate his own truth one day." He answered nothing directly but said, "I am not Satan. I am a pretty black boy. This is my pretty girl. I have been here a great while."[13] I sat still and answered nothing to these expressions, but when he directed himself to me again, "Oh! You black rogue, I do not love you," I replied through God's grace, "I hate thee." He rejoined, "But you had better love me." These manner of expressions filled some of the company there present with great consternation. Others put on boldness to speak to him, at which I was displeased and advised them to see their call clear, fearing least by his policy and many apish expressions he used, he might insinuate himself and raise in them a fearlessness of spirit of him. I no sooner turned my back to go to the fire, but he called out again, "Where is that black rogue gone?" I, seeing little good to be done by discourse and questioning many things in my mind concerning it, I desired the company to join in prayer unto God. When we went about that duty and were kneeled down, with a voice louder than before something, he cried out, "Hold your tongue. Hold your tongue. Get you gone, you black rogue. What are you going to do? You have nothing to do with me," et cetera. But through God's goodness was silenced, and she lay quiet during the time of prayer, but as soon as it was ended, began afresh, using the former expressions, at which some ventured to speak to him, though I think imprudently. One told him God had him in chains. He replied, "For all my chains, I can knock thee on the head when I please."[14] He said he would carry her away that night. Another answered, "But God is stronger than thou." He presently rejoined that, " 'Tis a lie. I am stronger than God." At which blasphemy I again advised them to be wary of speaking, counseled them to get serious parsons to watch with her, and left her, commending her to God.

On Tuesday following, she confessed that the Devil entered into her the 2nd night after her first taking. That when she was going to bed, he entered in (as she conceived) at her mouth and had been in her ever since and professed that if there were ever a Devil in the world, there was one in her, but in what manner he spake in her she could not tell. On Wednesday night, she must forthwith be carried down to the bay in all haste, she should never be well till an assembly of ministers was met together to pray with and for her, and in particular Mr. Cobbet. Her friends advised with me about it. I signified to them that I apprehended. Satan never made any good motion, but it was out of season, and that it was not a thing now feasible, the season being then extreme cold and the snow deep. That if she had been taken in the woods with her fits she must needs perish. On Friday in the evening she was taken again violently and then the former voice (for the sound) was heard in her again, not speaking, but imitating the crowing of a cock, accompanied with many other gestures, some violent, some ridiculous, which occasioned my going to her, whereby signs she signified that the Devil threatened to carry her away that night. God was again then sought for her and when in prayer that expression was used, that God had proved Satan a liar in preserving her once when he had threatened to carry her away that night and was entreated so to do again. The same voice, which had ceased 2 days before, was again heard by the bystanders 5 times distinctly to cry out, "Oh, you are a rogue," and then ceased. But the whole time of prayer, sometimes by violence of fits, sometimes by noises she made, she drowned her own hearing from receiving our petition, as she afterward confessed.

Since that time she hath continued for the most part speechless, her fits coming upon her sometimes often, sometimes with greater intermission and with great varieties in the manner of them, sometimes by violence, sometimes by making her sick, but (through God's goodness) so abated in violence that now one person can as well rule her, as formerly 4 or 5. She is observed always to fall into her fits when any strangers go to visit her, and the more go, the more violent are her fits. As to the frame of her spirits, he hath bin more averse lately to good counsel than heretofore, that sometimes she signifies a desire of the company of ministers.

On Thursday last in the evening, she came a season to her speech, and (as I received from them with her) again disowned a covenant with the Devil, disowned that relation about the knife fore mentioned, declared the occasion of her fits to be discontent, owned the temptations to murder, declared that though the Devil had power of her body, she hoped he should not of her soul, that she had rather continue so speechless than have her speech, and make no better use of it than formerly she had, expressed that she was sometimes disposed to do mischief, and was as if some had laid hold of her to enforce her to it and had double strength to her own, that she knew not whither the Devil were in her or no. If he were, she knew not when or how he entered, that when she was taken speechless, she fared as if a string was tied about the roots of her tongue and reached down into her vitals and pulled her tongue down, and then most when she strove to speak.

On Friday in the evening she was taken with a passion of weeping and sighing, which held her till late in the night. At length she sent for me, but then unreasonableness of the weather and my own bodily indisposedness prevented. I went the next morning, when she strove to speak something but could not, but was taken with her fits, which held her as long as I tarried, which was more than an hour, and I left her in them. And thus she continues speechless to this instant, January 15, and followed with fits, concerning which state of hers I shall suspend my own judgment and willingly leave it to the censure of those that are more learned, aged, and judicious. Only I shall leave my thoughts in respect of 2 or 3 questions which have risen about her, namely,

1. Whether her distemper be real or counterfeit: I shall say no more to that but this, the great strength appearing in them and great weakness after them will disclaim the contrary opinion. For though a person may counterfeit much, that such a strength is beyond the force of dissimulation.[15]

2. Whither her distemper be natural or diabolical, I suppose the premises will strongly enough conclude the latter, that I will add these 2 further arguments:[16]

1.   The actings of convulsion, which these come nearest to, are (as persons acquainted with them observe) in many, that the most essential parts of them quite contrary to these actings.

2.   She hath no ways wasted in body or strength by all these fits, though so dreadful, but gathered flesh exceedingly,[17] and hath her natural strength when her fits are off, for the most part.

3. Whether the Devil did really speak in her: to that point which some have much doubted of, this much I will say to countermand this apprehension.

1.   The manner of expression I diligently observed and could not perceive any organ, any instrument of speech (which the philosopher makes mention of) to have any motion at all, that her mouth was sometimes shut without opening, sometimes open without shutting or moving, and then both I and

others saw her tongue (as it used to be when she was in some fits, when speechless) turned up circularly to the roof of her mouth.

2. The labial letters, diverse of which were used by her, namely, B. M. P., which cannot be naturally expressed without motion of the lips, which must needs come within our ken, if observed, were uttered without any such motion, she had used only linguals, gutturals, et cetera, the matter might have been more suspicious.

3. The reviling terms then used were such as she never used before nor since, in all this time of her being thus taken. She hath bin always observed to speak respectively concerning me.

4. They were expressions which the Devil (by her confession) aspersed me and others withal, in the hour of temptation. Particularly she had freely acknowledged that the Devil was wont to appear to her in the house of God and divert her mind and charge her she should not give ear to what the black coated rogue spake.

5. We observed when the voice spake, her throat was swelled formidably as big at least as one's fist. These arguments I shall leave to the censure of the judicious.

4. Whether she have covenanted with the Devil or no: I think this is a case unanswerable. Her declarations have been so contradictory one to another that we know not what to make of them and her condition is such as administers many doubts. Charity would hope the best. Love would also fear the worst, but this much is clear, she is an object of pity, and I desire that all that hear of her would compassionate her forlorn state. She is (I question not) a subject of hope, and therefore all means ought to be used for her recovery. She is a monument of divine severity and the Lord grant that all that see or hear may fear and tremble. Amen.[18]

                                                                    S. W.

REBECCA FOWLER, CALVERT COUNTY, MARYLAND 1685

One of the rare Chesapeake witches, Fowler was accused of being led by the Devil to injure a man named Francis Sandsbury using witchcraft and sorcery. She was hanged. Usually Chesapeake witchcraft cases were milder than their New England equivalents, often limited to bad-mouthing and rumor. Accused witches in the South were fewer in number and were usually acquitted. Fowler is thought to be the only witch executed in the Maryland colony, though a man named John Cowman was accused of witchcraft, condemned, and then begged a stay of execution.[1]

Court Records of Rebecca Fowler[2]

At a meeting of the provincial court on the 29th day of September, 1685, Rebecca Fowler was indicted by a grand jury.

For that she, the said Rebecca Fowler, the last day of August in the year of our Lord, 1685, and at diverse other days and times, as well before and after, having not the fear of God before her eyes, but being led by the instigation of the Devil certain evil and diabolical arts, called witchcrafts, enchantments, charms, and sorceries, then wickedly, devilishly, and feloniously, at Mount Calvert Hundred[3] and several other places in Calvert County of her malice forethought feloniously did use, practice, and exercise, in, upon, and against one Francis Sandsbury, late of Calvert County aforesaid, laborer, and several other persons of the said county, whereby the said Francis Sandsbury and several others, as aforesaid, the last day of August, in the year aforesaid and several other days and times as well before as after, at Mount Calvert hundred and several other places in the said county, in his and their bodies were very much the worse, consumed, pined, and lamed again the peace, et cetera, and against the form of the statute in this case made and provided.

To this indictment Rebecca pleaded not guilty. She was tried before a jury who rendered the following verdict:

We find that Rebecca Fowler is guilty of the matters of fact charged in the indictment against her and if the court finds the matters contained in the indictment make her guilty of witchcraft, charms, and sorceries, et cetera, then they find her guilty. And if the court finds those matters contained in the indictment do not make her guilty of witchcraft, charms, sorceries, et cetera, then they find her not guilty.

In view of this finding of the jury, judgment was "respited" until the court had time to further consider the case. After the court reconvened a few days later, Rebecca was again brought to the bar and the judges having "advised themselves of and upon the premises, it is considered by the court that the said Rebecca Fowler be hanged by the neck until she be dead, which was performed the ninth day of October aforesaid."

GOODWIFE GLOVER, BOSTON, MASSACHUSETTS, 1688

Cotton Mather, theologian son of Increase Mather, presided over the possession of John Goodwin's children, ultimately resulting in the execution of an Irish laundress named Glover for having bewitched them. The experience led Cotton Mather to write Memorable Providences, Relating to Witchcrafts and Possessions *(1689), which in some respects formed a follow-up to his father's previous work, while also making him disposed to view the behavior of the afflicted girls in the Salem panic definitely the result of witchcraft. The Goodwin case resembles the Knapp possession, though in this case a responsible witch was identified and convicted. Goodwife Glover raises the intriguing question of witches and ethnicity, for at her trial she was reported to speak only in Gaelic.[1] While for the most part accused witches in North America were of English background and Puritan religion, Glover's case, taken together with witches from other backgrounds and regions, suggests that witchcraft, as a cultural belief, was not limited to the Puritan realm.*

The Case of the Goodwin Children[2]

Section 1. There dwells at this time, in the south part of Boston, a sober and pious man, whose name is John Goodwin, whose trade is that of a mason and whose wife (to which a good report gives a share with him in all the characters of virtue) has made him the father of six (now living) children. Of these children, all but the eldest, who works with his father at his calling, and the youngest, who lives yet upon the breast of its mother, have labored under the direful effects of a (no less palpable than) stupendous witchcraft. Indeed, that exempted son had also, as was thought, some lighter touches of it in unaccountable stabs and pains now and then upon him, as indeed every person in the family at some time or other had, except the godly father and the sucking infant, who never felt any impressions of it. But these four children mentioned were handled in so sad and strange a manner, as has given matter of discourse and wonder to all the country, and of history not unworthy to be considered by more than all the serious or the curious readers in this New English world.

Section 2. The four children (whereof the eldest was about thirteen and the youngest was perhaps about a third part so many years of age) had enjoyed a religious education and answered it with a very cowardly ingenuity. They had an observable affection unto divine and sacred things and those of them that were capable of it seemed to have such a resentment of their eternal concernments as is not altogether usual. Their parents also kept them to a continual employment, which did more than deliver them from the temptations of idleness, and as young as they were, they took a delight in it, maybe as much as they should have done. In a word, such was the whole temper and carriage of the children that there cannot easily be anything more unreasonable than to imagine that a design to dissemble could cause them to fall into any of their odd fits, though there should not have happened, as there did, a thousand things, wherein it was perfectly impossible for any dissimulation of theirs to produce what scores of spectators were amazed at.

Section 3. About midsummer in the year 1688, the eldest of these children, who is a daughter, saw cause to examine their washerwoman upon their missing of some linen, which 'twas feared she had stolen from them, and of what use this linen might be to serve the witchcraft intended, the thief's tempter knows! This laundress was the daughter of an ignorant and a scandalous old woman in the neighborhood, whose miserable husband before he died had sometimes complained of her that she was undoubtedly a witch,[3] and that whenever his head was laid, she would quickly arrive unto the punishments due to such a one. This woman in her daughter's defense bestowed very bad language upon the girl that put her to the question, immediately upon which the poor child became variously indisposed in her health, and visited with strange fits beyond those that attend an epilepsy or a catalepsy[4] or those that they call the diseases of astonishment.[5]

Section 4. It was not long before one of her sisters and two of her brothers were seized, in order one after another with effects like those that molested her. Within a few weeks, they were all four tortured everywhere in a manner very grievous, that it would have broken a heart of stone to have seen their agonies. Skillful physicians were consulted for their help, and particularly our worthy and prudent friend Dr. Thomas Oakes, who found himself so affronted by the distempers of the children that he concluded nothing but a hellish witchcraft could be the original of these maladies. And that which yet more confirmed such apprehension was that for one good while, the children were tormented just in the same part of their bodies all at the same time together, and though they saw and heard not one another's complaints, though likewise their pains and sprains were swift like lightning, yet when (suppose) the neck or the hand or the back of one was racked, so it was at that instant with the other two.

Section 5. The variety of their tortures increased continually, and though about nine or ten at night they always had a release from their miseries and ate and slept all night for the most part indifferently well, yet in the daytime they were handled with so many sorts of ails that it would require of us almost as much time to relate them all as it did of them to endure them. Sometimes they would be deaf, sometimes dumb, and sometimes blind, and often all this at once. One while their tongues would be drawn down their throats; another while they would be pulled out upon their chins to a prodigious length. They would have their mouths opened unto such a wideness that their jaws went out of joint, and anon they would clap together again with a force like that of a strong spring lock. The same would happen to their shoulder blades and their elbows and hand wrists and several of their joints. They would at times lie in a benumbed condition and be drawn together as those that are tied neck and heels, and presently be stretched out, yea, drawn backward, to such a degree that it was feared the very skin of their bellies would have cracked. They would make most piteous outcries that they were cut with knives and struck with blows that they could not bear. Their necks would be broken, so that their neck bone would seem dissolved unto them that felt after it, and yet on the sudden, it would become again so stiff that there was no stirring of their heads. Yea, their heads would be twisted almost round, and if main force at any time obstructed a dangerous motion which they seemed to be upon, they would roar exceedingly. Thus they lay some weeks most pitiful spectacles, and this while as a further demonstration of witchcraft in these horrid effects, when I went to prayer by one of them that was very desirous to hear what I said, the child utterly lost her hearing till our prayer was over.

Section 6. It was a religious family that these afflictions happened unto, and none but a religious contrivance to obtain relief would have been welcome to them. Many superstitious proposals were made unto them by persons that were I know not who nor what, with arguments fetched from I know not how much necessity and experience. But the distressed parents rejected all such counsels with a gracious resolution to oppose devils with no other weapons but prayers and tears unto him that has the chaining of them, and to try first whether graces were not the best things to encounter witchcrafts with. Accordingly, they requested the four ministers of Boston, with the minister of Charlestown, to keep a day of prayer at their thus haunted house, which they did in the company of some devout people there. Immediately upon this day, the youngest of the four children was delivered and never felt any trouble as afore. But there was yet a greater effect of these our applications unto our God!

Section 7. The report of the calamities of the family for which we were thus concerned arrived now unto the ears of the magistrates, who presently and prudently applied themselves, with a just vigor, to enquire into the story. The father of the children complained of his neighbor, the suspected ill woman whose name was Glover, and she, being sent for by the justices, gave such a wretched account of herself, that they saw cause to commit her unto the jailer's custody. Goodwin had no proof that could have done her any hurt, but the hag had not power to deny her interest in the enchantment of the children. And when she was asked whether she believed there was a God, her answer was too blasphemous and horrible for any pen of mine to mention. An experiment was made whether she could recite the Lord's Prayer, and it was found that though clause after clause was most carefully repeated unto her, yet when she said it after them that prompted her,[6] she could not possibly avoid making nonsense of it, with some ridiculous depravations. This experiment I had the curiosity since to see made upon two more, and it had the same event. Upon commitment of this extraordinary woman, all the children had some present ease, until one (related unto her) accidentally meeting one or two of them, entertained them with her blessing, that is, railing, upon which three of them fell ill again, as they were before.

Section 8. It was not long before the witch thus in the trap was brought upon her trial, at which, through the efficacy of a charm, I suppose, used upon her by one or some of her cruel, the court could receive answers from her in one but the Irish, which was her native language, although she understood the English very well, and had accustomed her whole family to none but that language in her former conversation, and therefore the communication between the bench and the bar was now chiefly conveyed by two honest and faithful men that were interpreters. It was long before she could with any direct answers plead unto her indictment. And when she did plead, it was with confession rather than denial of her guilt. Order was given to search the old woman's house, from whence there were brought into the court several small images or puppets or babies made of rags and stuffed with goat's hair and other such ingredients. When these were produced, the vile woman acknowledged that her way to torment the objects of her malice was by wetting of her finger with her spittle and streaking of those little images. The abused children were then present, and the woman still kept stooping and shrinking as one that was almost pressed to death with a mighty weight upon her. But one of the images being brought unto her, immediately she started up after an odd manner and took it into her hand. But she had no sooner taken it than one of the children fell into sad fits, before the whole assembly. This the judges had their just apprehensions at and carefully causing the repetition of the experiment found again the same event of it. They asked her whether she had any to stand by her. She replied she had, and looking very pertly in the air, she added, "No, he's gone." And she then confessed that she had one who was her prince, with whom she maintained I know not what communion. For which cause, the night after, she was heard expostulating with a devil for his thus deserting her, telling him that because he had served her so basely and falsely, she had confessed all. However, to make all clear, the court appointed five or six physicians one evening to examine her very strictly, whether she were not crazed in her intellectuals and had not procured to herself by folly and madness the reputation of a witch.[7] Diverse hours did they spend with her, and in all that while no discourse came from her but what was pertinent and agreeable, particularly, when they asked her what she thought would become of her soul, she replied, "You ask me a very solemn question, and I cannot well tell what to say to it." She owned herself a Roman Catholic and could recite her Pater Noster in Latin very readily,[8] but there was one clause or two always too hard for her, whereof she said she could not repeat it if she might have all the world. In the up-shot, the doctors returned her compos mentis, and sentence of death was passed upon her.

Section 9. Diverse days were passed between her being arraigned and condemned. In this time one of her neighbors had been giving in her testimony of what another of her neighbors had upon her death related concerning her. It seems one Howen about six years before, had been cruel bewitched to death, but before she died, she called one Hughes unto her, telling her that she laid her death to the charge of Glover, that she had seen Glover sometimes come down her chimney, that she should remember this, for within this six years she might have occasion to declare it. This Hughes now preparing her testimony, immediately one of her children, a fine boy, well grown toward youth, was taken ill, just in the same woeful and surprising manner that Goodwin's children were. One night particularly, the boy said he saw a black thing with a blue cap in the room, tormenting of him, and he complained most bitterly of a hand put into the bed to pull out his bowels. The next day the mother of the boy went unto Glover in the prison and asked her why she tortured her poor lad at such a wicked rate. This witch replied that she did it because of wrong done to herself and her daughter. Hughes denied (as well she might) that she had done her any wrong. "Well then," said Glover, "Let me see your child and he shall be well again." Glover went on and told her of her own accord, "I was at your house last night." Says Hughes, "In what shape?" Says Glover, "As a black thing with a blue cap." Says Hughes, "What did you do there?" Says Glover, "With my hand in the bed I tried to pull out the boy's bowels but I could not." They parted, but the next day Hughes, appearing at court, had her boy with her, and Glover, passing by the boy, expressed her good wishes for him, though I suppose his parent had no design of any mighty respect unto the hag, by having him with her there. But the boy had no more indispositions after the condemnation of the woman.

Section 10. While the miserable old woman was under condemnation, I did myself twice give a visit unto her. She never denied the guilt of the witchcraft charged upon her but she confessed very little about the circumstances of her confederacies with the devils, only, she said, that she used to be at meetings, which her prince and four more were present at. As for those four, she told who they were, and for her prince, her account plainly was that he was the Devil. She entertained me with nothing but Irish, which language I had not learning enough to understand without an interpreter.[9] Only one time, when I was representing unto her that and how her prince had cheated her, as herself would quickly find, she replied, I think in English, and with passion too, "If it be so, I am sorry for that!" I offered many questions unto her, unto which, after long silence, she told me she would fain give me a full answer, but they would not give her leave. It was demanded, "They! Who is that they?" And she returned that they were her spirits, or her saints (for they say the same word in Irish signifies both). And at another time, she included her two mistresses, as she called them in that they, but when it was enquired who those two were, she fell into a rage, and would be no more urged. I set before her the necessity and equity of her breaking her covenant with hell and giving herself to the Lord Jesus Christ by an everlasting covenant. To which her answer was that I spoke a very reasonable thing, but she could not do it. I asked her whether she would consent or desire to be prayed for. To that she said if prayer would do her any good, she could pray for herself. And when it was again propounded, she said she could not unless her spirits (or angels) would give her leave.[10] However, against her will I prayed with her, which if it were a fault it was in excess of pity. When I had done, she thanked me with many good words; but I was no sooner out of her sight than she took a stone, a long and slender stone, and with her finger and spittle fell to tormenting it, though whom or what she meant, I had the mercy never to understand.

Section 11. When this witch was going to her execution, she said the children should not be relieved by her death, for others had a hand in it as well as she, and she named one among the rest, whom it might have been thought natural affection would have advised the concealing of. It came to pass accordingly that the three children continued in their furnace as before, and it grew rather seven times hotter than it was. All their former ails pursued them still, with an addition of ('tis not easy to tell how many) more, but such as gave more sensible demonstrations of an enchantment growing very far toward a possession by evil spirits.

Section 12. The children in their fits would still cry out upon they and them as the authors of all their harm, but who that they and them were, they were not able to declare. At last, the boy obtained at some times a sight of some shapes in the room. There were three or four of them, the names of which the child would pretend at certain seasons to tell, only the name of one who was counted a sager hag than the rest. He still so stammered at that, he was put upon some periphrasis in describing her. A blow at the place where the boy beheld the specter was always felt by the boy himself in the part of his body that answered what might be stricken at, and this though his back were turned, which was once and again so exactly tried, that there could be no collusion in the business. But as a blow at the apparition always hurt him, so it always helped him too. For after the agonies, which a push or stab of that had put him to were over (as in a minute or 2 they would be), the boy would have a respite from his fits a considerable while and the hobgoblins[11] disappeared. It is very credibly reported that a wound was this way given to an obnoxious woman in the town, whose name I will not expose, for we should be tender in such relations lest we wrong the reputation of the innocent by stories not enough enquired into.

SALEM

Explanations for and interpretations of the Salem witch crisis vary so widely that they can in many respects be seen as more reflective of the times in which the historians are writing about Salem than of Salem itself in 1692. Whether explained away as a delusion of Satan, in the first decades of the eighteenth century,[1] when North American intellectual and religious life was beginning to morph in response to the Scientific Revolution; in the nineteenth century, as an embarrassing relic of medieval thought,[2] when history as a field was in the grips of professionalization; or as a shocking aftereffect of eating moldy rye bread, in the 1970s,[3] when Freudian psychoanalysis began to influence the practice of the humanities and drugs played an increased role in popular culture, Salem has always been a screen on which to project presentist interpretations. These various readings of the Salem episode are attractive primarily because they are easily dismissed: Satan made dangerous inroads once but not again; the Middle Ages are well behind us; and bread mold is easily controlled. None of these proximate causes suggest that Salem was a usual or predictable phenomenon and they all reinforce the comforting thought that such a widespread government-sanctioned panic cannot possibly happen again.

Recent scholarship presents a more nuanced and resilient interpretive picture. Paul Boyer and Stephen Nissenbaum argue in their 1974 book, Salem Possessed, that the largest and most fatal North American witch crisis can be understood as a land-based rivalry between two loose family groups, the Porters and the Putnams. Within this rivalry reside kernels of class resentment, coalescing around the divisive figure of the village minister, Samuel Parris, and the cultural differences between a growing port town (Salem Town) and its more insular rural *counterpart (Salem Village). The Boyer and Nissenbaum argument represents a starting point for an understanding of what went awry in Salem Village, though its narrow focus requires greater elaboration.*

That elaboration begins to appear in 1987's The Devil in the Shape of a Woman *by Carol Karlsen. Part of the broader trend toward cultural history and its attendant emphasis on questions of class and gender, Karlsen's writing focuses on an all-important question that had preoccupied writers on witchcraft during the early modern period, but which had eluded Boyer and Nissenbaum: namely, what to make of the fact that most witches were women. In Karlsen's view, female witches tended to be middle-aged women who were socially conspicuous in some way and challenged the rigid gender hierarchy of Puritan New England. Karlsen's point is a vital one for an understanding of Salem but still leaves questions unanswered. Why this particular community? Why then?*

Answers to this last set of questions take shape in Mary Beth Norton's 2003 account, In the Devil's Snare. *Norton rightly points out that the Salem witch crisis might be better understood as the Essex County witch crisis, as its complex web of accusations and suspected witches extended well outside of Salem Village and deep into the surrounding countryside. She broadens the focus beyond the intricacies of village life, instead placing the Salem episode in context with the Indian wars across the Maine frontier. Norton demonstrates that many of the afflicted girls had direct ties to the violence at the Eastward, and that the language that is used to describe the Devil during the trial testimony overlaps with the language used to describe the native population. The Salem Villagers were a "People of God, settled in those which were once the Devil's territories,"⁴ and the strain, at the personal, political, and psychological levels, on a community so deeply touched with violence and uncertainty, could only find its expression in that culture, at that time, in a witch trial.*

Seen within the wider context of English witch-hunting with other North American examples, the Salem witch crisis can no longer be explained away as an anomaly. Every aspect of the Salem crisis—the region in which it took place, the personalities that emerge from the historical record, the outcomes for the accused and the accusers, even the scale of the trial—had an antecedent that can clearly be identified and that was sometimes even known to the participants themselves. Salem's unique element was the expressed idea of a covenanted conspiracy of witches, a parallel anti-Christian community within the visible Christian one, with accounts of witches' Sabbaths that find their roots in English folk magical belief.[5] Even the concept of conspiracy, which opened the scale of inquiry to include as many as 150 people before the panic was brought to a close, finds its source in English witch-hunting manuals, which suggest that a witch can be reliably identified by another confessed conspirator.

So, what caused it? What elusive factor sent a widespread community of pious New Englanders into a witch-fearing terror that would result in the death of nineteen innocent people at the hands of the state? Was it superstition? Rotten bread? Indians? Gender panic? Satan himself?

In a sense, Salem was caused by all of these things (or rather, all of them except for rotten bread). The signal fact about Salem is that the panic did not take place in a vacuum. The Salem witch crisis exists as a set of interrelated phenomena along a historical continuum with both a past and, just as important, a future. Rather than being an aberrant expression of North American fears and attitudes about witchcraft, it should instead be seen as the ultimate *expression of it. And therein lies the most alarming aspect of the Salem witch crisis—if Salem is not aberrant then it cannot be comfortably consigned to the past. Within this slippery historical continuum of behavior, precedent, practice, and response, witchcraft in North American religious and intellectual life becomes less safe to think about. This lack of safety, this persistent reminder of the inhumanity that a small community and its learned and trusted government can show its own members, lingers among us, a threat of what we could at any time still become.*

WARRANT FOR THE APPREHENSION OF SARAH GOOD, AND OFFICER'S RETURN MONDAY, FEBRUARY 29, 1692

*The warrant for Sarah Good marked the legal begin-
ning of the Salem witch trials.[1] She, Sarah Osburn, and
Tituba were the first three women in Salem accused of
witchcraft. In many respects, Good and Osburn were
the usual suspects, as witchcraft trials went.[2] Good was
a beggar. She was married with children, but did not
conform to standard religious practice, missing church
regularly because she had no suitable clothes. She was
on the margin and disreputable; with her these infamous
trials began.*

Salem, February the 29th, 1691/2[3]

Whereas Mrs.[4] Joseph Hutcheson, Thomas Putnam, Edward
Putnam,[5] and Thomas Preston, yeomen of Salem Village in the
county of Essex, personally appeared before us, and made complaint on behalf of Their Majesty against Sarah Good, the wife
of William Good of Salem Village above said, for suspicion of
witchcraft by her committed, and thereby much injury done to
Elizabeth Parris, Abigail Williams, Anna Putnam, and Elizabeth
Hubert,[6] all of Salem Village aforesaid sundry times within this
two months and lately also done at Salem Village contrary to the
peace of our sovereign lord and lady William and Mary, King
and Queen of England, et cetera. You are therefore in Their Majesties' names hereby required to apprehend and bring before us
the said Sarah Good, tomorrow about ten of the clock in the

forenoon at the house of Lieutenant Nathaniel Ingersoll in Salem Village or as soon as may be then and there to be examined relating to the above said premises and hereof you are not to fail at your peril.

Dated: Salem, February 29th, 1691/2, John Hathorne to Constable George Locker;

assistant: Jonathan Corwin

[verso]

I brought the person of Sarah Good, the wife of William Good, according to the tenor of the within warrant as is attested by me

George Locker, constable, 1 March 1691/2

WARRANT FOR THE APPREHENSION OF SARAH OSBURN AND TITUBA, AND OFFICER'S RETURN MONDAY, FEBRUARY 29, 1692

Sarah Osburn and Tituba Indian were the next two women accused.[1] Sarah Osburn also represented the sort of woman one might conventionally expect to see accused. She had stopped going to church. She lived with a much younger man. Tituba, on the other hand, was a slave in Parris's house, where the first two girls were afflicted.[2]

With this warrant we begin to see the spread of Parris's investigation, but its pattern still fell within the norms of North American and English witch trials. If we compare Salem at this moment with its nearest analogues, the Bury St. Edmunds trial for example, the tendency in early modern Anglophone witch trials was for a small knot of women to be accused, and for the trial to remain focused on those women. In February 1692, the Salem episode still looked fairly typical in terms of its scale and the number of individuals involved.

Warrant for Sarah Good and Tituba

Salem, February, the 29th day, 1691/2

Whereas Mrs.[3] Joseph Hutcheson, Thomas Putnam, Edward Putnam, and Thomas Preston, yeomen of Salem Village in the county of Essex, personally appeared before us, and made complaint on behalf of Their Majesties against Sarah Osburn, the wife of Alexander Osburn[4] of Salem Village aforesaid, and Tituba, an Indian woman servant of Mr. Samuel Parris of said place also, for suspicion of witchcraft by them committed and thereby much injury done to Elizabeth Parris, Abigail Williams, Anna Putnam, and Elizabeth Hubert[5] all of Salem Village, contrary to the peace and laws of our sovereign lord and lady, William and Mary of England, et cetera, king and queen.

You are therefore in Their Majesties' names hereby required to apprehend and forthwith or as soon as may be bring before us the above said Sarah Osburn, and Tituba Indian, at the house of Lieutenant Nathaniel Ingersoll in said place and if it may be by tomorrow about ten of the clock in the morning then and there to be examined relating to the above said premises. You are likewise required to bring at the same time Elizabeth Parris, Abigail Williams, Anna Putnam, and Elizabeth Hubert or any other person or persons that can give evidence in the above said case and hereof you are not to fail. Dated: Salem, February 29th, 1691/2, John Hathorne to Constable Joseph Herrick, constable in Salem; assistant: Jonathan Corwin

[verso]

According to this warrant I have apprehended the persons within mentioned and have brought them accordingly and have made diligent search of images and such like but can find none.

Salem Village, this 1st March, 1691/92, me, Joseph Herrick,[6] constable

EXAMINATIONS OF SARAH GOOD, SARAH OSBURN, AND TITUBA
TUESDAY, MARCH 1, 1692

The examinations of Sarah Good and Sarah Osburn[1] continued within the normal bounds of witch trials; they were asked about their long-standing reputations for unusual or disagreeable behavior, like missing church or arguing with neighbors. The trials took a unique turn, however, in the examination and subsequent confession of Tituba. In this first examination, Tituba, like the other women, denied being a witch but then almost immediately confessed, blaming Good and Osburn for making her do it. She described the other witches who are part of the conspiracy, but did not name them save for Good and Osburn. The Devil who made her do it is described as a man in a tall hat with white hair and black clothes. More than one historian has pointed out that this description could apply quite well to her owner (and possible tormentor), Samuel Parris.

Most important, according to A Discourse of the Damned Art of Witchcraft *by William Perkins reproduced above, the word of a confessed witch is sufficient evidence to condemn another accused witch. So Tituba, through her confession and naming, condemned Good and Osburn as well as pointed to a wider group of witches as yet undiscovered. Tituba's confession marks the moment at which the Salem trial branches into a different kind of legal and social event: from it stemmed the concept of a conspiracy with an unknown number of conspirators.*

Another important distinction is that the examinations were conducted in public. Generally, examinations of accused witches would be conducted in private to determine if evidence was sufficient to move to a public trial. In this case, the examinations themselves became unstable and, as historian Mary Beth Norton describes it, "explosive," between the magistrates, who assumed the guilt of the accused; the accused themselves, who had to figure out how to answer the charges against them; the afflicted, whose torments grew more theatrical and acute with the presence of an audience; and the audience itself, tossing in unsolicited comments and inducements as the examinations took place.[2] The spectacle of these examinations must have been staggering. Even reading the transcripts today is a riveting exercise.

The Examination

The examination of Sarah Good before the worshipful assistants John Hathorn, Jonathan Corwin.

[Hathorne]: Sarah Good, what evil spirit have you familiarity with?
[Sarah Good]: None.
[Hathorne]: Have you made no contract with the Devil?
[Sarah Good]: Good answered no.
[Hathorne]: Why do you hurt these children?
[Sarah Good]: I do not hurt them. I scorn it.
[Hathorne]: Who do you employ, then, to do it?
[Sarah Good]: I employ no body.
[Hathorne]: What creature[3] do you employ then?
[Sarah Good]: No creature, but I am falsely accused.
[Hathorne]: Why did you go away muttering from Mr. Paris, his house?
[Sarah Good]: I did not mutter, but I thanked him for what he gave my child.[4]
[Hathorne]: Have you made no contract with the Devil?
[Sarah Good]: No.

[Hathorne]: Desire the children all of them to look upon her and see if this were the person that hurt them?

*And so they all did look upon her and said this was one of the persons that did torment them. Presently they were all tormented.*5

[Hathorne]: Sarah Good, do you not see now what you have done? Why do you not tell us the truth? Why do you thus torment these poor children?

[Sarah Good]: I do not torment them.

[Hathorne]: [illegible] Who do you employ, then?

[Sarah Good]: I employ nobody. I scorn it.

[Hathorne]: How came they thus tormented?

[Sarah Good]: What do I know? You bring others here and now you charge me with it.

[Hathorne]: Why? Who was it?

[Sarah Good]: I do not know but it was some you brought into the meetinghouse with you.

[Hathorne]: You were brought into the meetinghouse.

[Sarah Good]: But you brought in two more.

[Hathorne]: Who was it, then, that tormented the children?

[Sarah Good]: It was Osburn.

[Hathorne]: What is it that you say when you go muttering away from persons' houses?

[Sarah Good]: If I must tell I will tell.

[Hathorne]: Do tell us then.

[Sarah Good]: If I must tell I will tell. It is the commandments, I may say, my commandments, I hope.

[Hathorne]: What commandment is it?

[Sarah Good]: If I must tell you I will tell. It is a psalm.

[Hathorne]: What psalm?

After a long time she [Sarah Good] muttered over some part of a psalm.

[Hathorne]: Who do you serve?

[Sarah Good]: I serve God.

[Hathorne]: What God do you serve?

[Sarah Good]: The God that made heaven and earth.

Though she was not willing to mention the word God, her answers were in [a] very wicked, spiteful manner reflecting and retorting against the authority with base and abusive words and many lies she was taken in.[6] *It was here said that her hus-band had said that he was afraid that she either was a witch or would be one very quickly. The worsh*[7] *Mr. Harthon*[8] *asked him his re[scored out] reason why he said so of her, whether he had ever seen anything by her and he answered, no, not in this nature. But it was her bad carriage to him and indeed, said he, I may say with tears that she is an enemy to all good.*[9]

Sarah Osburn, her examination

[Hathorne]: What evil spirit have you familiarity with?

[Sarah Osburn]: None.

[Hathorne]: Have you made no contract with the Devil?

[Sarah Osburn]: I no I never saw the Devil in my life.

[Hathorne]: Why do you hurt these children?

[Sarah Osburn]: I do not hurt them.

[Hathorne]: Who do you employ then to hurt them?

[Sarah Osburn]: I employ nobody.

[Hathorne]: What familiarity have you with Sarah Good?

[Sarah Osburn]: None. I have not seen her these 2 years.

[Hathorne]: Where did you see her then?

[Sarah Osburn]: One day agoing to town.

[Hathorne]: What communications had you with her?

[Sarah Osburm]: I had none, only how do you do or so. I did not know her by name.

[Hathorne]: What did you call her then?

Osburn made a pa [scored out] stand at that at last said she called her Sarah.

[Hathorne]: Sarah Good saith that it was you that hurt the children.

[Sarah Osburn]: I do not know that the Devil goes about in my likeness to do any hurt.[10]

Mr. Harthon desired all these children to stand up and look upon her and see if they did know her, which they all did and every one of them said that she [scored out] this was one of the women that did afflict them and that they had constantly seen her in [the] very habit that she was now in.[11] *The evidence do stand that she said this morning that she was more like to be bewitched than that she was a witch.*

Mr. Harthon asked her what made her say so.

She answered that she was frighted one time in her sleep and either saw or dreamed that she saw a thing like an Indian all black,[12] which did pinch her in her neck and pulled her by the back part of her head to the door of the house.

[Hathorne]: Did you never see anything else?

[Sarah Osburn]: No. It was said by some in the meetinghouse that she had said that she would never believe that lying spirit any more.

[Hathorne]: What lying spirit is this? Hath the Devil ever deceived you and been false to you?

[Sarah Osburn]: I do not know the Devil. I never did see him.

[Hathorne]: What lying spirit was it, then?

[Sarah Osburn]: It was a voice that I thought I heard.

[Hathorne]: What did it propound to you?

[Sarah Osburn]: That I should go no more to meeting but she [scored out] I said I would and did go the next Sabbath day.

[Hathorne]: Were you never tempted further?

[Sarah Osburn]: No.

[Hathorne]: Why did you yield thus far to the Devil as never to go to meeting since.

[Sarah Osburn]: Alas I have been sick and not able to go.

Her husband and others said that she had not been at meeting these year and two months.[13]

The [scored out] examination of Tituba

[Hathorne]: Tituba, what sp[scored out] evil spirit have you familiarity with?

[Tituba]: None.

[Hathorne]: Why do you hurt these children?

[Tituba]: I do not hurt them.

[Hathorne]: Who is it then the de [scored out]

[Tituba]: The Devil for ought I ken[14] [scored out] know.

[Hathorne]: Did you never see the [illegible] Devil?

[Tituba]: The Devil came to me and bid me serve him.

[Hathorne]: Who have you seen?

[Tituba]: 4 women and [scored out] sometimes hurt the children.

[Hathorne]: Who were they?

[Tituba]: Goody Osburn and Sarah Good and I do not know who the others were. Sarah Good and Osburn would have me hurt the children, but I would not.

She further saith there was a tall man of Boston that she did see.

[Hathorne]: When did you see them?

[Tituba]: Last night at Boston.[15]

[Hathorne]: What did they say to you?

[Tituba]: They said, hurt the children.

[Hathorne]: And did you hurt them? No [scored out]

[Tituba]: No. There is 4 women and one man. They hurt the s[scored out] children and then lay all upon here[16] and they tell me if I will not hurt the children they will hurt me.

[Hathorne]: But did you not hurt them.

[Tituba]: Yes, but I will hurt them no more.

[Hathorne]: Are you not sorry that you did hurt them?

[Tituba]: Yes.

[Hathorne]: And why then do you hurt them?

[Tituba]: They say hurt children or we will do worse to you.

[Hathorne]: What have you seen?

[Tituba]: A man come to me and say serve me.

[Hathorne]: What service?

[Tituba]: Hurt the children and last night there was an appearance that said K[scored out] kill the children and if I would not go on hurting the children they would do worse to me.

[Hathorne]: What is this appearance you see?

[Tituba]: Sometimes it is like a hog and sometimes like a great dog.

This appearance she saith she did see 4 times.

[Hathorne]: What did it say to you?

[Tituba]: It s[scored out] the black dog said serve me but I said I am afraid. He said if I did not he would do worse to me.

[Hathorne]: What did you say to it?

[Tituba]: I will serve you no longer. Then he said he would hurt me and then he looks like a man and threatens to hurt me. She said that this man had a yellow bird that kept with him and he told me he had more pretty things that he would give me if I would serve him.

[Hathorne]: What were these pretty things?

[Tituba]: He did not show me them.

[Hathorne]: What else have you seen?

[Tituba]: Two cats: a red cat and a black cat.[17]

[Hathorne]: What did they say to you?

[Tituba]: They said, serve me.

[Hathorne]: When did you see them last? [scored out]

[Tituba]: Last night and they said serve me but I she [scored out] said I would not.

[Hathorne]: What service?

[Tituba]: She said hurt the children.

[Hathorne]: Did you not pinch Elisabeth Hubbard this morning?

[Tituba]: The man brought her to me and made her [scored out] pinch her.

[Hathorne]: Why did you go to Thomas Putnam's last night and hurt his child?[18]

[Tituba]: They pull and haul me and make go.

[Hathorne]: And what would they have you do?

[Tituba]: Kill her with a knife.

Left[19] Fuller and other said at this [time] when the child saw these persons and was tormented by them that she did complain of a knife that they would have her cut her head off with a knife.

[Hathorne]: How did you go?

[Tituba]: We ride upon sticks[20] and are there presently.

[Hathorne]: Do you go through the trees or over them?

[Tituba]: We see nothing but are there presently.

[Hathorne]: Why did you not tell your master?

[Tituba]: I was afraid. They said they would cut off my head if I told.

[Hathorne]: Would you not have hurt others if you could?

[Tituba]: They said they would hurt others but they could not [scored out]

[Hathorne]: What attendants hath Sarah Good?

[Tituba]: A yellow bird and she would have given me one.

[Hathorne]: What meat did she give it?

[Tituba]: It did suck her between her fingers.

[Hathorne]: Did not you hurt Mr. Currin's child?

[Tituba]: Goody Good and Goody Osburn told that they did hurt Mr. Curren's child and would have had me hurt him too but I did not.

[Hathorne]: What hath Sarah Osburn?

[Tituba]: Yesterday she had a thing with a head like a woman with 2 legs and wings.

Abigail Williams that lives with her uncle Mr. Parris said that she did see this same creature with Goody Osburn and yesterday being [scored out from "with"] and it turned into the shape of Goody Osburn.

[Hathorne]: What else have you seen with Goody Osburn?

[Tituba]: Another thing hairy. It goes upright like a man. It hath only 2 legs.

[Hathorne]: Did you not see Sarah Good upon Elizabeth Williams [scored out] Hubbard last Saturday?

[Tituba]: I did see her set a wolf upon her to afflict her.

The persons with this maid did say that she did complain of a wolf.[21]

[Tituba]: She further said that she saw a cat with Good at another time.

[Hathorne]: What clothes doth the man we [scored out] go in?

[Tituba]: He goes in black clothes. A tall man with white hair, I think.[22]

[Hathorne]: How doth the woman go?

[Tituba]: In a white hood and a black hood with a top knot.

[Hathorne]: Do you see who it is that torments it that hurts them now?

[Tituba]: I am blind now I cannot see.

Salem Village, March the 1st, 1691/2, written by Ezekiel Cheevers

TWO EXAMINATIONS OF TITUBA, AS RECORDED BY JONATHAN CORWIN TUESDAY, MARCH 1 AND WEDNESDAY, MARCH 2, 1692

If the expansion of the Salem witch trials was ignited by Tituba's confession, then we must ask her reason for confessing and condemning these other women. It is tempting to say that Tituba confessed to save herself, but when she did, she did not know that she would be spared because of it. Usually in an early modern witch trial, if one confessed it would only hurry one to the gallows, as was the case with Ursula Kemp one hundred years before. It has been argued that Parris beat Tituba's confession out of her; the descriptions of her body, when it was examined looking for her witch's teat, also include evidence of bruising. We may never fully understand why she confessed. She was a slave and a woman in a rigidly hierarchal society. Her questioning was leading at best and aggressive at worst. Tituba confessed for the same reason that people confess to crimes they did not commit today—because she had been hounded into it by people in a position of power.

What we can understand is how she confessed, which may tell us something about why. Tituba's confession displays a deep knowledge of English witchcraft: the covenanting with the Devil, the spirit familiars in the forms of animals, riding on a stick to the Sabbath, and sending out a spirit to do harm (often against children) are wholly consistent with English thinking about witchcraft. These details are perfectly consistent with English witchcraft

*manuals—too consistent. For someone who could not
read (Tituba made her mark rather than sign her name)
this kind of knowledge could only have come from someone else. Such details about witchcraft were scholastic,
rather than common folk knowledge. These details coming from the mouth of an illiterate slave from Barbados
strongly suggests coercion both in the act of the confession, as well as instruction in what specifically to say.*

The First Examination of Tituba[1]

Tituba the Indian Woman's Examination, March 1, 1691/2

[Q]: Why do you hurt these poor children? What harm have
they done unto you?

[A]: They do no harm to me. I no hurt them at all.

[Q]: Why have you done it?

[A]: I have done nothing. I can't tell when the Devil works.

[Q]: What, doth the Devil tell you that he hurts them?

[A]: No. He tells me nothing.

[Q]: Do you never see something appear in some shape?

[A]: No. Never see anything.

[Q]: What familiarity have you with the Devil, or what is it that
you converse withal? Tell the truth. Who it is that hurts them?

[A]: The Devil for aught I know.

[Q]: What appearance or how doth he appear when he hurts
them? With what shape or what is he like that hurts them?

[A]: Like a man. I think yesterday I being in the lentoe chamber
I saw a thing like a man, that told me serve him and I told him
no, I would not do such thing.[2]

*She charges Goody Osburn and Sarah Good as those that hurt
the children, and would have had her do it. She saith she hath
seen four, two of which she knew not.[3] She saw them last night
as she was washing the room.*

[A]: They told me hurt the children and would have had me
go to Boston. There was five of them with the man. They told me if
I would not go and hurt them they would do so to me. At first I did
agree with them but afterward I told them I do so no more.

[Q]: Would they have had you hurt the children the last night?

[A]: Yes, but I was sorry and I said I would do so no more, but
told I would fear God.

[Q]: But why [scored out] did not you do so before?

[A]: Why, they tell me I had done so before and therefore I must go on. These were the four women and the man, but she knew none but Osburn and Good; only the others were of Boston.[4]

[Q]: At first being with them, what then appeared to you? What was it like that got you to do it?

[A]: One like a man just as I was going to sleep came to me. This was when the children was first hurt. He said he would kill the children and she would never be well and he said if I would not serve him, he would do so to me.

[Q]: Is that the same man that appeared before to you? That appeared the last night and told you this?

[A]: Yes.

[Q]: What other likenesses besides a man hath appeared to you?

[A]: Sometimes like a hog. Sometimes like a great black dog. Four times.

[Q]: But what d [torn] they say unto you?

[A]: They told me serve him and that was a good way. That was the black dog. I told him I was afraid. He told me he would be worse than to me.

[Q]: What did you say to him then after that?

[A]: I answered, I will serve you no longer. He told me he would do me hurt then.

[Q]: What other creatures have you seen?

[A]: A bird.

[Q]: What bird?

[A]: A little yellow bird.

[Q]: Where doth it keep?

[A]: With the man who hath pretty things here besides.[5]

[Q]: What other pretty things?

[A]: He hath not showed them yet unto me, but he said he would show them me tomorrow, and he told me if I would serve him, I should have the bird.

[Q]: What other creatures did you see?

[A]: I saw two cats, one red, another black as big as a little dog.

[Q]: What did these cats do?

[A]: I don't know. I have seen them two times.

[Q]: What did they say?

[A]: They say serve them.

[Q]: When did you see them?

[A]: I saw them last night.

[Q]: Did they do any hurt to you or threaten you?

[A]: They did scratch me.

[Q]: When?

[A]: After prayer, and scratched me because I would not serve them and when they went away, I could not see. But they stood before the fire.

[Q]: What service do they expect from you?

[A]: They say more hurt to the children.

[Q]: How did you pinch them when you hurt them?

[A]: The other pull me and haul me to pinch the child and I am very sorry for it.

[Q]: What made you hold your arm when you were searched? What had you there?

[A]: I had nothing.

[Q]: Do not those cats suck you?

[A]: No, never yet. I would not let them, but they had almost thrust me into the fire.

[Q]: How do you hurt those that you pinch? Do you get those cats or other things to do it for you? Tell us, how is it done?

[A]: The man sends the cats to me and bids me pinch them and I think I went over to Mr. Griggs's and have pinched her this day in the morning. The man brought Mr. Griggs's maid[6] to me and made me pinch her.

[Q]: Did you ever go with these women?

[A]: They are very strong and pull me and make me go with them.

[Q]: Where did you go?

[A]: Up to Mr. Putnam's and make me hurt the child.

[Q]: Who did make you go?

[A]: A man that is very strong and these two women, Good and Osburn. But I am sorry.

[Q]: How did you go? What do you ride upon?

[A]: I rid upon a stick or pole and Good and Osburn behind me. We ride taking hold of one another and don't know how we go for I saw no trees nor path, but was presently there, when we were up.

[Q]: How long since you began to pinch Mr. Parris's children?

[A]: I did not pinch them at the first, but he made me afterward.

[Q]: Have you seen Good and Osburn ride upon a pole?

[A]: Yes and have held fast by me. I was not at Mr. Griggs's but once, but it maybe sent something like me, neither would I have gone, but that they tell me they will hurt me. Last night they tell me I must kill somebody with the knife.

[Q]: Who were they that told you so?

[A]: Sarah Good and Osburn and they would have had me kill Thomas Putnam's child last night.

The child also affirmed that at the same time they would have had her cut her own throat [scored out from "her"] of her own head for if she would not they told her Tituba would cut it off and complained at the same time of a knife cutting of her when her master hath asked her about these thing[torn] she saith they will not let her tell, but tell her if she tells her head shall be cut off.

[Q]: Who [torn] you so?

[A]: The man, Good, and Osburn's wife. Goody Good came to her last night when her master was at prayer and would not let her hear and she could not hear a good while.7 Good hath one of these birds, the yellow bird, and would have given me it, but I would not have it and in prayer time she stopped my ears and would not let me hear.

[Q]: What should you have done with it?

[A]: Give it to the children. Which yellow bird hath been several times seen by the children. I saw Sarah Good have it on her hand when she came to her when Mr. Parris was at prayer. I saw the bird suck Good between the forefinger and long finger upon the right hand.

[Q]: Did you never practice witchcraft in your own country?8

[A]: No. Never before now.

[Q]: Did you [lost] see them do it now while you are examining?

[A]: No, I did not see them but I saw them hurt at other times. I saw Good have a cat beside the yellow bird which was with her.

[Q]: What hath Osburn got to go with her?

[A]: Something. I don't know what it is. I can't name it. I don't know how it looks. She hath two of them. One of them hath wings and two legs and a head like a woman.

The children saw the same but yesterday which afterward turned into a woman.

[Q]: What is the other thing that Goody Osburn hath?

[A]: A thing all over hairy, all the face hairy and a long nose and I don't know how to tell how the face looks. With two legs, it goeth upright and is about two or three foot high and goeth upright like a man and last night it stood before the fire in Mr. Parris's hall.

[Q]: Who was that appeared like a wolf to Hubbard as she was going from Proctures?[9]

[A]: It was Sarah Good and I saw her send the wolf to her.

[Q]: What clothes doth the man appear unto you in?

[A]: Black clothes sometimes, sometimes serge coat or other color, a tall man with white hair, I think.

[Q]: What apparel do the women wear?

[A]: I don't know what color.

[Q]: What kind of clothes hath she?

[A]: A black silk hood with a white silk hood under it with topknots. Which woman I know not but have seen her in Boston when I lived there.

[Q]: What clothes the little woman?

[A]: A serge coat with a white cap, as I think.

The children having fits at this very time, she was asked who hurt them.[10] She answered Goody Good and the children affirmed the same, but Hubbard being taken in an extreme fit after she was asked who hurt her and she said she could not tell, but said they blinded her and would not let her see and after that was once or twice taken dumb herself.

The Second Examination of Tituba[11]

Second Examination, March 2, 1691/2[12]

[Q]: What covenant did you make with that man that came to you? What did he tell you?

[A]: He tell me he God and I must believe him and serve him six years and he would give me many fine things.[13]

[Q]: How long ago was this?

[A]: About six weeks and a little more. Friday night before Abigail was ill.

[Q]: What did he say you must do more? Did he say you must write anything? Did he offer you any paper?

[A]: Yes. The next time he come to me and showed me some fine things. Something like creatures, a little bird something like green and white.

[Q]: Did you promise him then when he spake to you then? What did you answer him?

[A]: I then said this. I told him I could not believe him God. I told him I ask my master and would have gone up but he stopped me and would not let me.

[Q]: What did you promise him?

[A]: The first time I believe him God and then he was glad.

[Q]: What did he say to you then? What did he say you must do?

[A]: This: he tell me they must meet together.

[Q]: When did he say you may meet together?

[A]: He tell me Wednesday next at my master's house, and then they all meet together and that night I saw them all stand in the corner, all four of them, and the man stand behind me and take hold of me to make me stand still in the hall.

[Q]: Time of night?

[A]: A little before prayer time.

[Q]: What did this man say to you when he took hold of you?

[A]: He say go into the other room and see the children and do hurt to them and pinch them. And then I went in and would not hurt them a good while. I would not hurt Betty. I loved Betty, but they haul me and make me pinch Betty and the next Abigail and then quickly went away altogether a [illegible] I had pinched them.

[Q]: Did they pinch?

[A]: No. But they all looked on and see me pinch them.

[Q]: Did you go into that room in your own person and all the rest?

[A]: Yes, and my master did not see us, for they would not let my master see.

[Q]: Did you go with the company?

[A]: No. I stayed and the man stayed with me.

[Q]: What did he then to you?

[A]: He tell me my master go to prayer and he read in book and he ask me what I remember, but don't you remember anything.

[Q]: Did he ask you no more but the first time to serve him or the second time?

[A]: Yes. He ask me again. And that I serve him six years and he Com[illegible] the next time and show me a book.

[Q]: And when would he come then?

[A]: The next Friday and show [illegible] me a book in the day-time, betimes in the morning.

[Q]: And what book did he bring? A great or little book?

[A]: He did not show it me, nor would not but had it in his pocket [illegible].

[Q]: Did not he make you write your name?

[A]: No, not yet for my [his] mistress called me into the other room.

[Q]: What did he say you must do in that book?

[A]: He said write and set my name to it.

[Q]: Did you write?

[A]: Yes. Once I made a mark in the book and made it with red like blood.

[Q]: Did he get it out of your body?

[A]: He said he must get it out the next time he come again. He give me a pin tied in a stick to do it with, but he no let me blood with it as yet but intended another time when he come again.

[Q]: Did you see any other marks in his book?

[A]: Yes, a great many. Some marks red, some yellow. He opened his book. A great many marks in it.

[Q]: Did he tell you the names of them?

[A]: Yes, of two, no more: Good and Osburn, and he say they make them marks in that book and he showed them me.

[Q]: How many marks do you think there was?

[A]: Nine.[14]

[Q]: Did they write their names?

[A]: They made marks. Goody Good said she made her mark, but Goody Osburn would not tell. She was cross to me.

[Q]: When did Good tell you she set her hand to the book?

[A]: The same day I came hither to prison.

[Q]: Did you see the man that morning?

[A]: Yes, a little in the morning and he tell me, tell nothing. If I did he would cut my head off.

[Q]: Tell us, Tr[torn] how many women did use to come when you rode abroad?

[A]: Four of them: these two, Osburn and Good, and those two strangers.

[Q]: You say that there was nine. Did he tell you who they were?

[A]: No. He no let me see but he tell me I should see them the next time.

[Q]: What sights did you see?

[A]: I see a man, a dog, a hog and two cats, a black and red, and the strange monster was Osburn's that I mentioned before. This was the hairy imp. The man would give it to me, but I would not have it.

[Q]: Did he show you in the book which was Osburn's and which was Good's mark?

[A]: Yes. I see their marks.

[Q]: But did he tell the names of the others?

[A]: No, sir.

[Q]: And what did he say to you when you made your mark?

[A]: He said serve me and always serve me. The man with the two women came from Boston.

[Q]: How many times did you go to Boston?

[A]: I was going and [illegible]en came back again. I was never at Boston.

[Q]: Who came back with you again?

[A]: The man came back with me and the women go away. I was not willing to go.

[Q]: How far did you go? To what town?

[A]: I never went to any town. I see no trees, no town.

[Q]: Did he tell you where the nine lived?

[A]: Yes. Some in Boston and some here in this town, but he would not tell me who they were.[15]

THE SUSPICION OF MARTHA CORY
MONDAY, MARCH 21, 1692

Martha Cory was the wife of Giles Cory and was the first woman accused whose accusation might be termed atypical. She was a full church member at a time when church membership was tantamount to social rank and respect, and meant probable membership in the elect who would advance to heaven. She was married, and not in a scandalous or volatile way. She was moneyed. Once Tituba's confession planted the seed of the idea that there was a conspiracy in town, suspicion was then free to spread to members of the community who might otherwise have been thought to be above reproach.

Most striking in Martha Cory's examination was her incredulity that this was really happening to her. In the course of her examination, she claimed that the children were "distracted," that is, crazy. She laughed during the proceedings. She did not claim to know whether there were or were not witches "in the country." The magistrates, in turn, pointed to Tituba's confession as evidence that witches were around, privileging the word of a slave woman over that of a churchwoman.

Martha Cory had publicly suspected that the afflicted girls were lying from the beginning, but her doubt, rather than being heard as a voice of reason within the community, would have been taken by doctrinaire Puritans as an error of faith. To doubt the existence of witches or the Devil was to go against the truth as laid out in the Bible. It was Martha Cory's very skepticism that made her worthy of suspicion and led to her eventual hanging.

Martha Cory's Examination[1]
21 March, 1691/2

[Mr. Hathorne]: You are now in the hands of authority. Tell me now why you hurt these persons.

[Martha Cory]: I do not.

[Mr. Hathorne]: Who doth?

[Martha Cory]: Pray give me leave to go to prayer.

This request was made sundry times.

[Mr. Hathorne]: We do not send for you to go to prayer.

[Mr. Hathorne]: But tell me why you hurt these?

[Martha Cory]: I am an innocent person; I never had to do with witchcraft since I was born. I am a Gospel woman.

[Mr. Hathorne]: Do not you see these complaints of you?

[Martha Cory]: The Lord open the eyes of the magistrates and ministers. The Lord show his power to discover the guilty.

[Mr. Hathorne]: Tell us who hurts these children.

[Martha Cory]: I do not know.

[Mr. Hathorne]: If you be guilty of this fact do you think you can hide it?

[Martha Cory]: The Lord knows.

[Mr. Hathorne]: Well, tell us what you know of this matter.

[Martha Cory]: Why, I am a Gospel woman, and do you think I can have to do with witchcraft too?[2]

[Mr. Hathorne]: How could you tell then that the child was bid to observe what clothes you wore when some came to speak with you?

Cheever interrupted her and bid her not begin with a lie and so Edward Putman declared the matter.[3]

[Mr. Hathorne]: Who told you that?

[Martha Cory]: He said the child said.

[Cheever]: You speak falsely.

Then Edward Putman read again.[4]

[Mr. Hathorne]: Why did you ask if the child told what clothes you wore?

[Martha Cory]: My husband told me the others told.

[Mr. Hathorne]: Who told you about the clothes? Why did you ask that question?

[Martha Cory]: Because I heard the children told what clothes the other wore.

[Mr. Hathorne]: Goodman Cory, did you tell her?

The old man denied that he told her so.

[Mr. Hathorne]: Did you not say your husband told you so?

[Martha Cory]: -

[Mr. Hathorne]: Who hurts these children now? Look upon them.

[Martha Cory]: I cannot help it.

[Mr. Hathorne]: Did you not say you would tell the truth? Why you asked that question: how come you to the knowledge?

[Martha Cory]: I did but ask.

[Mr. Hathorne]: You dare thus to lie in all this assembly.[5]

[Mr. Hathorne]: You are now before authority. I expect the truth. You promised it. Speak now and tell what clothes. [scored out] who told you what clothes?

[Martha Cory]: Nobody.

[Mr. Hathorne]: How came you to know that the children would be examined what cloth you wore?

[Martha Cory]: Because I thought the child was wiser than anybody if she knew.[6]

[Mr. Hathorne]: Give an answer. You said your husband told you.

[Martha Cory]: He told me the children said I afflicted them.

[Mr. Hathorne]: How do you know what they came for? Answer me this truly. Will you say how you came to know what they came for?

[Martha Cory]: I had heard speech that the children said I afflicted them[scored out] troubled them and I thought that they might come to examine.

[Mr. Hathorne]: But how did you know it?

[Martha Cory]: I thought they did.

[Mr. Hathorne]: Did not you say you would tell the truth? Who told you what they came for?

[Martha Cory]: Nobody.

[Mr. Hathorne]: How did you know?

[Martha Cory]: I did think so.

[Mr. Hathorne]: But you said you knew so.

[Children]: There is a man whispering in her ear.[7]

[Mr. Hathorne]: What did he say to you?

[Martha Cory]: We must not believe all that these distracted children say.[8]

[Mr. Hathorne]: Cannot he tell [scored out] you tell what that man whispered?

[**Martha Cory**]: I saw nobody.

[**Mr. Hathorne**]: But did not you hear?

[**Martha Cory**]: No.

Here was extreme agony of all the afflicted.[9]

[**Mr. Hathorne**]: If you expect mercy of God, you must look for it in God's way by confession.

[**Mr. Hathorne**]: Do you think to find mercy by aggravating your sins?

[**Martha Cory**]: A true thing.

[**Mr. Hathorne**]: Look for it then in God's way.

[**Martha Cory**]: So I do.

[**Mr. Hathorne**]: Give glory to God and confess then.

[**Martha Cory**]: But I cannot confess.

[**Mr. Hathorne**]: Do not you see how these afflicted do charge you?

[**Martha Cory**]: We must not believe distracted persons.

[**Mr. Hathorne**]: Who do you improve[10] to hurt them.

[**Martha Cory**]: I improved none.

[**Mr. Hathorne**]: Did not you say our eyes were blinded? You would open them?

[**Martha Cory**]: Yes, to accuse the innocent.

Then Crossly[11] *gave in evidence.*

[**Mr. Hathorne**]: Why cannot the girl stand before you?

[**Martha Cory**]: I do not know.

[**Mr. Hathorne**]: What did you mean by that?

[**Martha Cory**]: I saw them fall down.

[**Mr. Hathorne**]: It seems to be an insulting speech as if they could not stand before you.

[**Martha Cory**]: They cannot stand before others.

[**Mr. Hathorne**]: But you said they cannot stand before you.

[**Mr. Hathorne**]: Tell me what was that turning upon the spit by you?

[**Martha Cory**]: You believe the children that are distracted. I saw no spit.

[**Mr. Hathorne**]: Here are more than two that accuse you for witchcraft. What do you say?

[**Martha Cory**]: I am innocent.

Then Mr. Hathorne read farther of Crossly's evidence.

[**Mr. Hathorne**]: What did you mean by that the Devil could not stand before you?

She denied it.

[Mr. Hathorne]: 3 or 4 sober witnesses confirmed it.[12]

[Martha Cory]: What can I do? Many rise up against me.

[Mr. Hathorne]: Why, confess!

[Martha Cory]: So I would if I were guilty.

[Mr. Hathorne]: Here are sober persons. What do you say to them?

[Mr. Hathorne]: You are a Gospel woman. Will you lie?[13]

Abigail cried out, Next Sabbath is sacrament day, but she shall not come there.

[Martha Cory]: I do not care.

[Mr. Hathorne]: You charge these children with distraction. It is a note of distraction when persons vary in a minute, but these fix upon you. This is not the manner of distraction.[14]

[Martha Cory]: When all are against me, what can I help it?

[Mr. Hathorne]: Now tell me the truth, will you? Why did you say that the magistrates' and ministers' eyes were blinded. You would open them.

She laughed and denied it.[15]

[Mr. Hathorne]: Now tell us how we shall know.

[Mr. Hathorne]: Who doth hurt these if you do not?

[Martha Cory]: Can an innocent person be guilty?

[Mr. Hathorne]: Do you deny these words?

[Martha Cory]: Yes.

[Mr. Hathorne]: Tell who hurts these. We came to be a terror to evildoers.

[Mr. Hathorne]: You say you would open our eyes. We are blind.

[Martha Cory]: If you say I am a witch.

[Mr. Hathorne]: You said you would show us.

She denied it.

[Mr. Hathorne]: Why do you not now show us?

[Martha Cory]: I cannot tell. I do not know.

[Mr. Hathorne]: What did you strike the maid at Mr. Thomas Putman's with?

[Martha Cory]: I never struck her in my life.

[Mr. Hathorne]: Here are two that see you strike her with an iron rod.

[Martha Cory]: I had not hand in it.

[Mr. Hathorne]: Who had?

[Mr. Hathorne]: Do you believe these children are bewitched?

[Martha Cory]: They may for aught I know I have no hand in it.

[Mr. Hathorne]: You say you are no witch. Maybe you mean you never covenanted with the Devil. Did you never deal with any familiar?

[Martha Cory]: No, never.

[Mr. Hathorne]: What bird was that the children spoke of?

Then witnesses spoke.

[Mr. Hathorne]: What [illegible] bird was it?

[Martha Cory]: I know no bird.

[Mr. Hathorne]: It may be. You have engaged you will not confess, but God knows.

[Martha Cory]: So he doth.

[Mr. Hathorne]: Do you believe you shall go unpunished?

[Martha Cory]: I have nothing to do with witchcraft.

[Mr. Hathorne]: Why was you not willing your husband should come to the former session here?

[Martha Cory]: But he came for all.

[Mr. Hathorne]: Did not you take the saddle off?

[Martha Cory]: I did not know what it was for.

[Mr. Hathorne]: Did you not know what it was for?

[Martha Cory]: I did not know that it would be to any benefit.

Somebody said that she would not have them help to find out witches.[16]

[Mr. Hathorne]: Did you not say you would open our eyes? Why do you not?

[Martha Cory]: I never thought of a witch.

[Mr. Hathorne]: Is it a laughing matter to see these afflicted persons?

She denied it.

[Mr. Hathorne]: Several prove it.

[Martha Cory]: They are all against me and I cannot help it.

[Mr. Hathorne]: Do not you believe there are witches in the country.

[Martha Cory]: I do not know that there is any.

[Mr. Hathorne]: Do not you know that Tituba confessed it?[17]

[Martha Cory]: I did not hear her speak.

[Mr. Hathorne]: I find you will own nothing without several witnesses and yet you will deny for all.

It was noted when she bit her lip several of the afflicted were bitten.

When she was urged upon it that she bit her lip saith she, What harm is there in it.

[Mr. Noyes]: I believe it is apparent she practiceth witchcraft in the congregation. There is no need of images.

[Mr. Hathorne]: What do you say to all these things that are apparent?

[Martha Cory]: If you will all go hang me, how can I help it?

[Mr. Hathorne]: Were you to serve the Devil ten years? Tell how many.[18]

She laughed.

The children cried, There was a yellow bird with her.

When Mr. Hathorne asked her about it, she laughed.

When her hands were at liberty, the afflicted persons were pinched.

[Mr. Hathorne]: Why do not you tell how the Devil comes in your shapes and hurts these? You said you would.

[Martha Cory]: How can I know how?

She laughed again.

[Mr. Hathorne]: What book is that you would have these children write it?

[Martha Cory]: What book? Where should I have a book? I showed them none, nor have none nor brought none.

The afflicted cried out there was a man whispering in her ears.

[Mr. Hathorne]: What book did you carry to Mary Walcott?

[Martha Cory]: I carried none. If the Devil appears in my shape.

Then Needham said that Parker some time ago thought this woman was a witch.

[Mr. Hathorne]: Who is your God?

[Martha Cory]: The God that made me.

[Mr. Hathorne]: Who is that God?

[Martha Cory]: The God that made me.

[Mr. Hathorne]: What is his name?

[Martha Cory]: Jehovah.

[Mr. Hathorne]: Do you know any other name?

[Martha Cory]: God Almighty.

[Mr. Hathorne]: Doth he tell you that you pray to that he is God Almighty?

[Martha Cory]: Who do I worship but the God that made?

[Mr. Hathorne]: How many Gods are there?

[Martha Cory]: One.

[Mr. Hathorne]: How many persons?

[Martha Cory]: Three.

[Mr. Hathorne]: Cannot you say so? There is one God in three blessed persons.

[Torn]

[Mr. Hathorne]: Do not you see these children and women are rational and sober as their neighbors? When your hands are fastened.

Immediately they were seized with fits and the standers by said she was squeezing her fingers.

Her hands being eased by them that held them on purpose for trial.

Quickly after, the marshal said she hath bit her lip and immediately the afflicted were in an uproar.

[Torn]

[Mr. Hathorne]: You hurt these. Or who doth?

She denieth any hand in it.

[Mr. Hathorne]: Why did you say if you were a witch you should have no pardon?

[Martha Cory]: Because I am a [torn] woman.

Salem Village, March the 21st, 1691/2

The Reverend Mr. Samuel Parris being desired to take in writing the examination of Martha Cory, hath returned it as aforesaid. Upon hearing the aforesaid and seeing what we did then see, together with the charges of the persons then present we committed Martha Cory, the wife of Giles Cory of Salem Farms, unto the jail in Salem as mittimus then given out.

John Hathorne. Assistant, Jonathan Corwin.

THE ACCUSATION OF
REBECCA NURSE
THURSDAY, MARCH 24, 1692

The accusation of Rebecca Nurse, like that of Martha Cory, represented a complete break with convention in New England witch trials. Rebecca Nurse was universally well liked and, like Martha Cory, was a full church member. Unlike the other accused witches who were women of middle age, therefore posing at least a theoretical threat of bringing physical harm against their accusers, Nurse's possible malfeasance would have been confined wholly to the spectral realm. Rebecca Nurse at the time of the trials was sick and bedridden.[1] Only through spectral means, such as sending her spirit out in a different shape, could she harm anyone, opening the legal problem of spectral evidence in the course of the Salem witch trials. Theologians remained undecided over whether the Devil could assume the shape of an innocent person.

Rebecca Nurse's accusation stemmed from the reported spectral sufferings of Ann Putnam Jr., the daughter of Thomas Putnam. The Putnams and the extended Nurse family had been in conflict for several years over the boundaries of their land, and so Ann would have heard her spoken of often in the course of family discussions and complaints. In fact, it has been suggested that Ann Carr Putnam, the mother of Ann Jr., supplied the name to the apparition that Ann Jr. reported seeing.[2]

Unlike Martha Cory, who was dismissive during her examination, Rebecca Nurse appeared calm and godly, expressing empathy for the afflicted girls. Nurse believed in the reality of their bewitchment, even if she claimed to be an "innocent person" herself. Her empathy did not

*save her, in the end, from the gallows, any more than
Cory's contempt.*

Rebecca Nurse's Examination[3]

The Examination of Rebecca Nurse at Salem Village,
24 March, 1691/2

[Mr. Hathorne]: What do you say (speaking to one afflicted)?
Have you seen this woman hurt you?

[Afflicted girl]: Yes, she beat me this morning.

[Mr. Hathorne]: Abigail, have you been hurt by this woman?

[Abigail]: Yes.

Ann Putnam in a grievous fit cried out that she hurt her.

[Mr. Hathorne]: Goody Nurse, here are two, Ann Putnam
the child and Abigail Williams, complain of your hurting them.
What do you say to it?

[Rebecca Nurse]: I can say before my eternal father I am innocent, and God will clear my innocency.

[Mr. Hathorne]: Here is never a one in the assembly but desires
it, but if you be guilty, may God discover you.

Then Henry Kenny rose up to speak.

[Mr. Hathorne]: Goodman Kenny, what do you say?

*Then he entered his complaint and farther said that since
this Nurse came into the house, We was seized twice with an
amazed[4] condition.*

[Mr. Hathorne]: Here are not only these but here is the wife
of Mr. Thomas Putnam who accuseth you by credible information and that both of tempting her to iniquity and of greatly
hurting her.

[Rebecca Nurse]: I ha[scored out] am innocent and clear and
have not been able to get out of doors these 8 or 9 days.

[Mr. Hathorne]: Mr. Putnam, give in what you have to say.

Then Mr. Edward Putnam gave in his relate.

[Mr. Hathorne]: Is this true Goody Nurse?

[Rebecca Nurse]: I never afflicted no child never in my life.

[Mr. Hathorne]: You see these accuse you. Is it true?

[Rebecca Nurse]: No.

[Mr. Hathorne]: Are you an innocent person relating to this
witchcraft?

Here Thomas Putnam's wife cried out, Did you not bring the black man with you? Did you not bid me tempt God and die? How oft have you eat and drunk your own damaon?[5]

[Mr. Hathorne]: What do you say to them?

[Rebecca Nurse]: Oh, Lord help me, *and spread out her hands, and the afflicted were grievously vexed.*

[Mr. Hathorne]: Do you not see what a solemn condition these are in? When your hands are loose the persons are afflicted.

Then Mary Walcott (who often heretofore said she had seen her, but never could say or did say that she either bit or pinched her or hurt her) and also Elizabeth Hubbard[6] under the like circumstances both openly accused her of hurting them.

[Mr. Hathorne]: Here are these 2 grown persons now accuse you. What say you? Do not you see these afflicted persons and hear them accuse you?

[Rebecca Nurse]: The Lord knows I have not hurt them. I am an innocent person.

[Mr. Hathorne]: It is very awful to all to see these agonies and you an old professor[7] thus charged with contracting with the Devil by the effects of it and yet to see you stand with dry eyes when these are so many what.

[Rebecca Nurse]: You do not know my heart.

[Mr. Hathorne]: You would do well if you are guilty to confess and give glory to God.

[Rebecca Nurse]: I am clear as the child unborn.

[Mr. Hathorne]: What uncertainty there may be in apparitions I know not, yet this with me strikes hard upon you that you are at this very present charged with familiar spirits. This is your bodily person they speak to. They say now they see these familiar spirits come to your bodily person. Now what do you say to that?

[Rebecca Nurse]: I have none, sir.

[Mr. Hathorne]: If you have confessed and give glory to God, I pray God clear you if you be innocent, and if you are guilty discover you. And therefore give me an upright answer. Have you any familiarity with these spirits?

[Rebecca Nurse]: No, I have none but with God alone.

[Mr. Hathorne]: How came you sick for there is an odd discourse of that in the mouths of many.

[Rebecca Nurse]: I am sick at my stomach.

[Mr. Hathorne]: Have you no wounds?

[Rebecca Nurse]: I have none but old age.

[Mr. Hathorne]: You do know whether you are guilty and have familiarity with the Devil and now when you are here present to see such a thing as these testify a black man whispering in your ear and birds about you, what do you say to it?

[Rebecca Nurse]: It is all false. I am clear.

[Mr. Hathorne]: Possibly you may apprehend you are no witch, but have you not been led aside by temptations that way?[8]

[Rebecca Nurse]: I have not.

[Mr. Hathorne]: What a sad thing is it that a church member here and now an[9] others of Salem should be thus accused and charged.

Mrs. Pope fell into a grievous fit and cried out, A sad thing sure enough. *And then many more fell into lamentable fits.*

[Mr. Hathorne]: Tell us. Have not you had visible appearances more than what is common in nature?

[Rebecca Nurse]: I have none nor never had in my life.

[Mr. Hathorne]: Do you think these suffer voluntary or involuntary?

[Rebecca Nurse]: I cannot tell.

[Mr. Hathorne]: That is strange. Everyone can judge.

[Rebecca Nurse]: I must be silent.

[Mr. Hathorne]: They accuse you of hurting them, and if you think it is [torn] but by design you must look upon them as murderers.

[Rebecca Nurse]: I cannot tell what to think of it.

Afterward when she was somewhat insisted on, she said, I do not think so. *She did not understand aright what was said.*

[Mr. Hathorne]: Well, then, give an answer now. Do you think these suffer against their wills or not?

[Rebecca Nurse]: I do not think these suffer against their wills.

[Mr. Hathorne]: Why did you never visit these afflicted persons?

[Rebecca Nurse]: Because I was afraid I should have fits too.

Not upon the motion of her body had [scored out] fits followed upon the complainants abundantly and very frequently.

[Mr. Hathorne]: Is it not an unaccountable case that when yes[scored out] you are examined these persons are afflicted?

[Rebecca Nurse]: I have got nobody to look to but God.

Again upon stirring her hands, the afflicted persons were seized with violent fits of torture.

[**Mr. Hathorne**]: Do you believe these afflicted persons are bewitched?

[**Rebecca Nurse**]: I do think they are.[10]

[**Mr. Hathorne**]: When this witchcraft came upon the stage there was no suspicion of Tituba *(Mr. Parris's Indian woman)*. She professed much love to that child Betty Parris, but it was her apparition did the mischief, and why should not you also be guilty, for your apparition doth hurt also.

[**Rebecca Nurse**]: Would you have me bely[11] my your [scored out] self.

She held her neck on one side, and accordingly so were the afflicted taken.

The authority requiring it Samuel Parris read what he had in character[12] taken from Mr. Thomas Putman's wife in her fits.

[**Mr. Hathorne**]: What do you think of this?

[Verso]

This is a true account of the sum of her examination, but by reason of great noises by the afflicted and many speakers many things are pretermitted.[13]

Memorandum

Nurse held her neck on one side and Elizabeth Hubbard (one of the sufferers) had her neck set in that posture. Whereupon another patient, Abigail Williams, cried out, Set up Goody Nurse's head. The maid's neck will be broke and when some set up Nurse's head Aaron Wey observed that Betty Hubbard's was immediately righted.

Salem Village, March 24th, 1691/2

The Reverend Mr. Samuel Parris being desired to take in writing the examination of Rebecca Nurse hath returned it aforesaid.

Upon hearing the aforesaid and seeing what we then did see together with the charges of the persons then present were committed Rebecca Nurse, the wife of Frances Nurse of Salem Village, unto Their Majesties' jail in Salem as a Mittimus then given out, and [scored out] in order to further examination.

John Hathorne. Assistant, Jonathan Corwin

WARRANT FOR THE APPREHENSION OF RACHEL CLINTON, WITH SUMMONS FOR WITNESSES, AND OFFICER'S RETURN TUESDAY, MARCH 29, 1692

This warrant was the first that did not directly issue from the authorities in Salem Village. Rachel Clinton had actually suffered a bad reputation for decades.[1] She had an unfortunate marriage and was disinherited, plummeting from the top of society to the bottom, and at this point lived in Ipswich. Thus, the accusation of Rachel, who, on the one hand, was a usual suspect as far as witches were concerned but on the other hand was outside the power struggles of Salem Village, marked a crucial turning point in the transition of the Salem panic from small-scale community battle to large-scale outbreak. With this warrant, the Salem panic began to extend into the rest of Essex County.

Warrant Against Rachel Clinton[2]

To the constable of Ipswich

Whereas there is complaint exhibited to the honored court now Const[illegible] holden at Ipswich in behalf of Their Majesties against Rachel, formerly the wife of Laurence Clinton of Ipswich, on grounded suspicion of witchcraft and whereas recognizance is entered for prosecution.

You are hereby required in Their Majesties' names forthwith

or s[illegible] soon as may be to apprehend, seize, and bring before the honored court to be holden at Ipswich the said Rachel Clinton on the next morrow[scored out] morning at eight a clock in order to an orderly examination and conviction and hereof fail not at your peril and for so doing this shall be your warrant of which you are to make a true return as the law directs.

Ipswich, March 29th, 1692, Curiam Thomas Wade, clerk, to the constable of Ipswich

You are hereby required in Their Majesties' names to summons, warn, and require to appear at the court to be holden at Ipswich on the morrow morning. Namely, Mary Fuller Senior and Mary Fuller Junior and Alexander Thomson Junior and Richard Fits and Doctor John Brigham and Thomas Manning and Nathaniel Burnham, all of Ipswich, and Thomas Knowlton Junior and Mary Thorne to give in their several evidences before the court to clear up the grounds of suspicion of Rachel Clinton's being a witch and hereof fail not at your peril but make a true return under your hand as the law directs.

Curiam Thomas Wade, clerk

[verso]

I have served this Sp[scored out] warrant or read it to Rachel Clinton this morning and seized her body and left her in the hands of Samuel Ordway here in the courthouse against your honors shall call for her.

And I have read the several warrants, one the other side written this morning. Save only Richard Fits and Mary Thorne. And Richard Fits I could not find and Mary Thorne is not well, as witness, my hand, Joseph Fuller, constable of Ipswich, dated this 29th March, 1691/2.

Warrant against Rachel Clinton returned.[3]

DEPOSITION OF THOMAS KNOWLTON JR. VERSUS RACHEL CLINTON

Rachel Clinton was without question an angry woman. In this deposition, we learn that Clinton had been forced into begging to sustain herself after her husband abandoned her. Clinton went to the house of John Rogers, who was out of town in Boston, and over the protests of the maid, began to peek around the house looking for milk and meat. The maid asked Thomas Knowlton to assist in removing Rachel from Rogers's house. As he did this, Clinton denounced him, calling him "hellhound" and "whoremasterly rogue" and a "limb of the Devil."

This account is incredibly vibrant, exposing how dangerous it was to be an angry woman in the early modern period, especially at the fringes of society. Rachel Clinton's frustrations at being without food led to her being accused of witchcraft.

Knowlton's Deposition[1]

[Torn]he deposition of Thomas Knowlton, aged 50 years, saith that about 3 weeks ago that Mr. John Rogers and his wife were gone to Bosto[torn] That Rachel, the wife of Laron Clinton that is now suspected to be a witch, went to Mr. Rogers's house and told Mr. Rogers's maid that she must have some meat and milk and the said Rachel went into seve[torn]al rooms of the said house, as Mr. Rogers's maid told me and then sent for me, this deponent, to get her away out of the hous[torn] And when I came into the house there was Rachel Clinton and when she sa[illegible]we me come in she, the said Rachel, went away scoldi[torn][2] and railing. Calling of me, the said Thomas, hellhound and whoremasterly rogue and said I was a limb of the Devil and she said[torn] she had rather see the Devil than see me, the said Thomas. And that Samuel Aires and Thomas Smith, tailor, can testify to the same languages that Rachel used or called the said Knowlton. And after this the said Rachel took up a stone and threw it toward me and it fell short three or four yards from me, said Knowlton, a[torn] so came rolling to me and just touched the toe of my shoe[torn] And presently my great toe was in a great rage as if the nail were held up by a pair of pinchers up by the roots.

And further the said Thomas Knowlton testifieth and saith that about 3 months ago that my daughter Mary Ded [torn][illegible]e and cried out in a dreadful manner that she was p[torn][3] of her side with pins as she thought. Being asked who pric[torn] her, she said she could not tell and when she was out of her fits, I, this deponent, asked her whether she gave Rach[torn][4] any pins and she said she gave Rachel about seven and after this she had one fit more of being pricked and then there came into our house Cornelius Kent and John Best, a[torn] saw Mary Knowlton in a solemn condition, crying as if she would be pricked to death and then said Kent and Best and my son Thomas went over and threatened said Rachel that if ever she pricked said Mary Knowlton again they would knock out her brains and ever since my girl hath been well.

BRIDGET BISHOP
TUESDAY, APRIL 19, 1692

Bridget Bishop, though she was accused a few months after Sarah Good, Sarah Osburn, and Tituba Indian, was the first person executed. She was accused of the murder of her first husband by witchcraft and of spectrally coming into the bedchamber of Marshal Herrick. The account of her entry into his bedchamber illustrates the sexual threat embodied by witches, particularly the threat that they posed to male authority.

Bridget Bishop was also an example of the spread of the accusations outside the main purview of the small community of Salem Village. She was a woman of dubious character, living in Salem Town, who was not personally acquainted with any of the afflicted girls, nor did she have a stake in any of the ongoing conflict between the various factions in Salem Village. Instead, she was a woman who had been tried as a witch once before and who had stoked the suspicion of her neighbors for years.[1]

The use of conventional courtroom arguments, like proof by negation ("if you don't know what a witch is, how do you know that you are not a witch?"), illustrates that the existence of witchcraft was treated in the court system like any other common felony. Witchcraft was a real enough phenomenon in the colonial New England intellectual world that it could be argued as any other criminal act.

The Examination of Bridget Bishop[2]

The Examination of Bridget Bishop at Salem Village
19 April, 1692
by John Hathorne and Jonathan Corwin, esquires

As soon as she came near all fell into fits.

[Q]: Bridget Bishop, you are now brought before authority to give account of what witchcrafts you are conversant in.

[A]: I take all this people *(turning her head and eyes about)* to witness that I am clear.

[Q]: Hath this woman hurt you *(speaking to the afflicted)*?

A[illegible]g Hubb[?]d[scored out] Elizabeth Hubbard, Ann Putnam, Abigail Williams, and Mercy Lewis affirmed she had hurt them.

[Q]: You are here accused by 4 or 5 for hurting them. What do you say to it?

[A]: I never saw these persons before; nor I never was in this place before.

Mary Walcott says that her brother Jonathan stroke her appearance and she saw that ha[scored out] he had tore her coat in striking, and she heard it tear.

Upon sea[scored out] some search in the court, a rent that seems to answer what was alleged was found.

[Q]: They say you bewitched your first husband to death.[3]

[A]: If it please your worship, I know nothing of it.

She shake her head and the afflicted were tortured.

The like again upon the motion of her head.

Sam. Braybrook affirmed that she told him today that she had been accounted a witch these 10 years, but she was no witch. The Devil cannot hurt her.

[A]: I am no witch.

[Q]: Why if you have not wrote in the book, yet tell me how far you have gone? Have you not to do with familiar spirits?

[A]: I have no familiarity with the Devil.

[Q]: How is it, then, that your appearance doth hurt these?

[A]: I am innocent.

[Q]: Why you seem to act witchcraft before us, but the motion of your body, which has in[scored out] seems to have influence upon the afflicted.

[A]: I know nothing of it. I am innocent to a witch. I know not what a witch is.

[Q]: How do you know then that you are not a witch? And yet not know what a witch is? [scored out from "and yet"]

[A]: I do not understand [scored out] know what you say.

[Q]: How can you know you are no witch, and yet not know what a witch is?⁴

[A]: I am clear: if I were any such person you should know it.

[Q]: You may threaten, but you can do no more than you are permitted.

[A]: I am innocent of a witch.

[Q]: What do you say of those murders you are charged with?

[A]: I hope I am not guilty of murder.

Then she turned up her eyes and they [scored out] the eyes of the afflicted were turned up.

[Q]: It may be you do not know that any have confessed today, who have been examined before you, that they are witches.

[A]: No, I know nothing of it.

John Hutchinson and John Hewes in open court affirmed that they had told her.⁵

[Q]: Why look you, you are taken now in a flat lie.

[A]: I did not hear them.

Note Sam. Gold saith that after this examination he asked said Bridget Bishop if she were not troubled to see the afflicted persons so tormented, said Bishop answered no, she was not troubled for them. Then he asked her whether she thought they were bewitched. She said she could not tell what to think about them. Will Good and John Buxton Junior was by and he supposeth they heard her also.

Salem Village, April the 19th, 1692, Mr. Samuel Parris being desired to take into writing the examination of Bridget Bishop, hath delivered it as aforesaid. And upon hearing the same, and seeing what we did then see, together wit[torn] the charge of the afflicted persons th[torn] present, we committed said Bridg[torn] Oliver.

John Hathorne.

THE NOTORIOUS
GILES CORY
TUESDAY, APRIL 19, 1692

Giles Cory, husband of accused witch Martha Cory, is one of the most notorious Salem witches because he was not only a man, but a man who was crushed to death between stones rather than hanged. With his case, we can see the spreading of the accusations not only across class lines, but also within families. Cory died because he refused to enter a plea, and the punishment of "peine forte et dure," or "pain long and difficult," was imposed in an attempt to compel him to plead.[1]

Giles Cory, however, was no gentle and retiring soul. In 1675 he had kicked a servant to death, a crime which had largely gone forgotten in his community, but which reasserted itself in the public memory once Ann Putnam began to report seeing him in her spectral visitations.[2] Even choosing the death that would come from being pressed to death required a certain stoniness of character. Robert Calef, writing his later skeptical account of the Salem trials, reported that the pressure on his body was so great that his "Tongue being prest out of his Mouth, the Sheriff with his Cane forced it in again, when he was dying."[3]

The Examination of Giles Cory[4]

The examination of Giles Cory, at a court at Salem Village, held by John Hathorne and Jonathan Corwin, esquires, April 19, 1692.

[Q]: Giles Cory, you are brought before authority upon high suspicion of sundry acts of witchcraft; now tell us the truth in this matter.

[A]: I hope through the goodness of God I shall, for that matter I never had no hand in, in my life.

[Q]: Which of you have seen this man hurt you?

Mary Wolcott, Mercy Lewis, Ann Putman Jr., and Abigail Williams affirmed he had hurt them.

[Q]: Hath he hurt you too? *Speaking to Elizabeth Hubbard.*

She going to answer was prevented by a fit.

[Q]: Benjamin Gold, hath he hurt you?

[Gold]: I have seen him several times, and been hurt after it, but cannot affirm that it was he.

[Q]: Hath he brought the book to any of you?

Mary Wolcott and Abigail Williams and others affirmed that he brought the book to them.

[Q]: Giles Cory, they accuse you, or your appearance, of hurting them and bringing the book to them. What do you say? Why do you hurt them? Tell us the truth.

[A]: I never did hurt them.

[Q]: It is your appearance hurts them, they charge you; tell us what you have done.

[A]: I have done nothing to damage them.

[Q]: Have you never entered into contract with the Devil?

[A]: I never did.

[Q]: What temptations have you had?

[A]: I never had temptations in my life.

[Q]: What, have you done it without temptations?[5]

[Q]: What was the reason *(said Goodwife Bibber)* that you were frighted in the cow-house? *And then the questioner was suddenly seized with a violent fit.*

Samuel Braybrook, Goodman Bibber, and his daughter testified that he had told them this morning that he was frighted in the cow-house.

Cory denied it.

[Q]: This was not your appearance but your person, and you told them so this morning. Why do you deny it? What did you see in the cow-house?

[A]: I never saw nothing but my cattle.

Diverse witnessed that he told them he was frighted.

[Q]: Well, what do you say to these witnesses? What was it frighted you?

[A]: I do not know that ever I spoke the word in my life.

[Q]: Tell the truth. What was it frighted you?

[A]: I do not know anything that frighted me.

All the afflicted were seized now with fits and troubled with pinches. Then the court ordered his hands to be tied.

[Q]: What, is it not enough to act witchcraft at other times, but must you do it now in the face of authority?

[A]: I am a poor creature, and cannot help it.

Upon the motion of his head again, they had their heads and necks afflicted.

[Q]: Why do you tell such wicked lies against witnesses, that heard you speak after this manner, this very morning?

[A]: I never saw anything but a black hog.

[Q]: You said that you were stopped once in prayer. What stopped you?

[A]: I cannot tell. My wife came toward me and found fault with me for saying living to God and dying to sin.

[Q]: What was it frighted you in the barn?

[A]: I know nothing frighted me there.

[Q]: Why, here are three witnesses that heard you say so today.

[A]: I do not remember it.

Thomas Gold testified that he heard him say that he knew enough against his wife that would do her business.[6]

[Q]: What was that you knew against your wife?

[A]: Why that of living to God, and dying to sin.

The marshal and Bibber's daughter confirmed the same, that he said he could say that that would do his wife's business.

[A]: I have said what I can say to that.

[Q]: What was that about your ox?

[A]: I thought he was hipt.[7]

[Q]: What ointment was that your wife had when she was seized? You said it was ointment she made by Major Gidney's direction.

He denied it, and said she had it of Goody Bibber, or from her direction.

Goody Bibber said it is not like that ointment.

[Q]: You said you knew, upon your own acknowledgment, that she had it of Major Gidney.

He denied it.

[Q]: Did not you say, when you went to the ferry with your wife, you would not go over to Boston now, for you should come yourself the next week?

[A]: I would not go over, because I had not money.

The marshal testified he said as before.

One of his hands was let go, and several were afflicted.

He held his head on one side, and then the heads of several of the afflicted were held on one side. He drew in his cheeks, and the cheeks of some of the afflicted were sucked in.

John Bibber and his wife gave in testimony concerning some temptations he had to make away with himself.[8]

[Q]: How doth this agree with what you said, that you had no temptations?

[A]: I meant temptations to witchcraft.

[Q]: If you can give way to self-murder, that will make way to temptation to witchcraft.

Note. There was witness by several that he said he would make away with himself, and charge his death upon his son.

Goody Bibber testified that the said Cory called said Bibber's husband damned, devilish rogue.

Other vile expressions testified in open court by several others.

Salem Village, April 19, 1692

Mr. Samuel Parris being desired to take in writing the examination of Giles Cory, delivered it in, and upon hearing the same, and seeing what we did see at the time of his examination, together with the charge of the afflicted persons against him, we committed him to Their Majesties' jail.

    John Hathorne

EXAMINATIONS OF ABIGAIL HOBBS IN PRISON WEDNESDAY, APRIL 20, 1692

In this examination, confessed witch Abigail Hobbs accused George Burroughs, the previous minister in Salem Village, of being a witch. After his time in Salem, Burroughs had moved to Falmouth, Maine, where Hobbs knew him when she was living there with her family. Abigail claimed that Burroughs had brought her puppets to stick with thorns, including a puppet of his wife, which was a reference to the image magic that appeared frequently in accounts of early modern English folk magic. This examination elucidates the fact that the Salem Villagers would have seen the presence of witches in their midst as part of an overarching attack on their godly settlement by the Devil, who was also responsible for the attacks on their settlements by Catholic Indians and French, and who was recruiting witches to Maine in league with the Wabanaki tribe.

With the naming of George Burroughs, a man and a respected minister, as a witch, we also begin to see the rapid ascent of the accusations up the social hierarchy.[1] By this time in the trials, the inquiry had expanded far beyond the normal confines of a North American (or even English) witch trial. The accusations were reaching people whose reputations would normally have made them immune to suspicion. They have also extended well beyond the confines of the village. Though Burroughs would have left a reputation behind him when he left Salem Village, it is his questionable

*reputation and involvement in the Maine violence that
drew suspicion.*

Hobbs Accuses George Burroughs[2]

Abigail Hobbs's Examination, 20 April 1692 in Salem Prison.
This examinant declares that Judah White, a Jersey maid that
lived with Joseph Ingersoll at Casco but now lives at Boston, with
whom this examinant was very well formerly acquainted, came
to her yesterday in apparition, as she was g[scored out from "as"]
together with Sarah Good, as this examinant was going to examination, and advised her to fly, and not to go to be examined. She
told them that she would go. They charged her if she did go to
examination not to confess anything. She said she would confess
all that she knew. They told her also Goody Osburn was a witch.
This Judah White came to her in fine clothes, in a sad[3] colored
silk [illegible] mantel, with a topknot and a hood. She confesseth
further that the Devil, in the shape of a man, came to her and
would have her to afflict Ann Putnam, Mercy Lewis, and Abigail
Williams, and brought their images with him in wood like them,
and gave her thorns, and bid her prick them into those images,
which she did accordingly into each of them one.[4] And then the
Devil told her they were afflicted, which accordingly they were
and cried out they were hurt by Abigail Hobbs. She confesseth
she was at the great meeting in Mr. Parris's pasture when they
administered the sacrament, and did eat of the red bread and
drink of the red wine at the same time.[5]

Abigail Hobbs's Examination at Salem Prison, May 12, 1692
[Q]: Did Mr. Burroughs[6] bring you any of the poppets of his
wife's to stick pins into?
[A]: I do not remember that he did.
[Q]: Did he of any of his children or of the Eastward soldiers?[7]
[A]: No.
[Q]: Have you known of any that have been killed by witch-
craft?
[A]: No. Nobody.
[Q]: How came you to speak of Mr. Burroughs's wife yester-
day?
[A]: I don't know.

[Q]: Is that true about Davis's son of Casco? And of those of the village?

[A]: Yes, it is true.

[Q]: What service did he put you upon? And who are they you afflicted?

[A]: I cannot tell who, neither do I know whether they died.

[Q]: Were they stranger to you, that Burroughs would have you afflict?

[A]: Yes.

[Q]: And were they afflicted accordingly?

[A]: Yes.

[Q]: Can't you name some of them?

[A]: No. I cannot remember them.

[Q]: Where did they live?

[A]: At the Eastward.

[Q]: Have any vessels been cast away by you?

[A]: I do not know.

[Q]: Have you consented to the afflicting of any other besides those of the village?

[A]: Yes.

[Q]: Who were they?

[A]: I cannot tell. But it was of such who lived at the fort side of the river about half a mile from the fort, toward Captain Bracketts.

[Q]: What was the hurt you did to them by consent?

[A]: I don't know.

[Q]: Was the[illegible] anything brought to y [torn] ke them?

[A]: Yes.

[Q]: Did [scored out] Q. What did you stick into the [illegible]?

[A]: Thorns.

[Q]: [torn] of them die?

[A]: Yes. [torn] of them was Mary.

[Q]: [torn] Did you stick the thorns?

[A]: I do not know.

[Q]: Was it about [illegible] [torn]

[A]: Yes, and I stuck it right in.

Q. What provoked you? Had she displeased you?

[A]: Yes, by some words she spoke of me.

[Q]: Who brought the image to you?

[A]: It was Mr. Burroughs.

[Q]: How did he bring it to you?

[A]: In his own person. Bodily.

[Q]: Where did he bring it to you?

[A]: Abroad a little way off from the house.

[Q]: And what did he say to you then?

[A]: He told me he was angry with that family.

[Q]: How many years since was it?

[A]: Before this Indian war.[8]

[Q]: How did you know Mr. Burroughs was a witch?

[A]: I don't know.

She owned again she had made two covenants with the Devil, first for two years, and after that for four years, and she confesseth herself to have been a witch these six years.

[Q]: Did the maid complain of pain about the place you stuck the thorn in?

[A]: Yes. But how long she lived I don't know.

[Q]: How do you know Burroughs was angry with Lawrence's family?

[A]: Because he told me so.

[Q]: Where did any other live that you afflicted?

[A]: Just by the other toward James Andrews's, and they died also.

[Q]: How many? Were they more than one?

[A]: Yes.

[Q]: And who brought those poppets to you?

A. Mr. Burroughs.

[Q]: What did you stick into them?

[A]: Pins, and he gave them to me.

[Q]: Did you keep those poppets?

[A]: No, he carried them away with him.

[Q]: Was he there himself with you in bodily person?

[A]: Yes, and so he was when he appeared to tempt me to set my hand to the book, he then appeared in person, and I felt his hand at the same time.

[Q]: Were they men, women or children you killed?

[A]: They were both boys and girls.

[Q]: Were you angry with them yourself?

[A]: Yes, though I don't know why now.

[Q]: Did you know Mr. Burroughs's wife?

[A]: Yes.
[Q]: Did you know of any poppets pricked to kill her?
[A]: No, I don't.
[Q]: Have you seen several witches at the Eastward?
[A]: Yes. But I don't know who they were.

SUSANNAH MARTIN AND HER POOR REPUTATION MONDAY, MAY 2, 1692

Susannah Martin, a widow from Amesbury only a few years younger than Rebecca Nurse, had suffered a poor reputation as a witch for over two decades.[1] She mounted her own defense in theological terms, articulating the controversial belief that the Devil could appear in whatever shape he would like, including the shape of an innocent person. In her claim that "he that appeared in same shape as glorified saint can appear in anyone's shape," she spoke to some of the doubts that theologians were beginning to express as the course of the trials started to rapidly expand. "Glorified saint" in Martin's telling refers to the Bible's witch of Endor, who conjured an image meant to be the spirit of Samuel.[2] If Samuel could be represented by witchcraft, then certainly Susannah Martin could have been. Like Martha Cory, Susannah Martin also expressed contempt for the proceedings.

At Martin's examination we learn that the makeup of the group of afflicted has started to shift. What began as a collection of young girls bolstered by the word of a few teenagers now included a number of adults, most notably John Indian, Tituba's husband. His affliction undermines the fun, but unsound, theory that ergot poisoning caused the girls' fits: as a grown man, he would not have had the same symptoms of convulsive ergotism as an adolescent girl.

Susannah Martin Defending Herself[3]

The Examination of Susannah Martin, 2 May 1692
As soon as she came in many had fits.

[Q]: Do you know this woman?

Abigail Williams saith, It is Goody Martin. She hath hurt me often.

Others by fits were hindered from speaking.

Elizabeth Hubbard said she hath not been hurt by her.

John Indian said he hath not seen her.

Mercy Lewis pointed to her and fell into a little fit.

Ann Putman threw her glove in a fit at her.

The examinant laughed.

[Q]: What do you laugh at?.

[A]: Well I may at such folly.

[Q]: Is this folly? The hurt of these persons?

[A]: I never hurt man, woman, or child.

Mercy Lewis cried out, She hath hurt me a great many times and pulls me down.

Then Martin laughed again.

Mary Walcott saith, This woman hath hurt me a great many times.

Susannah Sheldon also accused her of afflicting her.

[Q]: What do you say to this?

[A]: I have no hand in witchcraft.

[Q]: What did you do? Did not you give your consent?[4]

[A]: No, never in my life.

[Q]: What ails this people?

[A]: I do not know.

[Q]: But what do you think?

[A]: I do not desire to spend my judgment upon it.

[Q]: Do not you think they are bewitched?

[A]: No, I do not think they are.

[Q]: Tell me your thoughts about them.

[A]: Why, my thoughts are my own, when they are in, but when they are out they are another's.

[Q]: You said their master. Who do you think is their master?

[A]: If they be dealing the black art, you may know as well as I.[5]

[Q]: Well, what have you done toward this?

[A]: Nothing.

[Q]: Why it is you, or your appearance.

[A]: I cannot help it.

[Q]: That may be your master.

[A]: I desire to lead myself according to the will of God [scored from "will"] word of God.

[Q]: Is this according to God's word?

[A]: If I were such a person I would tell you the truth.

[Q]: How comes your appearance just now to hurt these.

[A]: How do I know?

[Q]: Are not you willing to tell the truth?

[A]: I cannot tell. He that appeared in same shape as glorified saint can appear in anyone's shape.[6]

[Q]: Do you believe these do not say true?

[A]: They may lie for aught I know.

[Q]: May not you lie?

[A]: I dare not tell a lie if it would save my life.[7]

[Q]: Then you will speak the truth.

[A]: I have spoke nothing else. I would do them any good.

[Q]: I do not think you have such affections for them, whom just now you insinuated had the Devil for their master.

Elizabeth Hubbard was afflicted and then the marshal who was by her said she pinched her hand.

Several of the afflicted cried out they [torn] her upon the beam.

[Q]: Pray God discover you, if you be guilty.

[A]: Amen. Amen. A false tongue will never make a guilty person.[8]

You have been a long time coming to the court today. You can come fast enough in the night, *said Mercy Lewis.*[9]

No, sweetheart, *said the examinant.*

And then Mercy Lewis and all, or many of the rest, were afflicted.

John Indian fell into a violent fit and said, It was that woman, she bites, she bites *[and illegible] then she was biting her lips.*

[Q]: Have you not compassion for these afflicted?

[A]: No, I have none.

Some cried out there was the black man with her, and Goody Bibber, who had not accused her before, confirmed it.

Abigail William upon trial could not come near her. Nor Goody Bibber. Nor Mary Walcott.[10]

John Indian cried he would kill her if he came near her, but he [was?] flung down in his approach to her.

[Q]: What is the reason these cannot come near you?

[A]: I cannot tell. It may be the Devil bears me more malice than another.

[Q]: Do not you see h[illegible] God evidently [torn] you?

[A]: No, not a bit for that.

[Q]: All the congregation think so.

[A]: Let them think what they will.

[Q]: What is the reason these cannot come near you?

[A]: I do not know but they can if they will [illegible] else if you please, I will come to them.

[Q]: What is the black man whispering to you?

[A]: There was none whispered to me.

STATEMENT OF ELIZABETH HUBBARD VERSUS GEORGE BURROUGHS MONDAY, MAY 9, 1692

The shift in accusation from the local women of Salem Village to deposed minister George Burroughs marked a dramatic change in both tenor and scope for the Salem episode. This expansive transformation is one reason that Salem would be better understood as a regional panic rather than one tied to a specific community. Hubbard's testimony claimed that Burroughs had told her he was "above a wizard, for he was a conjurer."

In the historiographic tendency to interpret witch trials as proxies for other, real conflicts, the fact that witchcraft itself was a category of reality for early modern Christians gets lost. The villagers of Salem were undoubtedly responding to a series of circumstances that intersected in the crucible (to borrow a turn of phrase) of a witch trial. But for them the threat of witchcraft was not a substitute for, or an overlaid scrim atop, their frontier anxieties and destructive religious and class conflicts. For the Salem Villagers, and those Puritans in the surrounding communities who were as touched by the panic as the village itself was, witchcraft was an organizing principle of how the universe worked. George Burroughs was a wizard. He was an instrument in the Devil's arsenal for attacking the godly, an arsenal that also included Indian attacks and internal discord. Even those individuals who, like Susannah Martin or Martha Cory, evinced doubt as to the bewitchment of the afflicted girls, only expressed doubt in terms of the location of the Devil's agency. The reality of the Devil

*was never in question. The reality of his ability to effect
change in human lives was also never in question. For the
Salem magistrates in charge of the prosecutions, the idea
of a deposed minister as a ringleader of witches was a hall-
mark of the Devil's awesome, and God-granted, power in
the human realm.*

Hubbard versus Burroughs[1]

May the 9th, 1692

Elizabeth Hubbard, aged about 17 years, saith that the last second day at night, There appeared a little black-haired man to
me in blackish apparel. I asked him his name and he told his
name was Burroughs. Then he took a book out of his pocket
and opened it and bid me set my hand to it. I told him I would
not. The lines in this book was red as blood. Then he pinched
me twice and went away. The next morning he appeared to me
again and told me he was above a wizard for he was a conjurer
and so went away. But since that he hath appeared to me every
day and night often. And[scored out] and urged me very much to
set my hand to his book and to run away telling me if I would
do so I should be well and that I should need fear nobody and
withal tormented me several ways every time he came except that
time he told me he was a conjuror. This night he asked me very
much to set my hand to his book or else he said he would kill me,
withal torturing me very much by biting and pinching, squeezing
my body and running pins into me also. On the 9th May 1692,
being the time of his examination, Mr. George Burroughs or
his appearance did most grievously afflict and torment the bodies of Mary Walcott, Mercy Lewes, Ann Putnam, and Abigail
Williams for if he did but look upon them he would strike them
down or almost choke them to death. Also several times since he
has most dreadfully afflicted and tormented me with variety of
torments and I believe in my heart that Mr. George Burroughs is
a dreadful wizard and that he has very often tormented me and
also the above named persons by his acts of witchcraft.

Jurat in Curia

Elizabeth Hubbard declared the above written evidence to
be the truth upon her oath that she had taken. This she owned
before the jury of inquest, August 3, 1692.

ESTABLISHING THE COURT OF OYER AND TERMINER FOR SUFFOLK, ESSEX, AND MIDDLESEX COUNTIES FRIDAY, MAY 27, 1692

The Salem trials were conducted by a special tribunal that was established to deal with the legal backlog that had built up after the expiration of the Massachusetts Bay Charter. Oyer and Terminer means "to hear" and "to determine." The Glorious Revolution of 1688 was under way in Britain,[1] and in 1692 the newly restored monarchy had other priorities besides the legal problems of a small backwoods settlement. The lack of a charter, and therefore the lack of the legal authority to conduct a trial, explains the unusually long delay between the accusations first levied in January and the first trials, finally held in May. Normally in colonial courts, a trial would follow a complaint almost immediately. In other witch trials, the accused would have been executed within a month. By the time the Court of Oyer and Terminer was established and the witch trials could move forward, the jails in Salem and Boston were overflowing with accused witches. Together with the public nature of the preliminary examinations, it has been thought that the delay in holding a trial contributed to the massive spread of accusations across Essex County.

The Special Order for Oyer and Terminer[2]

Upon consideration that there are many criminal offenders now in custody, some whereof have lain long and many inconveniences attending the thronging of the jails at this hot season of the year, there being no judicatories or court of justice yet established.

Ordered: That a special commission of Oyer and Terminer be made out unto William Stoughton, John Richards, Nathaniel Saltonstall, Wait Winthrop, Bartholomew Gedney, Samuel Sewall, John Hathorne, Jonathan Corwin, and Peter Sergeant, esquires. Assigning them the said William Stoughton, John Richards, Nathanael Saltonstall, Wait Winthrop, Bartholomew Gedney, Samuel Sewall, John Hathorne, Jonathan Corwin, and Peter Sergeant, esquires, to be justices, or any five of them (whereof the said William Stoughton, John Richards, or Bartholomew Gedney, esquires, to be one), to enquire of, hear and determine for this time according to the law and custom of England and of this Their Majesties' province, all and all manner of crimes and offences had made, done or perpetrated within the counties of Suffolk, Essex, Middlesex and of either of them.

William Phips.

Captain Stephen Sewall of Salem is nominated and appointed to officiate as clerk of the special Court of Oyer and Terminer.

William Phips.

Mr. Thomas Newton is appointed to officiate as attorney for and on behalf of Their Majesties at the special Court of Oyer and Terminer.

William Phips.

MARTHA CARRIER, QUEEN OF HELL
TUESDAY, MAY 31, 1692

Truth be told, more people were accused in Andover, Massachusetts, than in Salem, Massachusetts. Andover's Martha Carrier, according to her accusers, was the center of that witch conspiracy, called, at one point, "Queen of Hell." Like most accused witches, Martha was not old but at thirty-eight, solidly middle aged, a woman not on the margins of her community, but at the height of her social power. In the accusation of Martha Carrier, the Salem panic entered its second major iteration, spreading well beyond the purview of Salem Village and igniting a regional fervor.

As with previous examinations, dramatic interjections of the afflicted girls and other bystanders pepper the narrative. Notably, the girls also said that they could see a "black man" speaking in her ear. Rather than necessarily implying African heritage, the word "black" here can be understood as a moral category, implying evil, but it could also refer to the actual appearance of the man, which the colonists used to denote the native people in New England. Such terminology reinforced the already established association between Satan and his native confederates in the Puritan mind.

THE EXAMINATION OF MARTHA CARRIER[1]

The Examination of Martha Carrier, 31 May 1692
[Q]: Abigail Williams, who hurts you?
[**Abigail Williams**]: Goody Carrier of Andover.

[Q]: Elizabeth Hubbard, who hurts you?

[Elizabeth Hubbard]: Goody Carrier.

[Q]: Susan Sheldon, who hurts you?

[Susan Sheldon]: Goody Carrier. She bites me, pinches me, and tells me she would cut my throat if I did not sign her book.

Mary Walcott said she afflicted her and brought the book to her.

[Q]: What do you say to this you are charged with?

[Martha Carrier]: I have not done it.

Susannah Sheldon cried, She looks upon the black man.

Ann Putman complained of a pin stuck in her.

[Q]: What black man is that?

[A]: I know none.

Ann Putman testified there was.

Mary Warren cried out she was pricked.

[Q]: What black man did you see?

[A]: I saw no black man but your own presence.[2]

[Q]: Can you look upon these and not knock them down?

[A]: They will dissemble if I look upon them.[3]

[Q]: You see you look upon them and they fall down.

[A]: It is false. The Devil is a liar.

[A]: I looked upon none since I came into the room but you.

Susannah Sheldon cried out in a trance, I wonder what could you murder. 13 persons?

Mary Walcott testified the same that there lay 13 ghosts.

All the afflicted fell into the most intolerable outcries and agonies.

Elizabeth Hubbard and Ann Putman testified the same that she had killed 13 at Andover.

[A]: It is a shameful thing that you should mind these folks that are out of their wits.[4]

[Q]: Do not you see them?

[A]: If I do speak you will not believe me.

You do see them, said the accusers.

[A]: You lie. I am wronged.

There is the black man whispering in her ear, said many of the afflicted.

Mercy Lewis in a violent fit was well upon the examinant's grasping her arm.

The tortures of the afflicted was so great that there was no enduring of it, so that she was ordered away and to be bound hand and foot with all expedition. The afflicted in the meanwhile almost killed to the great trouble of all spectators, magistrates and others.

Note. As soon as she was well bound they all had strange and sudden ease.

Mary Walcott told the magistrates that this woman told her she had been a witch this 40 years.

STATEMENT OF SARAH INGERSOLL AND ANN ANDREWS REGARDING SARAH CHURCHILL JUNE 1, 1692

Sarah Ingersoll's statement provides good evidence that the afflicted girls might have been intentionally faking, or at the very least subject to pressure from the magistrates not to recant once they had levied an accusation. Sarah Churchill, who was part of the group of accusing girls, was a servant in George Jacobs Sr.'s house. Churchill, according to Ingersoll, admitted that she had lied in her testimony and that she had been frightened into testifying by one of the ministers. She recognized that she had made a mistake initially but did not see a way to tell the truth once the lie had been told.

Statement Concerning Faked Afflictions[1]

The deposition of Sarah Ingersoll, aged about 30 years. Saith that seeing Sarah Church after her examination, she came to me crying and wringing her hands seeming to be much troubled in spirit. I asked her what she ailed. She answered she had undone herself. I asked her in what. She said in belying herself and others in saying she had set her hand to the Devil's book whereas she said she never did. I told her I believed she had set her hand to the book. She answered crying and said, No, no, no. I never. I never did. I asked then what had made her say she did. She answered because they threatened her and told her they would put her into the dungeon and put her along with Mr. Burroughs. And thus several times she followed me up and down telling me that she had undone herself in belying herself and others. I asked her why she did not [illegible] writ it. She told me because she had stood out so long in it that now she darest not. She said also that if she told Mr. Noyes but once she had sat her hand to the book he would believe her but if she told the truth and said she had not sat her hand to the book a hundred times he would not believe her.

Sarah Ingersoll
Anna Andrus

AFTER SALEM

By late 1692, voices critical of the Salem trials began to grow in number and influence. The last eight of the nineteen executed witches were hanged on September 22, but by that time several prominent ministers had already begun to question the assumption that the Devil could not assume the shape of an innocent person. In October of 1692, theologian Increase Mather published Cases of Conscience Concerning Evil Spirits Personating Men, *which claimed that spectral evidence of the kind used to condemn those executed was unreliable for the prosecution of witches. Later that same month, prominent merchant Thomas Brattle circulated a letter that sharply criticized the methods used by the Court of Oyer and Terminer. Partly in response to these two texts, Governor William Phips finally dissolved the Court on October 29, 1692.[1]*

The magnitude of the Salem witch crisis and the near-immediate reversal by some of the participants after the trials drew to a close—most notably Judge Samuel Sewall, afflicted girl Ann Putnam, and minister John Hale—can sometimes leave the impression that Salem formed a final conflagration of witch superstition that burned itself up in one great paroxysm, leaving North American legal, religious, and intellectual life abruptly free of early modern biases and misconceptions. Such an impression is hardly accurate. While no witch trial in North America—or Europe, for that matter—would ever again approach the magnitude and fatality of the Salem episode, witch belief did not disappear. It merely changed form.

Enough questions arose about the conduct of the legal proceedings at Salem that courts grew more cautious in their willingness to prosecute witches. The legal anxiety specifically concerned the vexing question of whether spectral evidence should be used only to open inquiry into a witch's crimes, or whether it should also be admissible in determining her ultimate guilt. The spectral evidence debate revolved around differing theological opinions on whether the Devil could assume the shape of an innocent person. Cotton Mather, drawing from the published accounts of the Bury St. Edmunds trial of 1662, felt that he could not, but that spectral evidence alone should not be the sole basis for conviction; his father, Increase Mather, argued that it was possible for the Devil to frame innocent people, and it would be better for a witch to go free than for an innocent person to be falsely convicted. Skeptics like Thomas Brattle argued that treating the actions of a person's shape as equivalent to the actions of the person was insupportable. With so many unsettling questions about the burden of proof in the Salem trial, the legal system no longer seemed able to deal credibly with witches. But the legal system's shortcomings did not necessarily imply a sudden shift in popular consciousness.

Gradually, over the course of the eighteenth century, witchcraft moved from being a legal problem to being a purely cultural one. One example of this transition appears in the passage of the Witchcraft Act of 1735, which redefined the crime from witchcraft, understood as a covenant with the Devil, to claiming to practice witchcraft, that is, to a matter of fraud. But if witchcraft was no longer a crime against God and man and was instead a matter of unscrupulous cunning folk taking advantage of credulous people, then belief in witchcraft hadn't exactly disappeared. Witches still stalked the Atlantic Anglophone eighteenth-century world, both in the form of Salem-related aftermath, in a few isolated trials, in newspaper stories, and eventually, in folklore.[2]

THE APOLOGY OF
SAMUEL SEWALL
JANUARY 14
1697

Samuel Sewall was the only judge involved in the Salem trials to apologize afterward for his involvement, although Nathaniel Saltonstall absented himself from the trials after the execution of Bridget Bishop in early June 1692.[1] Interestingly, Sewall came to his apology not because he stopped believing in witches and witchcraft. On the contrary, he felt only that Satan had misled him and the other judges as part of his ongoing attempts to derail the Christian community in which they all lived. Sewall started to reconsider his involvement after experiencing a series of wonders and marvels, which caused him to speculate what blemish on his soul might have made God unhappy with him. Sewall in this instance represents a fascinating turning point in North American intellectual history, a Harvard-trained Puritan whose very faith acts to underscore his eventual skepticism.[2] He delivered his apology in public, on a day of public fasting and prayer declared by the Massachusetts legislature.

Sewall's Apology[3]

Samuel Sewall, sensible of the reiterated strokes of God upon himself and family, and being sensible that as to the guilt contracted upon the opening of the late commission of Oyer and Terminer at Salem (to which the order of this day relates) he is, upon many accounts, more concerned than any that he knows of, desires to take the blame and shame of it, asking pardon of men.

And especially desiring prayers that God, who has an unlimited authority, would pardon that sin and all other his sins, personal and relative. And according to his infinite benignity and sovereignty, not visit the sin of him or of any other upon himself or any of his, nor upon the land. But that he would powerfully defend him against all temptations to sin, for the future and vouchsafe him the efficacious, saving conduct of his word and spirit.

THE APOLOGY OF THE
SALEM JURY
1697

*Following Samuel Sewall's public apology for his
involvement in the Salem trials, a number of jurors who
had been instrumental in the condemnations of witches
also jumped to make their own public apology. They
reaffirmed their intent to act rightly, but such rapid public distancing helped to push belief in witchcraft out of
the courtroom and into the more private, and less mea-
sured, court of public opinion.*

The Jury's Apology[1]

Some that had been of several juries have given forth a paper,
signed with our own hands in these words. We whose names are
underwritten, being in the year 1692 called to serve as jurors in
court in Salem, on trial of many who were by some suspected
guilty of doing acts of witchcraft upon the bodies of sundry
persons.

We confess that we ourselves were not capable to understand,
nor able to withstand the mysterious delusions of the powers
of darkness and prince of the air,[2] but were for want of knowledge in ourselves and better information from others, prevailed
with to take up with such evidence against the accused as on
further consideration and better information, we justly fear was
insufficient for the touching the lives of any, Deuteronomy 17.6,[3]
whereby we fear we have been instrumental with others, though
ignorantly and unwittingly, to bring upon ourselves and this people of the Lord, the guilt of innocent blood, which sin the Lord
saith in Scripture, he would not pardon, 2 Kings 24.4,[4] that is we
suppose in regard of His temporal judgments. We do, therefore,

hereby signify to all in general (and to the surviving sufferers in especial) our deep sense of and sorrow for our errors in acting on such evidence to the condemning of any person.

And do hereby declare that we justly fear that we were sadly deluded and mistaken, for which we are much disquieted and distressed in our minds, and do therefore humbly beg forgiveness, first of God for Christ's sake for this our error. And pray that God would not impute the guilt of it to ourselves nor others. And we also pray that we may be considered candidly and aright by the living sufferers as being then under the power of a strong and general delusion,[5] utterly unacquainted with and not experienced in matters of that nature.

We do heartily ask forgiveness of you all, whom we have justly offended and do declare, according to our present minds, we would none of us do such things again on such grounds for the whole world, praying you to accept of this in way of satisfaction for our offense, and that you would bless the inheritance of the Lord that He may be entreated for the land.

Foreman, Thomas Fisk	Thomas Perly, Senior
William Fiske	John Peabody
John Batcheler	Thomas Perkins
Thomas Fisk, Junior	Samuel Sather
John Dane	Andrew Elliott
Joseph Evelith	Henry Herrick, Senior

ROBERT CALEF, *MORE WONDERS OF THE INVISIBLE WORLD*
1700

Robert Calef was a Boston merchant who finally pub-
lished his account of the Salem episode a few short years
after the trials concluded, after the tide of public opin-
ion had already begun to turn. However, while he was
writing it over the 1690s, he was unable to find a North
American publisher for his account, which heavily criti-
cized Cotton Mather on several theological points and
called all the Salem trials into question. Calef's book
first appeared in London in 1700, but was widely cir-
culated in Massachusetts, and caused enough conster-
nation among the Puritan elite that Increase Mather
oversaw the burning of copies of the Calef book in Har-
vard Square.

More Wonders of the Invisible World[1]

In a time when not only England in particular, but almost all
Europe had been laboring against the usurpations of tyranny and
slavery, the English America has not been behind in a share in the
common calamitie. More especially, New England has met not
only with such calamities as are common to the rest but with several aggravations enhancing such afflictions, by the devastations
and cruelties of the barbarous Indians in their eastern borders, et
cetera.[2]

But this is not all. They have been harassed (on many accounts)
by a more dreadful enemy, as will herein appear to the considerate.
Were it as we are told in *Wonders of the Invisible World,*[3]

that the devils were walking about our streets with lengthened chains making a dreadful noise in our ears, and brimstone, even without a metaphor, was making a horrid and a hellish stench in our nostrils, and that the Devil exhibiting himself ordinarily as a black man had decoyed a fearful knot of proud, forward, ignorant, envious and malicious creatures to list themselves in his horrid service by entering their names in a book tendered unto them, and that they have had their meetings and sacraments and associated themselves to destroy the kingdom of our Lord Jesus Christ, in these parts of the world, having each of them their specters, or devils, commissioned by them, and representing of them, to be the engines of their malice, by these wicked specters seizing poor people about the country with various and bloody torments. And of those evidently preternatural torments some too have died. And that they have bewitched some even so far as to make them self-destroyers, and others in many towns here and there languished under their evil hands. The people thus afflicted miserably scratched and bitten, and that the same invisible furies did stick pins in them, and scald them, distort and disjoint them, with a thousand other plagues and sometimes drag them out of their chambers and carry them over trees and hills miles together, many of them being tempted to sign the Devil's laws.

These furies whereof several have killed more people perhaps than would serve to make a village.

If this be the true state of the afflictions of this country, it is very deplorable, and beyond all other outward calamities miserable. But if on the other side, the matter be as others do understand it, that the Devil has been too hard for us by his temptations, signs, and lying wonders, with the help of pernicious notions formerly imbibed and professed; together with the accusations of a parcel of possessed, distracted, or lying wenches, accusing their innocent neighbors, pretending they see their specters, that is, devils in their likeness afflicting of them, and that God in righteous judgment (after men had ascribed his power to witches, of commissioning devils to do these things) may have given them over to strong delusions to believe lies, et cetera. And to let loose the devils of envy, hatred, pride, cruelty, and malice against each other; yet still disguised under the mask of zeal for God, and left them to the branding one another with the odious name of witch; and upon the accusation of those above mentioned, brother to accuse and prosecute brother, children their parents, pastors and teachers their immediate flock unto death. Shepherds becoming wolves, wise men infatuated, people hauled to prisons, with a bloody noise pursuing to, and insulting over, the (true) sufferers at execution, while some are fleeing from that called justice, justice itself fleeing before such accusations, when once it did but begin to refrain further proceedings, and to question such practices, some making their escape out of prisons, rather than by an obstinate defense of their innocency, to run so apparent hazard of their lives. Estates seized, families of children and others left to the mercy of the wilderness (not to mention here the numbers prescribed dead in prisons or executed, et cetera).

All which tragedies, though begun in one town, or rather by one parish, has plaguelike spread more than through that country. And by its echo giving a brand of infamy to this whole country throughout the world. If this were the miserable case of this country in the time thereof, and that the Devil had so far prevailed upon us in our sentiments and actions, as to draw us from so much as looking into the scriptures for our guidance in these pretended intricacies, leading us to a trusting in blind guides, such as the corrupt practices of some other countries, or the bloody experiments of Bodin,[4] and such other authors. Then though our case be most miserable, yet it must be said of New England, thou has destroyed thyself, and brought this greatest of miseries upon thee.

And now whether the witches (such as have made a compact by explicit covenant with the Devil, having thereby obtained a power to commission him) have been the cause of our miseries, or whether a zeal governed by blindness and passion, and led by precedent, has not herein precipitated us into far greater wickedness (if not witchcrafts) than any have been yet proved against those that suffered, to be able to distinguish aright in this matter, to which of these two to refer our miseries is the present work. As to the former, I know of no sober man, much less reverend Christian, that being asked dares affirm and abide by it, that witches have that power; namely, to commission devils to kill and destroy. And as to the latter, it were well if there were not too much of truth in it, which remains to be demonstrated.

But here it will be said, what need of raking in the coals that lay buried in oblivion. We cannot recall those to life again that have suffered, supposing it were unjustly; it tends but to the exposing the actors, as if they had proceeded irregularly.

Truly, I take this to be just as the Devil would have it, so much to fear disobliging men, as not to endeavor to detect his wiles, that so he may the sooner, and with the greater advantages set the same on foot again (either here or elsewhere) so dragging us through the pond twice by the same cat. And if reports do not (herein) deceive us, much the same has been acting this present year in Scotland. And what kingdom or country is it that has not had their bloody fits and turns at it. And if this is such a catching disease, and so universal, I presume I need make no apology for my endeavors to prevent, as far as in my power, any more such bloody victims or sacrifices. Though indeed I had rather any other would have undertaken so offensive, though necessary, a task. Yet all things weighed, I had rather thus expose myself to censure, than that it should be wholly omitted. Were the notions in question innocent and harmless, respecting the glory of God, and well-being of men, I should not have engaged in them, but finding them in my esteem so intolerably destructive of both, this, together with my being by warrant called before the justices, in my own just vindication, I took it to be a call from God to my power, to vindicate his truths, against the pagan and popish assertions[5] which are so prevalent. For though Christians in general do own the scriptures to be their only rule of Faith and doctrine, yet these notions will tell us that the scriptures have not sufficiently, nor at all, described the crime of witchcraft, whereby the culpable might be detected, though it be positive in the command to punish it by death. Hence the world has been from time to time perplexed in the prosecution of the several diabolical mediums of heathenish and popish invention, to detect an imaginary crime (not but that there are witches, such as the law of God describes) which has produced a deluge of blood; hereby rendering the commands of God not only void but dangerous.

So also they own God's providence and government of the world, and that tempests and storms, afflictions and diseases are of his sending. Yet these notions tell us that the Devil has the power of all these and can perform them when commissioned by a witch thereto, and that he has a power at the witch's call to act and do, without and against the course of nature, and all natural causes, in afflicting and killing of innocents; and this is that so many have died for.

Also it is generally believed that if any man has strength, it is from God the almighty being. But these notions will tell us that the Devil can make one man as strong as many, which was one of the best proofs, as it was counted, against Mr. Burroughs the minister. Though his contemporaries in the schools during his minority could have testified that his strength was then as much superior to theirs as ever (setting aside incredible romances) it was discovered to be since. Thus rendering the power of God, and his providence of none effect.[6]

These are some of the destructive notions of this age, and however the asserters of them seem sometimes to value themselves much upon sheltering their neighbors from spectral accusations, they may deserve as much thanks as that tyrant that having industriously obtained an unintelligible charge against his subjects in matters wherein it was impossible they should be guilty, having thereby their lives in his power, yet suffers them of his mere grace to live, and will be called gracious Lord.

It were too Icarian[7] a task for one unfurnished with necessary learning and library to give any just account from whence so great delusions have sprung and so long continued. Yet as an essay from those scraps of reading that I have had opportunity of, it will be no great venture to say that signs and lying wonders have been one principal cause.

It is written of Justin Martyr, who lived in the second century, that he was before his conversion a great philosopher; first in the way of the Stoics and after of the Peripatetics, after that of the Pythagorean, and after that of the Platonists sects. And after, all proved of eminent use in the church of Christ. Yet a certain author speaking of one Apollonius Tyaneus has these words, "That the most Orthodox themselves began to deem him vested with power sufficient for a Deity; which occasioned that so strange a doubt from Justin Martyr, as cited by the learned Gregory, Fol. 37., etc. If God be the Creator and Lord of the World, how comes it to pass that Apollonius his Telisms, have so much over-ruled the course of things! For we see that they also have stilled the Waves of the Sea, and the raging of the Winds, and prevailed against the Noisome Flies, and Incursions of wild Beasts," et cetera. If so eminent and early a Christian were by these false shows in such doubt, it is the less wonder in our depraved times to meet with what is equivalent thereto. Besides this, a certain author informs me, that "Julian (afterward called the Apostate) being instructed in the philosophy and disciplines of the heathen by Libarius, his tutor, by this means he came to love philosophy better than the Gospel, and so by degrees turned from Christianity to heathenism."

This same Julian did, when apostate, forbid that Christians should be instructed in the discipline of the Gentiles, which (it seems) Socrates, a writer of the ecclesiastical history, does acknowledge to be by the singular providence of God, Christians having then begun to degenerate from the Gospel and to betake themselves to heathenish learning. And in the *Mercury* for the month of February 1695, there is this account, "That the Christian Doctors conversing much with the writings of the Heathen, for the gaining of Eloquence, A Counsel was held at Carthage, which forbad the reading of the Books of the Gentiles."

From all which it may be easily perceived, that in the primitive times of Christianity, when not only many heathens of the vulgar, but also many learned men and philosophers had embraced the Christian faith, they still retained a love to their heathen learning, which as one observes being transplanted into a Christian soil, soon proved productive of pernicious weeds, which overran the face of the church, hence it was so deformed as the Reformation found it.

Among other pernicious weeds arising from this root, the doctrine of the power of devils and witchcraft as it is now, and long has been understood, is not the least. The fables of Homer, Virgil, Horace, and Ovid, et cetera, being for the elegancy of their language retained then (and so are to this day) in the schools, have not only introduced, but established, such doctrines to the poisoning of the Christian world. A certain author expresses it thus, "that as the Christian schools at first brought men from heathenism to the Gospel, so these schools carry men from the Gospel to heathenism, as to their great perfection." And Mr. I. M.,[8] in his *Remarkable Providences*, gives an account that (as he calls it) an old counsel did anathematize all those that believed such power of the devils, accounting it a damnable doctrine. But as other evils did afterward increase in the church (partly by such education), so this insensibly grew up with them, though not to that degree, as that any counsel I have ever heard or read of has to this day taken of those anathemas. Yet after this the church so far declined that witchcraft became a principal ecclesiastical engine (as also that of heresy was) to root up all that stood in their way. And besides the ways of trial that we have still in practice, they invented some, which were peculiar to themselves, which, whenever they were minded to improve against any orthodox believer, they could easily make effectual: that deluge of blood which that scarlet whore has to answer for, shed under this notion, how amazing is it.

The first in England that I have read of, of any note since the Reformation, that asserts this doctrine, is the famous Mr. Perkins,[9] he, as also Mr. Gaul and Mr. Bernard, et cetera, seem all of them to have undertaken one task. They, taking notice of the multiplicity of irregular ways to try them by, invented by heathens and papists, made it their business and main work herein to oppose such as they saw to be pernicious. And if they did not look more narrowly into it, but followed the first, namely, Mr. Perkins, whose education (as theirs also) had forestalled him into such belief, whom they readily followed, it cannot be wondered at. And that they were men liable to err and so not to be trusted to as perfect guides will manifestly appear to him that shall see their several receipts laid down to detect them by their presumptive and positive ones. And consider how few of either have any foundation in scripture or reason, and how vastly they differ from each other in both, each having his art by himself, which forty or a hundred more may as well imitate, and give theirs, ad infinitum, being without all manner of proof.

But though this be their main design, to take off people from those evil and bloody ways of trial which they speak so much against, yet this does not hinder to this day, but the same evil ways or as bad are still used to detect them by, and that even among Protestants. And is so far justified that a reverend person has said lately here, How else shall we detect witches? And another being urged to prove by scripture such a sort of witch as has power to send devils to kill men replied that he did as firmly believe it as any article of his faith. And that he (the inquirer) did not go to the scripture to learn the mysteries of his trade or art. What can be said more to establish there heathenish notions and to vilify the scriptures, our only rule, and that after we have seen such dire effects thereof, as has threatened the utter extirpation of this whole country.

And as to most of the actors in these tragedies, though they are so far from defending their actions that they will readily own that undue steps have been taken, et cetera. Yet it seems they choose that the same should be acted over again, enforced by their example, rather than that it should remain as a warning to posterity, wherein they have missed it. So far are they from giving glory to God and taking the due shame to themselves.

And now to sum up all in a few words, we have seen a bigoted zeal stirring up a blind and most bloody rage, not against enemies or irreligious profligate persons but (in judgment of charity, and to view) against as virtuous and religious as any they have left behind them in this country, which have suffered as evildoers with the utmost extent of rigor (not that so high a character is due to all that suffered) and this by the testimony of vile varlets as not only were known before but have been further apparent since by their manifest lives, whoredoms, incest, et cetera. The accusations of these, from their spectral sight, being the chief evidence against those that suffered. In which accusations they were upheld by both magistrates and ministers, so long as they apprehended themselves in no danger.

And then though they could defend neither the doctrine nor the practice, yet none of them have in such a public manner as the case requires testified against either, though at the same time they could not but be sensible what a stain and lasting infamy they have brought upon the whole country, to the endangering the future welfare not only of this but of other places, induced by their example; if not, to an entailing the guilt of all the righteous blood that has been by the same means shed by heathens or papists, et cetera, upon themselves, whose deeds they have so far justified, occasioning the great dishonor and blasphemy of the name of God, scandalizing the heathen, hardening of enemies; and as a natural effect thereof, to the great increase of atheism.

A CASE OF POISONING IN
ALBANY, NEW YORK
1700

*Within Puritan North America, the native populations
were associated with the Devil in both figurative and literal ways. Salem, however, was not the only setting for
witch anxiety and uncertainty about the non-Christian
practices of native populations. The following account
conflates both confusions about native practice with lingering Protestant North American anxiety about terri-
torial clashes with Catholic French Canada.[1]*

An execution for witchcraft took place in Albany, in the year
1700, related in a communication of the Earl of Bellomont to the
lords of trade and plantations. As it is sufficiently concise for our
purpose, and graphically sketched, it follows in his own words.

Aquendero, the chief Sachem[2] of the Onondaga Nation, who
was prolocutor for all the five nations at the conference I had two
years ago at Albany, has been forced to fly from thence, and come
to live on Colonel Schuyler's land near Albany. Aquendero's son
is poisoned and languishes, and there is a sore broke out on one
of his sides, out of which there comes handfuls of hair, so that
they reckon he has been bewitched as well as poisoned.

I met with an old story from the gentlemen of Albany, which
I think worth relating. Decanniffore, one of the Sachems of the
Onondagas, married one of the Praying Indians[3] in Canada. This
woman was taught to poison as well as to pray. The Jesuits[4] had
furnished her with so subtle a poison and taught her a legerde-
main in using it, so that whoever she had a mind to poison, she
would drink to them a cup of water, and let drop the poison from
under her nails (which are always very long, for the Indians never
pare them) into the cup. This woman was so true a disciple to

the Jesuits that she has poisoned a multitude of our five nations that were best affected to us. She, lately coming from Canada in company of some of our Indians who went to visit their relations in that country who have taken sides with the French, and there being among others a Protestant Mohawk (a proper goodly young man), him this woman poisoned so that he died two days' journey short of Albany, and the magistrates of that town sent for his body and gave it a Christian burial. The woman comes to Albany, where some of the Mohawks happening to be, and among them a young man nearly related to the man that had been poisoned, who, espying the woman, cries out with great horror that there was that beastly woman that had poisoned so many of their friends, and it was not fit she should live any longer in this world to do more mischief; and so made up to her, and with a club beat out her brains.

JOHN HALE, *A MODEST ENQUIRY INTO THE NATURE OF WITCHCRAFT* 1702

John Hale was serving as a minister in Beverly, the town just north of Salem, and was one of the first Puritan ministers summoned to observe the behavior of the afflicted girls at Salem Village. He started out as a proponent of the trials, but his tenor changed as the accusations spread, finally touching Hale's own wife. His change of heart was penned in 1697 but published only after his death in 1700, and represents one of the early cacophony of voices that attempted to grapple with not only what Salem says about witchcraft in general but also what it says about justice.

A MODEST ENQUIRY INTO THE NATURE OF WITCHCRAFT[1]

Chapter 2. 1. In the latter end of the year 1691, Mr. Samuel Parris, pastor of the church in Salem Village, had a daughter of nine and a niece of about eleven years of age sadly afflicted of they knew not what distempers. And he made his application to physicians, yet still they grew worse. And at length one physician gave his opinion that they were under an evil hand. This the neighbors quickly took up and concluded they were bewitched. He had also an Indian manservant and his wife who afterward confessed that without the knowledge of their master or mistress, they had taken some of the afflicted persons' urine, and mixing it with meal had made a cake,[2] and baked it to find out the witch, as they said. After this, the afflicted persons cried out of the Indian woman, named Tituba, that she did pinch, prick, and grievously torment them, and that they saw her here and there, where nobody else could. Yea, they could tell where she was, and what she did, when out of their human sight. These children were bitten and pinched by invisible agents; their arms, necks, and backs turned this way and that way, and returned back again, so as it was impossible for them to do of themselves, and beyond the power of any epileptic fits or natural disease to effect. Sometimes they were taken dumb, their mouths stopped, their throats choked, their limbs wracked and tormented so as might move an heart of stone to sympathize with them, with bowels of compassion for them. I will not enlarge in the description of their cruel sufferings, because they were in all things afflicted as bad as John Goodwin's children at Boston in the year 1689. So that he that will read Mr. Mather's *Book of Memorable Providences,* page 3, et cetera, may read part of what these children, and afterward sundry grown persons suffered by the hand of Satan, at Salem Village and parts adjacent, anno 1691/2. Yet there was more in these sufferings than in those at Boston, by pins invisibly stuck into their flesh pricking with irons (as in part published in a book printed 1693, namely, *The Wonders of the Invisible World*). Mr. Parris, seeing the distressed condition of his family, desired the presence of some worthy gentlemen of Salem, and some neighbor ministers to consult together at his house, who, when they came and had enquired diligently into the sufferings of the afflicted, concluded they were preternatural and feared the hand of Satan was in them.

2. The advice given to Mr. Parris by them was that he should sit still and wait upon the providence of God to see what time might discover and to be much in prayer for the discovery of what was yet secret. They also examined Tituba, who confessed the making of a cake, as is above mentioned, and said her mistress in her own country was a witch, and had taught her some means to be used for the discovery of a witch and for the prevention of being bewitched, et cetera, but said that she herself was not a witch.

3. Soon after this, there were two or three private fasts at the minister's house, one of which was kept by sundry neighbor ministers, and after this, another in public at the village, and several days afterward of public humiliation, during these molestations, not only there, but in other congregations for them. And one general fast by order of the general court, observed throughout the colony to seek the Lord that he would rebuke Satan and be a light unto his

people in this day of darkness. But I return to the history of these troubles. In a short time after, other persons who were of age to be witnesses were molested by Satan, and in their fits cried out upon Tituba and Goody Osburn and Sarah Good, that they or specters in their shapes did grievously torment them. Hereupon some of their village neighbors complained to the magistrates at Salem, desiring they would come and examine the afflicted and accused together, the which they did. The effect of which examination was that Tituba confessed she was a witch and that she with the two others accused did torment and bewitch the complainers, and that these with two others whose names she knew not had their witch meeting together, relating the times when and places where they met, with many other circumstances to be seen at large. Upon this the said Tituba and Osburn and Sarah Good were committed to prison upon suspicion of acting witchcraft. After this the said Tituba was again examined in prison, and owned her first confession in all points, and then was herself afflicted and complained of her fellow witches tormenting of her for her confession and accusing them, and being searched by a woman, she was found to have upon her body the marks of the Devil's wounding of her.

4. Here were these things rendered her confession credible. (1.) That at this examination she answered every question just as she did at the first. And it was thought that if she had feigned her confession, she could not have remembered her answers so exactly. A liar, we say, had need of a good memory, but truth being always consistent with itself is the same today as it was yesterday. (2.) She seemed very penitent for her sin in covenanting with the Devil. (3.) She became a sufferer herself, and as she said for her confession. (4.) Her confession agreed exactly (which was afterward verified in the other confessors) with the accusations of the afflicted. Soon after these afflicted persons complained of other persons afflicting of them in their fits, and the number of the afflicted and accused began to increase. And the success of Tituba's confession encouraged those in authority to examine others that were suspected, and the event was that more confessed themselves guilty of the crimes they were suspected for. And thus was this matter driven on.

5. I observed in the prosecution of these affairs that there was in the justices, judges and others concerned, a conscientious endeavor to do the thing that was right. And to that end they consulted the presidents of former times and precepts laid down by

learned writers about witchcraft. As Keeble on the common law, Chapt. Conjuration, (an author approved by the twelve judges of our nation). Also Sir Mathew Hale's trial of witches, printed anno 1682. Glanville's collection of sundry trials in England and Ireland in the years 1658, '61, '63, '64, and '81.[3] Bernard's guide to jurymen, Baxter and R. Burton, their histories about witches and their discoveries. Cotton Mather's *Memorable Providences Relating to Witchcrafts,* printed anno 1689.

6. But that which chiefly carried on this matter to such an height was the increasing of confessors till they amounted to near about fifty. And four or six of them upon their trials owned their guilt of this crime, and were condemned for the same, but not executed. And many of the confessors confirmed their confessions with very strong circumstances: As their exact agreement with the accusations of the afflicted; their punctual agreement with their fellow confessors; their relating the times when they covenanted with Satan, and the reasons that moved them thereunto; their witch meetings, and that they had their mock sacraments of baptism and the supper, in some of them, their signing the Devil's book. And some showed the scars of the wounds which they said were made to fetch blood with to sign the Devil's book. And some said they had imps to suck them, and showed sores raw where they said they were sucked by them.

7. I shall give the reader a taste of these things in a few instances. The afflicted complained that the specters which vexed them urged them to set their hands to a book represented to them (as to them it seemed) with threatenings of great torments if they signed not, and promises of ease if they obeyed. Among these D. H.[4] did as she said (which sundry others confessed afterwards) being overcome by the extremity of her pains, sign the book presented, and had the promised ease; and immediately upon it a specter in her shape afflicted another person and said, I have signed the book and have ease, now do you sign, and so shall you have ease. And one day this afflicted person pointed at a certain place in the room, and said, there is D. H., upon which a man with his rapier struck at the place, though he saw no shape; and the afflicted called out, saying, you have wounded her side, and soon after the afflicted person pointed at another place, saying, there she is, whereupon a man struck at the place, and the afflicted said, you have given her a small prick about the eye. Soon after this, the said D. H. confessed herself to be made a witch by signing the Devil's book as above said; and declared that

she had afflicted the maid that complained of her, and in doing of it had received two wounds by a sword or rapier, a small one about the eye, which she showed to the magistrates, and a bigger on the side of which she was searched by a discreet woman, who reported that D. H. had on her side the sign of a wound newly healed. This D. H. confessed that she was at a witch meeting at Salem Village, where were many persons that she named, some of whom were in prison then or soon after upon suspicion of witchcraft. And the said G. B.[5] preached to them, and such a woman was their deacon, and there they had a sacrament.

8. Several others after this confessed the same things with D. H. In particular Goody F[6] said (inter alia[7]) that she with two others (one of whom acknowledged the same) rode from Andover to the same village witch meeting upon a stick above ground, and that in the way the stick brake, and gave the said F. a fall. Whereupon, said she, I got a fall and hurt of which I am still sore. I happened to be present in prison when this F. owned again her former confession to the magistrates. And then I moved she might be further questioned about some particulars. It was answered the magistrates had not time to stay longer; but I should have liberty to examine her farther by myself. The which thing I did, and I asked her if she rode to the meeting on a stick. She said yea. I enquired what she did for victuals. She answered that she carried bread and cheese in her pocket and that she and the Andover company came to the village before the meeting began, and sat down together under a tree and eat their food, and that she drank water out of a brook to quench her thirst.[8] And that the meeting was upon a plain grassy place, by which was a cart path, and sandy ground in the path, in which were the tracks of horses' feet. And she also told me how long they were going and returning. And some time after told me she had some trouble upon her spirit, and when I enquired what she said she was in fear that G. B. and M. C.[9] would kill her; for they appeared unto her (in specter, for their persons were kept in other rooms in the prison) and brought a sharp pointed iron like a spindle, but four square, and threatened to stab her to death with it because she had confessed her witchcraft and told of them that they were with her, and that M. C. above named was the person that made her a witch. About a month after, the said F. took occasion to tell me the same story of her fears that G. B. and E. C. would kill her, and that the thing was much for her spirits.

THE TRIAL OF GRACE SHERWOOD, PRINCESS ANNE COUNTY, VIRGINIA 1705–1706

Not all witches were found in New England, though the trial of Grace Sherwood in Virginia clearly bears the marks of legal anxiety following the Salem debacle. Sherwood had suffered a poor reputation for some time and was ultimately brought to trial. Several aspects of her trial will look familiar, most particularly the creation of a jury of women to search Sherwood's body for the telltale witch's teat where she would have suckled her familiar spirit. The jury went even further, resorting to a diagnostic technique very rarely used in North America: the ducking stool.[1] However, they felt unsure of their method or of the best way to interpret their results. Sherwood was found guilty, but without the fatal outcome that she would have incurred only a decade earlier. In effect, Sherwood marks the transition of belief in witchcraft from a legal concern to being a more purely social one.[2]

The record here given for the trial of Grace Sherwood for witchcraft was presented by the late J. P. Cushing, president of Hampden Sydney College, to the Virginia Historical and Philosophical Society, and published in their collections. While it throws some light on the state of society of that time, it evinces that persecution for witchcraft was not alone in our country confined to the Puritans of New England. There, it will be recollected, was shown a noble example of the strength of moral principle on the part of the accused, for they had only to declare themselves guilty and their lives were spared.[3] Rather than do this, many suffered death. Grace Sherwood met a milder fate. The place where she was ducked is a beautiful inlet making up from Lynnhaven Bay, which to this day is called Witch's Duck.[4]

Record of the trial of Grace Sherwood in 1705, Princess Anne County, for Witchcraft.

Princess Anne ss.

At a court held the 3rd of January 1705/6, present gentlemen: Mr. Beno (Benedict?) Burro, Colonel Moseley, Mr. John Cornick, Captain Hancock, Captain Chapman, justices

Whereas Luke Hill and uxor[5] summoned Grace Sherwood to this court in suspicion of witchcraft and she failing to appear, it is therefore ordered that attachment to the sheriff do issue to attach her body to answer the said summons next court.

Princess Anne ss.

At a court held the 6th February 1705/6, present: Colonel Mosely, Colonel Adam Thorrowgood, Captain Chapman, Captain Hancock, Mr. John Cornick, Mr. Richardson (came late), justices

Suit for suspicion of witchcraft brought by Luke Hill against Grace Sherwood is ordered to be referred till tomorrow.

Princess Anne ss.

At a court held the 7th February 1705/6, present gentlemen: Colonel Moseley, Lieutenant Colonel Thorrowgood, Mr. John Richardson, Mr. John Cornick, Captain Chapman, Captain Hancock, justices

Whereas a complaint was brought against Grace Sherwood upon suspicion of witchcraft by Luke Hill, et cetera, and the matter being after a long time debated and ordered that the said Hill pay all fees of this complaint and that the said Grace be here next court to be searched according to the complaint by a jury of women to decide the said Differ,[6] and the sheriff is likewise ordered to summon an able jury accordingly.

Princess Anne ss.

At a court held the 7th March 1705/6, Colonel Edward Mosely, Lieutenant L. Adam Thorrowgood, Major Henry Sprat, Captain Horatio Woodhouse, Mr. John Cornick, Captain Henry Chapman, Mr. William Smith, Mr. Jon Richardson, Captain George Hancock, justices

Whereas a complaint has been to this *Duq* court by Luke Hill and his wife that one Grace Sherwood of the county was and has been a long time suspected of witchcraft and has been as such represented wherefore the sheriff at the last court was ordered to summon a jury of women to the court to search her on the said suspicion, she assenting to the same. And after the jury was impaneled and sworn and sent out to make due inquiry and inspection into all circumstances, after a mature consideration, they bring in your verdict. Whereof the jury has searcheth Grace Sherwood and has found two things like teats with several other spots. Elizabeth Barnes, forewoman, Sarah Norris, Margaret Watkins, Hannah Dimis, Sarah Goddard, Mary Burgess, Sarah Sargent, Winifred Davis, Ursula Henley, Ann Bridges, Exable Waplies—Mary Cotle.

At a court held the 2nd May 1706, present: Mr. Jonathan Richardson, Major Henry Spratt, Mr. John Cornick, Captain Henry Chapman, Mr. William Smith, justices

Whereas a former complaint was brought against Grace Sherwood for suspicion of witchcraft, with by the attorney general's report to his excellency in counsel was too general and not charging her with any particular act therefore represented to them that Princess Ann Court might if they thought fit have her examined de novo[7] and the court being of opinion that there is great cause of suspicion does therefore order that the sheriff take the said Grace into his safe custody until she shall give bond and security for her appearance to the next court to be examined de novo and that the constable of that precinct go with this sheriff and search this said Grace's house and all suspicious places carefully for all images and such like things[8] as may any way strengthen the suspicion and it is likewise ordered that the sheriff summon an able jury of women. Also all evidences as can give in anything against her in evidence in behalf of our sovereign lady the queen to attend the next court accordingly.

Princess Ann ss.

At a court held the 6th June 1706, present, Mr. Jonathan Richardson, Captain Horatio Woodhouse, Mr. John Cornick, Captain Henry Chapman, Captain William Smith, Captain George Hancock, justices

Whereas Grace Sherwood of the county has been complained of as a person suspected of witchcraft and now being brought before this court in order for examination, they have therefore requested Mr. Maxmt. Bonah to present information against her as counsel in behalf of our sovereign lady the queen in order to her being brought to a regular trial.

Whereas an information in behalf of Her Majesty was presented by Luke Hill to y. court in pursuance to Mr. General Attorney Thomson's report on his excellency's order in Council the 16th April last about Grace Sherwood being suspected of witchcraft have thereupon sworn several evidences against her by which it doth very likely appear.

Princess Anne ss

At a court held the 7th of June 1706, Mr. Jonathan Richardson, Major Henry Spratt, Mr. John Cornick, Captain Chapman, Captain William Smith, Captain George Hancock, justices

Whereas at the last court an order was passed that the sheriff should summon an able jury of women to search Grace Sherwood on suspicion of witchcraft, which, although the same was performed by the sheriff, yet they refused,[9] and did not appear. It is therefore ordered that the same persons be again summoned by the sheriff for their contempt to be dealt with according to the utmost severity of the law and that a new jury of women be by him summoned to appear next court to search her on the aforesaid suspicion and that he likewise summon all evidences that he shall be informed of as material in the complaint and that she continue in the sheriff's custody unless she give good bond and security for her appearance at the next court and that she be of good behavior toward Her Majesty and all her liege people in the meantime.

Princess Ann ss

At a court held the 10th July 1706, present, Colonel Moseley, Captain Moseley, Captain Woodhouse, Mr. John Cornick, Captain Chapman, Captain William Smith, Mr. Richardson (came late), justices

Whereas Grace Sherwood being suspected of witchcraft has a long time waited for a fit opportunity for a further examination and by her consent and approbation of the court it is ordered that the sheriff take all such convenient assistance of boats and men as shall be by him thought fit to meet at Jonathan Harper's plantation in order to take the said Grace forthwith and put her into above man's depth and try her how she swims therein, always having care of her life to preserve her from drowning,[10] and as soon as she comes out that he request as many ancient and knowing women as possible he can to search her carefully for all teats, spots and marks about her body not usual on others and that as they find the same to make report on oath to the truth thereof to the court and further it is ordered that some women be requested to shift and search her before she go into the water that she carry nothing about her to cause any further suspicion.

Whereas on complaint of Luke Hill in behalf of Her Majesty that now is against Grace Sherwood for a person suspected of witchcraft and having had sundry evidences sworn against her, proving many circumstances and which she could not make any excuse or little or nothing to say in her own behalf, only seemed to rely on what the court should do and hereupon consented to be tried in the water and likewise to be searched again with experiments, being tried and she swimming when therein and bound contrary to custom and the Judgments of all the spectators and afterward being searched by five ancient women, who have all declared on oath that she is not like them nor no other woman that they knew of, having two things like teats on her private parts of a black color, being blacker than the rest of her body all with circumstance the court, weighing in their consideration, does therefore order that the sheriff take the said Grace into his custody and to commit her body to the common jail of this county, there to secure her by irons or otherwise, there to remain till such time as he shall be otherwise directed in order. For her coming to the common jail[11] of the county to be brought to a future trial there.

J. J. Burroughs, *county clerk*.

Princess Anne County Clerk's Office, 15 September 1832

MOB JUSTICE IN THE SOUTH
1712

*As the eighteenth century proceeded, witchcraft contin-
ued to recede from the legal realm and grew more arcane
and anecdotal. The following account suggests a small
frisson of witchcraft in South Carolina, citing as evidence
the continuation of anti-witchcraft laws on the books,
and an anecdote about suspected witches being seized by
a mob and burned. While impossible to substantiate, the
persistence of the anecdote nevertheless indicates the passage of witchcraft from the realms of legal legitimacy to
the hazy category of offenses to be addressed by the mob,
or to whispered rumor and social sanction. But, crucially,
mob justice is brought to bear when popular perception
holds that a problem will not receive sufficient redress
in the courts. Witchcraft had not vanished from North
American consciousness. Far from it; witchcraft had
merely changed venue from the courthouse to the street.[1]*

In South Carolina, as late as 1712, the law "against Conjuration,
Witchcraft, and dealing with evil and wicked Spirits," was declared
to be in force. It is quite probable that some cases of witchcraft had
occurred among some of the South Carolinians, which caused the
revival of the act of James the First; but what they were and how
extensive, we have no means at hand to determine, as their chroni-
clers are silent upon the subject. But this is very certain, and that is, if
they did not raise witches down there, they raised the Devil very early.

About this period some suspected of witchcraft were seized
upon by a sort of ruffianly vigilance committee and condemned to
be burned, and were actually roasted by fire, although we do not
learn that the injuries thus inflicted proved fatal. The parties so
tortured, or their friends, brought in action in the regular courts
for the recovery of damages, but the jury gave them nothing!

LITTLETON,
MASSACHUSETTS
1720

After Salem, belief in witchcraft persisted, though it tended to be met with rather more incredulity and caution than it had previously. The following account, a footnote to Governor Thomas Hutchinson's broader discussion of Salem in The History of the Province of Massachusetts-Bay: From the Charter of King William and Queen Mary in 1691, Until the Year 1750, *published in Boston in 1767, suggests in no uncertain terms that the afflicted girls were malingering. However, a large part of Hutchinson's project in addressing witchcraft was concerned with drawing explicit lines between his own rational time and the superstitious days of his forebears. Hutchinson's skepticism offsets the fact that in the following anecdote, the afflicted girls were universally believed until driven by their own Christian guilt to confess.[1]*

In the year 1720, at Littleton in the county of Middlesex, a family was supposed to be bewitched. One J. B. had three daughters, of 11, 9, and 5 years of age. The eldest was a forward girl, and, having read and heard many strange stories, would surprise the company where she happened to be with her manner of relating them. Pleased with the applause, she went from stories she had heard to some of her own framing, and so on to dreams and visions, and attained the art of swooning and of being to appearance for some time breathless. Upon her revival, she would tell of strange things she had met with in this and other worlds. When she met with the words, *God, Christ, the Holy Ghost,* in the Bible, she would drop down with scarce any signs of life in her. Strange noises were often heard in and upon the house; stones

came down the chimney and did great mischief. She complained
of the specter of Mrs. D—y, a woman living in the town; and
once, the mother of the girl struck at the place where the said
D—y was, and the girl said, You have struck her on the belly,
and upon enquiry it was found, that D—y complained of a hurt
in her belly about that time. Another time, the mother struck at a
place where the girl said there was a yellow bird, and she told her
mother she had hit the side of its head, again it again appeared
that D—y's head was hurt about the same time. It was common
to find her in ponds of water, crying out she should be drowned,
sometimes upon the top of the house, and sometimes upon the
tops of trees, where she pretended she had flown, and some fancied they had seen her in the air. There were often the marks of
blows and pinches upon her, which were supposed to come from
an invisible hand.

The second daughter, after her sister had succeeded so well,
imitated her in complaints of D—y, and outdid her in feats of
running up on the barn, climbing trees, et cetera, and, what was
most surprising, the youngest attempted the same feats, and in
some instances went beyond her sisters. The neighbors agreed
they were under an evil hand, and it was pronounced a piece of
witchcraft, as certain as that there ever had been any at Salem,
and no great pains were taken to detect the imposture. Physicians
had been at first employed but to no purpose. And afterward
ministers were called to pray over them but without success. At
length D—y, not long after the supposed blows, took to her bed,
and after some time died, and the two eldest girls ceased complaining. The youngest held out longer, but all persisted in it, that
there had been no fraud. The eldest, not having been baptized,
and being come to adult age, desired and obtained baptism, and
the minister then examined her upon her conduct in the affair,
and she persisted in her declarations of innocency. In 1728, having removed to Medford, she offered to join the church there, and
gave a satisfactory account of herself to the minister of the town;
but he knew nothing of the share she had had in this transaction.
The Lord's day before she was to be admitted, he happened to
preach from this text, "He that speaketh lies shall not escape."[2]
The woman supposed the sermon to be intended for her and
went to the minister, who told her nobody had made any objection against her; but being determined to confess her guilt, she

disclosed the fraud of herself and her sisters, and desired to make a public acknowledgment, in the face of the church; and accordingly did so. The two sisters, seeing her pitied, had become actors also with her, without being moved to it by her, but when she saw them follow her, they all joined in the secret and acted in concert. They had no particular spite against D—y, but it was necessary to accuse somebody, and the eldest having pitched upon her, the rest followed. The woman's complaints, about the same time the girl pretended she was struck, proceeded from other causes, which were not then properly enquired into. Once, at least, they were in great danger of being detected in their tricks; but the grounds of suspicion were overlooked, through the indulgence and credulity[3] of their parents. Manuscript of the Reverend Mr. Turell, minister of Medford.

BOSTON, MASSACHUSETTS
1728

This letter in a Boston newspaper describes a witch trial in Austria, and is remarkable because of the assumptions that the letter writer made about its readership. In this context, the witch trial was presented as something exotic and foreign, a proceeding with customs that must be explained to rational Bostonian readers. However, the witch ducking described very closely mirrors the practice undertaken in Grace Sherwood's trial in Virginia a scant twenty years earlier; it is not so very foreign after all. Further, the description of accused witches as including at least two prominent members of society, with allusion to their membership in a secret coven, would have inevitably stirred comparisons with Salem. To New Englanders hovering on the cusp of the Great Awakening,[1] beginning to engage with God on a more personal level, this account would have been both intriguing and reassuring, marking as it does the difference between their own religious outlook and those of their immediate predecessors.[2]

From a Written Letter, Vienna, August 25

Letters from Segedin in Hungary, of the 26th of July, import that several persons of both sexes convicted of witchcraft have been condemned to be burned alive, but before they were executed, they put them upon the following trials (according to the custom of the country). The first was to tie their hands and feet and throw them into the water, who as sorcerers used to do, swam like a piece of wood, after which they were put into scales when it appeared that a large woman weighed but an ounce, and her husband but 5 drams, and the other still lighter,[3] whereupon they were burned alive the 23rd past. There was among them a midwife who had baptized 2,000 children in the name of the Devil, and a man of 82 years old who was formerly a judge of that town.

NEW YORK, NEW YORK
1737

Attitudes about witchcraft had been changing in Britain as well, culminating in the passage of the Witchcraft Act of 1735, referenced in the following New York newspaper article. While witchcraft laws varied in North America from state to state, in Britain the 1735 law repealed the "Act against Conjuration, Witchcraft, and dealing with evil and wicked spirits" passed under King James I in 1604, which had established witchcraft as a felony under common law. For the first time, witchcraft was no longer to be held to be against the law as such, as it was now popularly thought to be a nonexistent crime. Instead, the new act would prosecute anyone who pretended to be practicing witchcraft, including dowsing for water, conjuring to find lost objects, or summoning spirits.

Such witch pretenders would be prosecuted as con artists and charlatans, rather than being charged with a felony punishable by death. What is remarkable about the passage of this law, however, is that the content of the supposed offenses stays essentially the same. Witchcraft, if we understand it to be a set of practices or beliefs, continues to exist under the 1735 law. In effect, the belief in witchcraft—its content, its reality, the existence of its practitioners—stays consistent, but the areas of perceived risk have changed.[1]

From the *White-Hall Evening-Post.*
London, July 21, 1737

SIR,

I send you enclosed a very remarkable letter concerning the late cruel usage of a poor old woman in Bedfordshire, who was suspected of being a witch. You will see by it that the late law for abolishing the act against witches has not abolished credulity of the country people; but I hope it has made proper provision for punishing their barbarity on such occasions. I am, *sir*, yours, et cetera, A. B.

Extract of a Letter about the Trial of a Witch.
OAKLEY,
THREE MILES FROM
BEDFORD

SIR,

The people here are so prejudiced in the belief of witches, that you would think yourself in Lapland, were you to hear their ridiculous stories. There is not a village in the neighborhood but has two or three. About a week ago I was present at the ceremony of ducking a witch, a particular account of which may not perhaps be disagreeable to you.

An old woman of about 60 years of age had long lain under an imputation of witchcraft, who, being willing (for her own sake and her children's) to clear herself, consented to be ducked; and the parish officers promised her a guinea if she should sink. The place appointed for the operation was in the River Oust by a mill. There were, I believe, 500 spectators. About eleven o'clock in the forenoon, the woman came, and was tied up in a wet sheet, all but her face and hands. Her toes were tied close together, as were also her thumbs, and her hands tied to the small of her legs. They fastened a rope about her middle, and pulled off her cap to search for pins, for their notion is, if they have but one pin about them, they won't sink.

When all preliminaries were settled, she was thrown in; but unhappily for the poor creature, she floated, though her head was all the while under water. Upon this there was a confused cry. "A witch! A witch! Drown her! Hang her!" She was in the water about 1 minute and a half and was taken out, half drowned. When she had recovered breath, the experiment was repeated twice more, but with the same success, for she floated each time, which was a plain demonstration of guilt to the ignorant multitude. For notwithstanding the poor creature was laid down upon the grass speechless and almost dead, they were so far from showing her any pity or compassion, that they strove who should be the most forward in loading her with reproaches. Such is the dire effect of popular prejudice! As for my part, I stood against the torrent, and when I had cut the strings which tied her, had her carried back to the mill, and endeavored to convince the people of the uncertainty of the experiment, and offered to lay five to one, that any woman of her age, so tied up in a close sheet, would float, but all to no purpose, for I was near being mobbed. Sometime after, the woman came out, and one of the company happened to mention another experiment to try a witch, which was to weigh her against the church Bible, for a witch, it seems, could not outweigh it. I immediately seconded that motion (as thinking it might be of service to the poor woman) and made use of an argument which (though as weak as * King James for their not sinking) had some weight with the people. For I told them that if she was a witch, she certainly dealt with the Devil; and as the Bible was undoubtedly the word of God, it must weigh more than all the works of the Devil. This seemed reasonable to several. And those that did not think it so, could not answer it. At last, the question was carried, and she was weighed against the Bible; which weighed about twelve pound. She outweighed it. This convinced some and staggered others, but the P—n, who believed through thick and thin, went away fully assured that she was a witch, and endeavored to inculcate that belief into all others.

I AM, *SIR*,
YOUR VERY HUMBLE SERVANT.

NEW YORK, NEW YORK
1741

The phrase "witch hunt" appears frequently in American political and cultural discourse, perhaps frequently enough to be leached of much of its impact. However, well before Joseph McCarthy's House Un-American Activities Committee, the idea of the witch hunt, or the witch trial, had already begun to stalk North American political discourse. In New York City during the winter of 1741, several fires were set across Manhattan, which the white inhabitants of the city took as a sign of an imminent violent slave uprising. The rush to discover who was responsible led to over a hundred black New Yorkers being imprisoned, seventeen put to death on the gallows, and—most chillingly—thirteen burned at the stake.[1]

The following newspaper editorial from a writer in New England draws an explicit parallel between the Salem trial—which the writer points out was the subject of much criticism from New York while it was under way—and the frenzy attendant on the slave revolt conspiracy trial in 1741. By the middle of the eighteenth century, the witch as a figure of fear, and the witch trial as an enterprise of unreason, had taken firm root in North American culture. Far from falling by the wayside under the purifying light of Enlightenment thought, the witch merely changed form, from a legal category to a cultural trope.[2]

Province of the Massachusetts
Bay, 1741.

Sir,

I am a stranger to you and to New York, and so must beg pardon
for the mistakes I may be guilty of in the subsequent attempt, the
design whereof is to put an end to the bloody tragedy that has
been, and I suppose is still acting among you, in regard of the
poor Negroes and the whites too.

I observe in one of the Boston newsletters, dated July 13,
that 5 Negroes were executed in one day at the gallows, a favor
indeed! For one the next day was burned at the stake, where he
impeached several others, and among them some whites, which,
with the former terrible executions among you upon this occasion, puts me in mind of our New England witchcraft in the year
1692, which, if I don't mistake, New York justly reproached us
for and mocked at our credulity about. But may it not now be
justly retorted, *Mutato nomine, de te Fabula Narratur*?[3] What
ground you proceed upon, I must acknowledge myself not sufficiently informed of. But finding that those five that were executed
in July denied any guilt, it makes me suspect that your present
case, and ours heretofore, are much the same, and that Negro
and specter evidence will turn out alike. We had near 50 confessors who accused multitudes of others, alleging time and place
and various other circumstances to render their confessions credible, that they had their meetings, formed confederacies, signed
the Devil's book, et cetera. And as long as confessions were
received and encouraged, accusations multiplied and increased:
But I am humbly of opinion that such confessions and the evidences founded thereon are not worth a straw, unless some certain overt act (that nobody else could perform) appear to confirm
the fame. For many times they are obtained by foul means, by
force or torture, by flattery or surprise, by over watch or distraction, by discontent with their circumstances, through envy
or malice, or in hopes of a longer time to live, or to die an easier
death, et cetera. For anybody would choose rather to be hanged
than to be burned.

It is true I have heard something of your forts being burned, but that might be by lightning from heaven, by accident, by some malicious person or persons of our own color. What other facts have been performed to petrify your hearts against the poor blacks, and some of your neighbors, the whites, I can't tell. Possibly there have been some murmurings among the Negroes, and a few mad fellows may have threatened and designed revenge for the cruelty and inhumanity they have met with, which is too rife in the English plantations, and not long since occasioned such another tremendous and unreasonable a massacre at Antigua. But two things seem to me almost as impossible as for witches to fly in the air, or change themselves into cats, namely, that the whites should join with blacks; or that the blacks (among whom there are no doubt some rational persons) should attempt the destruction of a city,[4] when it is impossible they should escape the just and direful vengeance of the countries round about, which would immediately pour in upon, and swallow them up quick. And therefore if nothing will put an end to this doleful tragedy till some of higher degree and better circumstances and characters are accused (which finished our Salem witchcraft), the sooner the better, lest all the poor people of your government perish in the merciless flames of an imaginary plot.

In the meantime don't be offended if out of friendship to my poor countrymen, and compassion to the Negroes (who are partakers of the same nature with us and ought to be treated with humanity), I entreat you not to go on to destroy your own estates by making bonfires of your Negroes, and thereby perhaps loading yourselves with greater guilt than theirs. For we have too much reason to fear that the divine vengeance does and will pursue us for our ill treatment to the bodies and souls of our poor slaves, and the meaner sort of people. And therefore let justice be done whenever you sit in judicature about their affairs.

All which is humbly submitted by a well-wisher to all human beings, and one that ever desires to be of the merciful side, et cetera.

PHILADELPHIA, PENNSYLVANIA 1787

By the end of the eighteenth century, witchcraft had largely become a fading memory to which the present may in general be favorably compared, dwelling only in folklore and in the isolated superstitions of uneducated people. Or so it would seem. The following anecdote, preserved in an anti-Federalist pamphlet as a point of evidence in support of the importance of legally securing the liberty of conscience in the Bill of Rights during the Constitutional Convention, suggests that belief in witches at the end of the eighteenth century instead was very much alive and well, and living in the hands of the mob. Belief in witches had not disappeared at all. It was not an obscure footnote to history. It was still real and it was still present and it was still threatening enough to warrant stoning a woman in the street to her death.[1]

Mr. Printer, In order that people may be sufficiently impressed with the necessity of establishing a bill of rights in the forming of a new constitution, it is very proper to take a short view of some of those liberties, which it is of the greatest importance for freemen to retain to themselves, when they surrender up a part of their natural rights for the good of society.

The first of these, which it is of the utmost importance for the people to retain to themselves, which indeed they have not even the right to surrender, and which at the same time it is of no kind of advantages to government to strip them of, is the liberty of conscience. I know that a ready answer is at hand to any objections upon this head. We shall be told that in this enlightened age, the rights of conscience are perfectly secure: There is no necessity of guarding them, for no man has the remotest thoughts of invading them. If this be the case, I beg leave to reply that now is the very time to secure them. Wise and prudent men always take care to guard against danger beforehand and to make themselves safe while it is yet in their power to do it without inconvenience or risk. Who shall answer for the ebbings and flowings of opinion or be able to say what will be the fashionable frenzy of the next generation? It would have been treated as a very ridiculous supposition, a year ago, that the charge of witchcraft would cost a person her life in the city of Philadelphia, yet the fate of the unhappy old woman called Corbmaker, who was beaten, repeatedly wounded with knives, mangled, and at last killed in our streets in obedience to the commandment which requires "that we shall not suffer a witch to live,"[2] without possibility of punishment or even of detecting the authors of this inhuman folly, should be an example to warn us how little we ought to trust to the unrestrained discretion of human nature.

MOLL PITCHER, LYNN, MASSACHUSETTS 1738–1813

Moll Pitcher, born in Marblehead (immediately east of Salem), who resided much of her life in Lynn (immediately south of Salem), embodies the shift of the witch in North American consciousness from a figure of fear to a figure of folklore. She made her living as a fortuneteller and was immortalized in a poem that bears her name by John Greenleaf Whittier. She was consulted on affairs of love and money by the educated and the uneducated alike, and her particular specialty concerned the outcomes of sea voyages. Whittier's representation of Pitcher is hardly complimentary, however: he writes that she was "A wasted, gray, and meagre hag / In features evil as her lot / She had the crooked nose of a witch."

In some respects, Moll Pitcher represents a consistency of Anglophone North Atlantic witch belief: in her function as a cunning woman in the early modern English sense, as an individual with particular occult skills available for a fee, and one able to stir both respect and fear in her community, Pitcher could just as easily have been born in 1538 as in 1738. However, her proximity to Salem, living among—and surely patronized by—people who felt the shadow of the Salem trials at their backs, renders Pitcher a curious character.

Most important, Moll Pitcher was born at the beginning of the consumer revolution in colonial North America. Though part of her skill, like the traditional cunning person, lay in conjuring to find lost property, scarcity was less of a grinding problem for average people by the 1730s than it had been a generation earlier. Pitcher's

*services could be seen as a boon, without the risk of being
as threatening as they would have been a generation previously.[1] Moll Pitcher simultaneously embodies folk magical belief, which had its roots in early modern practices
in Europe and the British Isles, while also ushering in
the figure of the witch in colonial North America, from
the confused waning category in the early part of the
eighteenth century to the fantastical fairy tale figure that
she would assume in the nineteenth century. That's a tall
order for one elderly New England woman to fill with
only some tea leaves to help her.[2]*

The reader should now be informed that the poetical extract
foregoing is from a poem commemorative of as great and notorious a witch as any that can be found described in the annals
of witchcraft, and that we are indebted to the bard of Lynn for
a graphic outline of her real history. But the reader should be
reminded that the amiable and excellent author of that work was
himself a poet, and that it is possible that his account may have
a tinge of poetry or be a little bordering on romance. With this
premonition it shall follow in his own words.

The celebrated Mary Pitcher, a professed fortune-teller, died
April 9th, 1813, aged 75. Her grandfather John Dimond lived
at Marblehead and for many years exercised the same pretentions. Her father, Captain John Dimond, was master of a vessel from that place and was living in 1770. Mary Dimond was
born in the year 1738. She was connected with some of the best
families in Essex County, and with the exception of her extraordinary pretentions, there was nothing disreputable in her life or
character. She was of the medium height and size for a woman,
with a good form and agreeable manners. Her head, phrenologi-
cally considered, was somewhat capacious, her forehead broad
and full, her hair dark brown, her nose inclining to long, and
her face pale and thin. There was nothing gross or sensual in her
appearance. Her countenance was rather intellectual and she had
that contour of face and expression which, without being posi-
tively beautiful is nevertheless decidedly interesting: a thoughtful, pensive, and sometimes downcast look, almost approaching
to melancholy, an eye, when it looked at you, of calm and keen
penetration, and an expression of intelligent discernment half

mingled with a glance of shrewdness. She took a poor man for a husband and then adopted what she doubtless thought the harmless employment of fortune-telling in order to support her children. In this she was probably more successful than she herself had anticipated and she became celebrated, not only throughout America but throughout the world for her skill. There was no port on either continent, where floated the flag of an American ship that had not heard of the fame of Moll Pitcher. To her came the rich and the poor, the wife and the ignorant, the accomplished and the vulgar, the timid and the brave. The ignorant sailor, who believed in the omens and dreams of superstition, and the intelligent merchant, whose ships were freighted for distant lands, alike sought her dwelling, and many a vessel has been deserted by its crew, and waited idly at the wharves for weeks in consequence of her unlucky predictions. Many persons came from places far removed to consult her on affairs of love or loss of property or to obtain her surmises respecting the vicissitudes of their future fortune. Every youth who was not assured of the reciprocal affection of his fair one and every maid who was desirous of anticipating the hour of her highest felicity repaired at evening to her humble dwelling, which stood on what was then a lonely road, near the foot of High Rock,[3] with the single dwelling of Dr. Henry Burchard nearly opposite, over whose gateway were the two bones of a great whale, disposed in the form of a Gothic arch. There for more than fifty years, in her unpretending mansion, did she answer the inquiries of the simple rustic from the wilds of New Hampshire, and the wealthy noble from Europe; and doubtless her predictions have had an influence in shaping the fortunes of thousands.

Notes

INTRODUCTION

1. Of course, to say that witchcraft has not persisted into our own time is not exactly true. Wicca as an organized religion began in the middle decades of the twentieth century and has only continued to grow. The ablest history of the establishment of this religion, and of the relationship that it has with early modern witchcraft, is elucidated in Ronald Hutton's *The Triumph of the Moon: A History of Modern Pagan Witchcraft* (Oxford: Oxford University Press, 1999).

WITCHES IN THE BIBLE

1. The Valley of the Son of Hinnom is both a literal place, located in Gehenna, outside of ancient Jerusalem, which was associated with apostate human sacrifice, and a figurative reference to hell. The blending of the figurative and the literal in this biblical account of the location of witchcraft, or in the idea of wickedness as having a concrete reality outside the body or the soul of the wicked person, will come to play a substantial role in the anxiety about witches in the North American landscape. The "observation of times" here alludes to the practice of astrology.

TRIAL OF URSULA KEMP, ST. OSYTH, ENGLAND, 1582

1. Gregory Durston, *Witchcraft and Witch Trials: A History of English Witchcraft and Its Legal Perspectives* (Chichester, England: Barry Rose Law, 2000), iv. Witchcraft in this period was both a legal and an ecclesiastic offense, and could be tried on both a civil and a religious basis. We will limit our inquiry to the treatment of witchcraft within the

legal system, which nevertheless turned to theological writing for its legitimacy.

2. Durston, *Witchcraft and Witch Trials*, v. The problematic traits of Kemp's personality, together with the long-standing complaints she has engendered in her neighbors, place her on a continuum of women who garner suspicion as a result of socially deviant behavior.

3. Durston, *Witchcraft and Witch Trials*, vi. The nature of the evidence entered against Kemp, which mainly consists of unsubstantiated gossip, suggests the fragility of social relationships in the early modern village, when networks of acquaintanceship could mean the difference between prosperity and ruin.

4. Durston, *Witchcraft and Witch Trials*, vii. Before the Scientific Revolution, the difference between correlated phenomena and causation between phenomena was not as widely understood as it is today. Close juxtaposition of two events could easily be mistaken for causation. Similarly, before the spread of the germ theory of disease, sickness could often strike with bewildering, and therefore suspicious, suddenness.

5. Durston, *Witchcraft and Witch Trials*, viii. The phenomenon of false confession poses some intriguing problems. A few North American cases seem to suggest that the confessing witch enjoys having a negative reputation. In other instances, most notoriously the probable forced confession of Tituba Indian at the outset of the Salem panic, confession appears as against the will of the confessor.

6. Durston, *Witchcraft and Witch Trials*, xi. Popular imagination assumes that witches were executed by burning at the stake. In English settlements, however, this was not the case. Witchcraft was a felony and was punished as a felony by hanging.

7. Durston, *Witchcraft and Witch Trials*, xii.

8. Excerpted from W.W., *A true and just recorde, of the information, examination and confessions of all the witches taken at S. Oses in the Countie of Essex*, originally published in London by Thomas Dawson, 1582. Images of the original document held at the Huntington Library may be viewed on Early English Books Online, http://gateway .proquest.com/openurl?ctx_ver=Z39.882003&res_id=xri:eebo&rft _id=xri:eebo:image:1960. As Early English Books Online is a subscription service, an alternate version may be found at http://gateway .proquest.com/openurl?ctx_ver=Z39.88=200&res=xri:eebo&rft _id=xri:eebo:image:1960.

9. The tragedy of a healthy four-month-old baby falling from a cradle and breaking its neck provides a focal point for the conflict between Ursula and Grace. Ursula has publicly questioned Grace's fitness for motherhood, whereas Grace has taken Ursula's regret— or lack of surprise—at the baby's death as an example of threat followed by maleficium, or evil done by supernatural means. Instead

NOTES TO PAGES 8–14

of expressing doubt about Grace's capacity, Ursula was instead making a prediction, which she then caused to come true.

10. To "lie in" means to take to bed in preparation for childbirth.

11. "Unwitching" someone was a skill for cunning folk, people of importance in the early modern village system, who offered occult services for a fee, marshaling folk magical belief to their own economic gain while sidestepping the label of "witch." See Owen Davies, *Popular Magic: Cunning-folk in English History* (New York: Bloomsbury, 2007), 29.

12. "Priuily" in the original, so "privily."

13. Michaelmas, or the feast of Saint Michael, one of the quarter days in England, usually falling around September 29. In English tradition, quarter days fell roughly on Lady Day, Midsummer Day, Michaelmas, and Christmas, and beginning in the Middle Ages were days on which lawsuits were settled and rents were due.

14. Ursula needs sand probably to scour her floors and she is offering to trade for it her labor dyeing a pair of women's stockings. Barter for goods and services was a more common mode of commerce between neighbors than the use of cash.

15. Modern usage treats "naughty" more mildly, connoting childlike misbehavior. However, the OED defines "naughty" in this period as "morally bad, wicked."

16. "Gyile" in the original.

17. Another reference to the cunning person, who blames Ursula for the sick Letherdall child. The cunning person's main task in the early modern English village was unbewitching, which often involved reinforcing assumptions held by the client about who the responsible witch might be.

18. Spirit familiars were thought to be small demons or imps that attended to a witch and helped with maleficium, or mischief done using spiritual means, in exchange for feeding from the witch's body. Even the name of one of these spirits, Tittey, alludes to the images of inverted motherhood common to folk beliefs about witches.

19. Saint John's-wort, which is still used by some today as a mood regulator.

20. "Wonderful" did not have today's positive association in this time period. Instead "wonderful" means astonishing. See OED, 1928.

21. Seven eight?

22. Ursula Kemp confessed to her various witchly activities in the apparent hopes of being treated leniently, but her hopes were in vain. In Salem a century later, confessions would help accused witches escape execution, but such an outcome was unusual. In previous examples of witch trials such as this one, confession was more likely to hasten conviction and punishment than it was to lead to any leniency.

REGINALD SCOT, *THE DISCOUERIE OF WITCHCRAFT*, 1584

1. Sydney Anglo, "Reginald Scot's *Discoverie of Witchcraft*: Skepticism and Sadduceeism" in *The Damned Art: Essays in the Literature of Witchcraft*, ed. Sydney Anglo (London: Routledge and Kegan Paul, 1977), 108.

2. Anglo, "Reginald Scot's *Discoverie of Witchcraft*," 117.

3. Scot represents a way station on the movement of witchcraft thought from the Continent to the British Isles, and eventually to North America. He turns his critical attention not only to witch trials contemporary to his own experience, but also to examples drawn from earlier Continental witch-hunting manuals such as the *Malleus Maleficarum* of 1486; writing as a Protestant, Scot sees some of the most notorious descriptions of witchcraft in the *Malleus* as examples of the venality so widespread in the Catholic Church.

4. Excerpted from Reginald Scot, *The discouerie of witchcraft vvherein the lewde dealing of witches and witchmongers is notablie detected* . . . Originally published in London by Henry Denham for William Brome, 1584. Images of the original document held at the Huntington Library may be viewed on Early English Books Online, http://gateway.proquest.com/openurl?ctx_ver=Z39.88-2003&res_id=xri:eebo&rft_id=xri:eebo:image:44. An alternate site is https://archive.org/details/discoverieofwitooscot.

5. This is widely read as a reference to Job 5:17, which states, "Behold, happy is the man whom God correcteth: therefore despise not thou the chastening of the Almighty." All Bible quotes are taken from the King James Bible (American version).

6. Matthew 11:28, "Come unto me, all thee that labor and are heavy laden, and I will give you rest."

7. Original reads "fraied."

8. Johan Brentius, 1499–1570, a Lutheran theologian.

9. This assertion derives from a number of biblical passages; among them Psalms 25 and 83, Ecclesiastes 43, Luke 8, Matthew 8, and Mark 4:41. "And they feared exceedingly, and said one to another, What manner of man is this, that even the wind and the sea obey him?" (Mark 4:41).

10. For "cousining," which meant "cheating."

11. John 10:21, "Others said, These are not the words of him that hath a devil. Can a devil open the eyes of the blind?"

12. Haggai 2:17, "I smote you with blasting and with mildew and with hail in all the labors of your hands; yet ye turned not to me, saith the LORD."

13. Eyewitness.

14. Foolish or insipid. See OED, 1897.

15. It is tempting to regard this passage as evidence that the vicar resorted to a cunning person to determine who was responsible for bewitching his son.

16. Syphilis.

17. In this case M. D. Lewen is likely an "ordinary" in the ecclesiastical sense, which the OED of 2004 defines as "A person who has, of his or her own right and not by the appointment of another, immediate jurisdiction in ecclesiastical cases, such as the archbishop in a province, or the bishop or bishop's deputy in a diocese."

18. Scot has no love for this licentious vicar, though his criticism is subtle. Even writers about witchcraft depend on the power of rumor and reputation as much as, if not more than, hard evidence.

19. Scot also notes the degree of risk inherent in the making of a witchcraft accusation at all. In colonial North America in the generation following, the mere spreading of a rumor of witchcraft was sufficient for the rumored witch to bring charges of slander against the rumor monger. Witches were so feared as a category that Scot admits that simply being accused could as often as not end in death for a suspected witch.

20. Original word reads "boten."

21. Stew or porridge.

22. Scot points out a surprising irony about suspected early modern witches, which is that usually they were living in poverty. In a time of scarcity, without structured public means of relief for the poor, begging was a sad necessity for some, while also imposing a hardship on the rest of the community.

23. A sudden-onset malady, usually taken to be a stroke.

24. Misdeeds and charms cover ignorance.

25. Defined by the OED, 1989 edition, as a "deceiver, cheat, impostor."

GEORGE GIFFORD, *A DIALOGUE CONCERNING WITCHES AND WITCHCRAFTES*, 1593

1. Alan Macfarlane, "A Tudor Anthropologist: George Gifford's *Discourse* and *Dialogue*," in *The Damned Art: Essays in the Literature of Witchcraft*, ed. Sydney Anglo (London: Routledge & Kegan Paul, 1977), 140.

2. Scott McGinnis, "'Subtiltie' Exposed: Pastoral Perspectives on Witch Belief in the Thought of George Gifford," *Sixteenth Century Journal* XXXIII/3 (2002): 665.

3. McGinnis, "'Subtiltie' Exposed," 672.

4. Gifford is less concerned with whether witches exist or not than with what witches mean. He recognizes that the witch as an idea serves

an important cultural role, either by offering a scapegoat for misfortune, or (in the role of the cunning person) by offering occult defense against misfortune. Gifford seems sympathetic to the fear and uncertainty that marked early modern English village life. He doesn't necessarily condemn belief in witchcraft as ignorant in the way that Scot does. Instead, Gifford wishes to channel that fear and hopelessness, leading believers in witchcraft to strengthen their belief in God.

5. Excerpted from George Gifford, *A dialogue concerning witches and witchcraftes In which is laide open how craftely the Diuell deceiueth not onely the witches but many other and so leadeth them awrie into many great errours.* Originally published in London. Printed by John Windet for Tobie Cooke and Mihil Hart, 1593. Images of the original document held at the Huntington Library may be viewed on Early English Books Online, http://gateway.pro quest.com/openurl?ctx_ver=Z39.88-2003&res_id=xri:eebo&rft _id=xri:eebo:image:5997. An alternate site is https://archive.org/ details/adialogueconceroogiffgoog. The physical document is located at Huntington Library, San Marino, California, call number 59292.

6. 2 Corinthians 7:10, "For godly sorrow worketh repentance to salvation not to be repented of: but the sorrow of the world worketh death."

7. A person who rails, or rants, OED, June 2008.

8. A gambler, or someone addicted to gambling with dice, OED, 1895.

9. English folk magic belief held that bewitchment established a sympathetic relationship between the witch and the bewitched animal. As such, a common method of unbewitching consisted of burning the afflicted animal alive. It was thought that burning the animal would convey the burning onto the witch responsible. See James George Frazer, *The Golden Bough: A Study in Magic and Religion* (New York: Macmillan, 1955), 308.

10. "Showing in a glass" is another way of saying "scrying," or looking for images in a highly reflective surface, such as a mirror, a dish of oil, or a polished ball of crystal. Scrying could be used to either see spirits or reveal the location of unknown information, such as the identity of people or objects. Scrying persists in popular culture today in the form of the crystal ball still seen in the windows of ostensible psychics in American cities—as recognizable a professional symbol as three gold balls for a pawn shop or a striped barber pole.

11. For "puckerel," meaning demon or imp; OED, 2007. This word is rare enough that one of the two OED examples is actually this usage of Gifford's.

12. The wearing of the first few words of the gospel of St. John on the body was considered to be a good luck charm. See Cora Linn Daniels and C. M. Stevans, eds., *Encyclopaedia of Superstitions,*

Folklore, and the Occult Sciences, vol. III (Chicago: JH Thewdale and Sons, 1903), 1635.

13. "Between two stools" is a proverbial expression from "between two stools the ass hits the ground," that is, stuck between two choices. See Bartlett J. Whiting, *Early American Proverbs and Proverbial Phrases* (Cambridge: Harvard University Press, 1977), 417–418.

14. This is the crux of Gifford's argument: not that maleficium is impossible, but that belief in witches and witchcraft is an error of faith, transferring confidence to the Devil that rightly belongs to God.

15. At the risk of subjecting Gifford to unfairly presentist criticisms, one cannot help but express amusement at the sharply circumscribed role of the nameless "wife." Other than serving as another untutored mouthpiece for common English folk magic beliefs, the wife serves no purpose whatsoever. Gifford's indifference underscores the paradoxical gender politics of witch fear during this period. Women are effectively invisible in Gifford's discourse, and yet pose the gravest threat when tempted by the Devil into witchery. Gifford will go on to worry about witches' being tempted into "whoredom" and "uncleanness," anxieties that allude to the sexual undertones of much anti-witch sentiment. The "wife" here fades into invisibility, yet the theoretical witches described by Daniel, Samuel, and M. B. stalk the narrative like avaricious devils.

16. Gifford has chosen accurate examples of the complaints that early modern English villagers often lodged against witches. To a modern reader, the sudden unexplained death of a healthy hen, or the failure of butter to come from churning, might seem meager in the grand scheme of things. But for subsistence farmers, the quotidian struggles of everyday life would have loomed very large indeed.

17. Gifford is likely alluding to Scot's skepticism. Puritan theologians like Gifford would have thought it irreligious to doubt the existence of witches, for to do so would go against the Bible's truth. Gifford doesn't wish to argue that witches do not exist. He only wishes to persuade his readers that their power is misunderstood, and is a delusion of Satan.

18. For "cavillers," defined as "one who cavils; a captious or frivolous objector, a quibbling disputant." OED, 1889.

19. Gifford is intrigued by the problem of self-confessed witches. How can spirit familiars be said not to exist when confessed witches like Ursula Kemp have confirmed that they do?

20. Possibly an archaic word for the plural of cow, though this incidence is much earlier than the OED examples. See OED, 1901.

21. Gifford's fictional dialogue also offers a reliable representation of witches' gender. In general, witches were thought to be women, but not always.

KING JAMES I, *DAEMONOLOGIE*, 1597

1. Stuart Clark, "King James's *Daemonologie*: Witchcraft and Kingship," in *The Damned Art: Essays in the Literature of Witchcraft* (London: Routledge and Kegan Paul, 1977), 156.

2. Clark, "King James's *Daemonologie*," 165.

3. Clark, "King James's *Daemonologie*," 168.

4. Excerpted from King James I, *Daemonologie in forme of a dialogue, diuided into three bookes*. Originally published in Edinburgh. Printed by Robert Walde-graue, printer to the King's Majestie, 1597. Images of the original document held at the Huntington Library may be viewed on Early English Books Online, http://gateway.proquest.com/openurl?ctx_ver=Z39.88-2003& res_id=xri:eebo&rft_id=xri:eebo:image:7990. An alternate site is https://archive.org/details/daemonologie25929gut.

5. Melancholia, or an excess of black bile, according to the Hippocratic principles of humorism. Here James addresses whether supposed effects of witchcraft are really caused by a physical or mental imbalance.

6. The Bible is at pains to distinguish between magicians, necromancers, sorcerers, and witches. Necromancy is the conjuring of the spirit of the dead to divine the future. Magicians are soothsayers using occult means, as in Genesis 41:8, "And it came to pass in the morning that his spirit was troubled; and he sent and called for all the magicians of Egypt, and all the wise men thereof: and Pharaoh told them his dream; but there was none that could interpret them unto Pharaoh." A biblical sorcerer is similar to a magician, as in Daniel 2:2, "Then the king commanded to call the magicians, and the astrologers, and the sorcerers, and the Chaldeans, for to shew the king his dreams." Witches consist of the slipperiest category of magic user in the Bible, defined principally by their negative qualities and their association with the Devil.

7. James takes on here the skeptical writers against witchcraft, most notably Reginald Scot, who doubt witchcraft's existence, rather than the writers of a more theological bent, like Gifford, who believe that witchcraft exists but who argue that its meaning and function are errors of faith.

8. The "Pythonisse," or Pythoness, is the witch of Endor, who conjures the image of Samuel for Saul. The OED defines "pythoness" as "a woman believed to be possessed by a spirit and to be able to foresee the future; a female soothsayer; a witch," and indicates that the word refers most often to either the biblical witch of Endor, or to the Delphic oracle.

9. James's account makes so much of the risks of feeble-mindedness or insanity that it almost seems to be overkill—he wishes to be taken

for an intellect and an authority so intently that he sets up straw men to bat down.

10. An antique term for medicine.

11. Referring to Acts 16:16–19, in which the apostle Paul meets a young woman "possessed with a spirit of divination," who follows him for several days before Paul commands the spirit to leave the woman in the name of Jesus Christ. The passage is commonly interpreted as an exorcism, but James here sees the soothsayer as an example of a "sorcerer or witch," and so further biblical proof of the reality of witchcraft.

12. "Terrene" is an archaic word for "earthy." See OED, 1911.

13. James suggests that skeptical writers have argued that the unfortunates who have admitted to being witches are suffering from an excess of melancholic humor, or black bile. However, James dismisses this objection on the grounds that many confessed witches do not conform to the agreed-upon traits of melancholics, who are thin and solitary. James sees confessed witches who are corpulent and loving of company and pleasures of the flesh. For this reason, James is convinced that confessed witches are not unfortunates suffering from mental disease but are instead engaged with the invisible world.

14. In response to Philopathes' question as to why, if witches really do command the power that we ascribe to them, they have not completely decimated the rest of the human population, Epistemon retorts that that is a ridiculous question, both because God has set limits on what the Devil is able to do, and also because the sobriety and vigilance of the faithful can keep the Devil's power at bay.

15. An acute gendering occurs in James's account of the difference between magicians and witches. Magicians have a greater sense of agency, for though they serve the same master as witches, they use the Devil to amass their own power and "popular honor and estimation." Witches, on the other hand, have been seduced to serve the Devil out of their own moral weakness, through their thwarted desire for revenge or out of greed. The difference between greed and the desire for "estimation" might appear academic, though one detects a certain nobility in the language James uses to describe magicians and contempt in the language reserved for witches. Both are evil; the only difference is the gender of the practitioner.

16. James here characterizes magicians as "scholars" of the Devil.

17. An archaic word synonymous with "next" or "afterward." See OED, 1919.

18. James refers to the "Devil's mark," or the "witches' teat," which was thought by early modern witch-hunters to be the only physical evidence of a witch's guilt.

19. An archaic word meaning elegant or tidy. See OED, 1891.

20. James repeats accounts found in other witch-hunting manuals that witches will convene in Sabbaths, which serve the dual purpose of exchanging diabolical knowledge while also perverting in their structure the worship of God.

21. "Urim and thummim" is an Old Testament Hebraic collocation, with "urim" signifying a reflective item worn on the breastplate of Jewish priests and used for divining God's will, and "thummim" signifying "perfection." OED, 2004. Essentially, the phrase can be taken to mean oracles or divination tools that are legitimate and God-sanctioned, in contrast to the entrails of beasts and other divination techniques associated with witchcraft and the Devil.

22. As the Christian might kiss the ring of a spiritual leader or a monarch, witches were often represented as sealing their covenant with Satan by kissing his rear end, thereby continuing the tangling of religious imagery with sexual imagery.

23. Likely a reference to Calcutta, and to the appearance and representation of Hindu gods in the form of animals. James underscores the idea that there are no alternatives to Christian faith; anything that does not adhere to the form and structure of the church of which he is the head is necessarily diabolical.

24. Exodus 33:22–23, "And it shall come to pass, while my glory passeth by, that I will put thee in a clift of the rock, and will cover thee with my hand while I pass by: And I will take away mine hand, and thou shalt see my back parts: but my face shall not be seen." This passage refers to the favor being shown Moses by God, in which Moses will be permitted to see a portion of his divine shape, but cannot be allowed to see God's face. James is suggesting that Satan, out of a desire to contort God's gestures in the structure of his Sabbaths, perverts the intent of this passage from Exodus by requiring all his minions to—quite literally—kiss his ass.

25. James estimates that for every man who is a practicing witch, one is likely to find twenty women.

26. James explains the particular appeal of witchcraft to women by considering the gender's inherent moral weakness, as signified both by their physical inferiority, as well as by the example of Eve, who was tempted by the serpent in the garden in Genesis 2, bringing Adam down with her. The assumption of women's innate sinfulness might at first appear surprising to a contemporary reader more familiar with the Victorian conception of womanhood as the guardian of the home and the center of moral worth for both men and family. However, that conception of gendered morality is of relatively recent vintage. As late as the eighteenth century women in the English world were held to be morally weaker, naturally wanton, and in need of spiritual and moral guidance from men. As

such, in both the sixteenth and seventeenth centuries, women were assumed to be at greater risk for temptation into sin, and therefore more likely to be enticed into witchcraft by the Devil.

27. The use of images for inflicting harm remotely appears in North American accounts of witchcraft as well, specifically the "poppets" referenced in trial testimony during the Salem panic.

28. The phrase "God's ape" refers to Satan's imitation and perversion of Christian and godly practice.

29. James cites John 9:1–12, in which Christ comes upon a man who was born blind and cures him by anointing the man's eyes with a poultice made of mud and Christ's spittle. Like other writers on witchcraft and demonology, James must grapple with explaining the magic and miracles that take place in the Bible as something other than the witchcraft that he is railing against.

30. Note the dismissive tone that James uses to discuss the mischief wrought by witches. It is both intensely gendered—women's trifles, such as making or breaking love ties, or engaging with questions of everyday health—and also not far from the way that witchcraft was represented in the English legal system at that time.

31. James argues that the Devil knows more about medicine than humans do and is able to see which humor dominates the body of a given individual, and thereby is able to tweak that individual to make him ill. Satan holds the blame for sickness in James's conception of the natural world.

32. "Roasting of the pictures" in this case means burning or destroying wax figurines to bring harm on living people. The alchemical worldview that predominated at this time rested on a complex pattern of correspondences between systems both large and small. Like was thought to affect like, and the structure of the universe was thought to be mirrored by the structure of the human body, which could itself be mirrored by external objects.

33. Greek and Roman physicians believed that health derived from the proper balance of four bodily fluids: blood, black bile, yellow bile, and phlegm. Humorism informed the science of medicine until well into the nineteenth century.

34. Ephesians 2:2, "Wherein in time past ye walked according to the course of this world, according to the prince of the power of the air, the spirit that now worketh in the children of disobedience." James is explaining that the Devil's ability to move into different forms, changing shape and entering into people's bodies, derives from this scriptural description of the Devil's constitution.

35. James addresses the question of why God would permit witches to exist, and concludes that they exist for three reasons. First, to punish the wicked for their sins (presumably of greed and pride);

second, to stimulate believers who have become weak in their faith to renew their efforts; and third, because he has the will to punish even the good if he so chooses, as he did with Job. In James's conception, witches have very clear theological purposes.

36. No one, according to James, can assume that he will be free of the Devil's torments, since God has preordained all suffering that every individual will undergo in his life.

37. Archaic word meaning "rumbling." See OED, 2011.

38. James shares Gifford's condemnation of the folk cures offered by cunning folk, not because he doesn't believe they work, but because to appeal to them would be "unlawful." This position can be attributed to the need James has of consolidating his power. He doesn't wish to grant any layperson special authority or dispensation when it comes to God.

39. Mark 3:22–23, "And the scribes which came down from Jerusalem said, He hath Beelzebub, and by the prince of the devils casteth he out devils. And he called them unto him, and said unto them in parables, How can Satan cast out Satan?"

WILLIAM PERKINS, *A DISCOURSE OF THE DAMNED ART OF WITCHCRAFT*, 1608

1. Brian P. Levack, ed., *The Witchcraft Sourcebook* (New York: Routledge, 2004), 94.

2. Professor Benjamin Ray, University of Virginia, electronic communication, May 14, 2011.

3. Malcolm Gaskill, "Witchcraft and Evidence in Early Modern England," *Past and Present* 198:1 (2008): 40.

4. Excerpted from William Perkins, *A discourse of the damned art of witchcraft so farre forth as it is reuealed in the Scriptures, and manifest by true experience.* Originally published in Cambridge. Printed by Cantrel Legge, 1608. Images of the original document held at the Huntington Library may be viewed on Early English Books Online, http://gateway.proquest.com/openurl?ctx_ver=Z39.88-2003&res _id=xri:eebo&rft_id=xri:eebo:image:14917. The physical document is located at Huntington Library, San Marino, California, call number 62889.

5. Perkins also condemns the use of cunning folk to guard against witchcraft. The continual reference to the problem of cunning folk in demonological writing from this time period suggests either that the practice was widespread or that early modern theologians at least feared that it was.

6. Perkins is calling out Reginald Scot in this instance. Like James, he regards disbelief in witchcraft as an ignorant and irreligious

position, and worries that learned men such as Scot are publishing tracts that pose a substantial spiritual hazard.

7. Notice also that Perkins, like James, assumes witches to have female gender.

8. Witchcraft is an "art," which is to say a practice governed by certain rules that can be mastered by study and practice. In defining witchcraft in affirmative terms, rather than negative terms (i.e., witchcraft as that which is not doctrinaire), Perkins grants witches a higher degree of agency than we saw in James. James represents witches as tools or dupes of Satan, who has appealed to their base desires. Perkins, on the other hand, recognizes that witchcraft is a system of mastery. Perkins's witches are skilled. They are not dupes. Also worth noting is Perkins's allusion to "certaine superstitious grounds and principles." Perkins is naming and clarifying the heretofore uneasy relationship between Christianity and folk practice. Witchcraft in a sense represents cultural knowledge and beliefs that are at odds with the church, be it purified or not.

9. Perkins locates the original author of magic as Satan himself.

10. Ephesians 6:12, "For we wrestle not against flesh and blood, but against principalities, against powers, against the rulers of the darkness of this world, against spiritual wickedness in high places."

11. 2 Corinthians 4:4, "In whom the god of this world hath blinded the minds of them which believe not, lest the light of the glorious gospel of Christ, who is the image of God, should shine unto them."

12. Perkins's witches take on a more powerful and frightening cast than in accounts by earlier writers. Witchcraft, he suggests, is the supreme law of the Devil's dominion, and witches have been specially trained in that law. Witches, in Perkins's conception, begin to appear as handmaidens of the Devil, skilled, trained, and powerful. Gone are the pitiful, weak creatures that Gifford suggests are dupes, and that Scot suggests are merely deluded.

13. 1 Samuel 15:23, "For rebellion is as the sin of witchcraft, and stubbornness is as iniquity and idolatry. Because thou hast rejected the word of the LORD, he hath also rejected thee from being king."

14. Perkins is a Puritan, and so his disdain for the sin of discontentment should come as no surprise. In his emphasis on such an easy risk we can see the influence that his thought would have on North American witch trials, a high proportion of which took place within Puritan communities. Eve's disobedience was a large part of her sin, but so was her thirst for knowledge; in effect, Perkins is critical of Eve's grasp for authority.

15. Perkins's choice of "scholar" as the designation of a person drawn to the study of witchcraft out of a desire to better him or herself, or out of hunger for material wealth, or desire for renown and respect,

is a telling one. He builds a picture of a witch as capable, in possession of both will and skill, in stark contrast to the representations of deluded victim witches found in Gifford, James, and Scot.

16. Perkins takes it as given that his reader will know the stories of popes as sorcerers that he is referencing here, though as a Puritan writer, he would associate much Catholic ritual and popery with diabolism and nondoctrinaire thinking. But to speak to one of his examples, Sylvester II, the first French pope, who reigned from 999 to 1003 CE, often appears in medieval illustrations in conversation with the Devil. Legend holds that Sylvester traveled at one time to Spain, where he studied magic and sorcery. This legend grew increasingly elaborate over time, finally suggesting that he had used magical technique to advance to the papacy. Perkins and other Puritan thinkers would have taken Sylvester for a perfect example of the moral depravity that had infected the Catholic Church, and as justification for its necessary purification. See Oscar G. Darlington, "Gerbert, the Teacher," *The American Historical Review*, 52 (1947): 462, note 28.

17. In effect, Perkins is arguing that his readers should be content with their lots in life. Overarching ambition and thirst for knowledge might drive one to know more than God sees fit to share with mankind, which can only be achieved by striking a diabolical bargain. Perkins's relationship with knowledge and expertise is shaky; on the one hand, he has admitted from the beginning that his argument will be built on other arguments and experiences of knowledgeable men, and yet he seems to suggest that curiosity, if left ungoverned, is a path to witchcraft.

JOAN WRIGHT, CHESAPEAKE REGION, VIRGINIA, 1626

1. Jon Butler, Grant Wacker, and Randall Daimler, *Religion in American Life: A Short History* (Oxford: Oxford University Press, 2011), 67.

2. Excerpted from John Bennett Boddie, *Colonial Surry* (Richmond, Virginia: Clearfield, 1948), 76–78. Asterisks appear in Boddie and signify gaps in the transcribed historical sources. Colonial records from the Southern colonies are not as complete as the records found in New England. In many cases early Southern colonial accounts persist only in the form of transcriptions made by historical societies in the nineteenth and twentieth centuries from primary source documents that have since been lost.

3. The joint stock company chartered by James I for the settlement of North America, which led to the founding of the Jamestown settlement.

4. Probably near modern-day Hampton, Virginia, on the coast south of Williamsburg.

5. Giles Allington wanted Joan Wright to help his wife while she was in labor.

6. By a sign or symbol that Goody Wright could read on Rebecca's forehead. "Goody" was a common diminutive form of "Good-wife," as later "Mrs." becomes short for "Missus" or "Mistress."

7. The gossip around Goody Wright touches upon many themes that have already emerged in the English witch cases preceding it. First is the uncertain reputation of Goody Wright, and specifically her potentially useful, yet potentially suspect, status as a cunning woman. She is skilled enough to be summoned to a laboring woman, but her left-handedness, which might be a literal or a figurative impugning of her character, causes another woman to be a better choice as a midwife. Further, her reading of impending death of a spouse in a young woman's face suggests that even if Goody Wright were referring to the girl's expression—perhaps Rebecca looked worried when speaking of her husband's health, and Goody Wright could tell she was worried—something about Goody Wright's character, or Rebecca's mentality, suggested that Goody Wright had unnatural knowledge of the future. Finally, the undercurrent of sexual licentiousness that emerges in theological accounts of witches appears in the odd threat that Goody Wright made against the servant, that if she stole wood again, she would make her dance stark naked.

8. Goodwife Wright can't win in this instance. On the one hand she is being consulted about Alice Beylie's husband, and whether he or Alice will die first. Such a question suggests that Goody Wright might be a source of authority the way a cunning woman would be. And yet despite this authority, Goody Wright has gotten in trouble for offering such an opinion, and so she declines to do so. It's impossible to say what Alice's motivations are for relaying this exchange—is she angry that Goody Wright knows who will die first but won't say? Even declining to answer leaves Goody Wright open to suspicion, and it is partly her implied authority that renders her suspect.

JANE JAMES, MARBLEHEAD, MASSACHUSETTS, 1646

1. John Putnam Demos, *Entertaining Satan: Witchcraft and the Culture of Early New England* (Oxford: Oxford University Press, 1982), 249.

2. Transcribed from *Records of the Quarterly Courts of Essex County*, Massachusetts State Archives, document 1-56-1.

MARGARET JONES, CHARLESTOWN, MASSACHUSETTS, 1648

1. David Hall, *Witch-hunting in Seventeenth-Century New England* (Boston: Northeastern University Press, 1991), 21.
2. Owen Davies, *Popular Magic: Cunning-folk in English History* (New York: Bloomsbury, 2007), 29–30.
3. Transcribed from *John Winthrop's Journal, History of New England, Volume 2, 1630–1649*, Winthrop Papers bound manuscripts, Massachusetts Historical Society. Microfilm reel 35, document 5.
4. Demos, *Entertaining Satan*, 402.
5. Margaret Jones is another possible example of cunning folk in the North American history of witchcraft. It is difficult not to read Winthrop's account of her crimes as a problem of effectiveness rather than substance. If Jones were thought to have a beneficial touch rather than a malignant one, would her reputation have suffered? Gifford and Perkins would have said she should be made to suffer either way. Is she a witch or a failed cunning woman?
6. For either "licorice" (sometimes spelled "liquorice") or "liquors," though precise determination is difficult to make.
7. Margaret Jones makes a mistake that will appear often in North American witchcraft trials, in that she makes a remark that could be construed in a neutral way—that is, that her patient shouldn't rely on anyone else because her medicine or care is the best—but which is later construed as a threat or prediction. The error lies in Margaret's claim to authority and seeming dismissal of the services that might be offered by her rivals. Margaret's accusers seem to share Perkins's uneasy relationship with authoritative speech and the appearance or claim of skill, particularly when coming from someone who, like Margaret Jones, does not occupy a position of power and respect within her community.
8. Margaret Jones knows secrets. Margaret Jones, in effect, knows too much. Her knowledge is unnatural, and Perkins would point to her knowledge as a sign of her seeking power and authority that God does not want her to have.
9. Margaret Jones is found to have a mysterious "teat" in her "secret parts," which more than one historian has suggested was likely the clitoris. See Elizabeth Reis, "The Devil, the Body, and the Feminine Soul in Puritan New England," *The Journal of American History* 82:1 (June 1995): 15–36.

10. To "use means" is another way of saying that she used technique, or witchcraft, that is, that Margaret Jones exercised some specific skill in the task of curing the unnamed woman in Winthrop's account.

11. Images of Hale's original text may be viewed via the University of Virginia's online Salem Witch Trials Documentary Archive and Transcription Project. http://salem.lib.virginia.edu/archives/ModestEnquiry/images.01/source/17.html.

12. Hall, *Witch-hunting in Seventeenth-Century New England*, 21.

13. Hale is suggesting that Margaret Jones was found out as a witch through the intervention of folk magic, namely, the idea that a bewitched object, if burned, would either punish or summon the witch responsible, because of the correspondence established between the witch's body and the bewitched object. In addition to having a personality that would make her an attractive prospect as a witch—her "rayling," which carried on right until her death, according to Winthrop—Jones also might have been an economically marginal figure, as evidenced by Hale's account of her past as a thief. Her gender, comportment, and economic status set Margaret Jones up as a fairly archetypal example, but even with witchcraft serving as a proxy for those other pressing issues, the presence of cunning-folk-informed magical practice remains paramount. Margaret Jones was undone by a charm.

RALPH AND MARY HALL, SETAUKET, NEW YORK, 1665

1. While Setauket is on Long Island and today belongs to New York, when Ralph and Mary Hall were tried the settlement was part of Connecticut. See Demos, *Entertaining Satan*, 409.

2. Judith Richardson, *Possessions: The History and Uses of Haunting in the Hudson Valley* (Cambridge: Harvard University Press, 2003), 18–19.

3. Transcription from unbound manuscript, handwritten by Judge Gabriel Furman, Witchcraft Collection, unbound manuscripts, #4620. Division of Rare and Manuscript Collections, Cornell University Library.

4. East Setauket, on the northern shore of Long Island.

5. This account echoes the language used by William Perkins, who characterizes witchcraft as an art. The tricky distinction with felony witchcraft is that it is both a crime of method and a crime of outcome. In this instance, Ralph and Mary Hall are accused of causing the death of their neighbor George Wood. But they are not accused of murder—they are accused of using "wicked and detestable arts" to bring about his death.

6. "Live voice," that is, in person.

7. Ralph and Mary Hall are fairly typical of North American accused witches if we consider the nature of their crimes, which specifically involve the harming of children and the negative impact on the health of a neighbor. Ralph Hall is the earliest example of a male witch that I have been able to find in colonial North America. Ralph's gender makes him somewhat special, as women vastly outweighed men both in the abstracted conception of who likely witches were, and in the actual historical record. Ralph Hall, however, was typical of male accused witches in that he was associated with—married to—a woman who was also accused. Notably, while the court agrees that Mary's actions are worthy of suspicion, they find that evidence against Ralph is insufficient for charging him. Instead, he is instructed to guarantee the appearance of his wife.

8. *Magnalia Christi Americana: the Ecclesiastical History of New England*, published by Cotton Mather in London in 1702. This text represented Mather's attempt to distance himself from some of what had happened at Salem and addresses the central theological problem of that trial, namely whether the Devil could assume the shape of an innocent person. Initially Mather had supposed that the Devil could assume the shape of anyone, innocent or guilty, in contrast to the belief of his father, Increase Mather. However, as the tide of public opinion about Salem turned in the decade immediately following the trial, Cotton Mather backed away from his earlier assertions.

9. The OED edition of 1916 defines "venefick" as "Practicing, or dealing in, poisoning; acting by poison; having poisonous effects," though the usage is rare enough that this passage quoted from the *Magnalia* is one of only three quoted examples. The OED holds the noun form of the word to be "One who practices poisoning as a secret art; a sorcerer or sorceress; a wizard or witch."

EUNICE COLE, HAMPTON, MASSACHUSETTS, LATER NEW HAMPSHIRE, 1647–1680

1. Demos, *Entertaining Satan,* 171.

2. Transcribed from *Records of the Quarterly Courts of Essex County,* Massachusetts State Archives, Document 1-93-1.

3. Transcribed from *Massachusetts Archives Collection,* Massachusetts State Archives, Document 135: 2, 2.

4. True copy by me.

5. A transcription of these documents has previously been published by David Hall, though a few words were left out. Hall does not

identify Thomas Mouton's wife's first name—Sobriety—though it is added in superscript in the original document. See Hall, *Witch-hunting in Seventeenth-Century New England*, 215.

6. At this point in Eunice Cole's career she has an established reputation as someone who is difficult to deal with. She also, as evidenced by her presentment for biting a constable, will express her anger in a physical way. But the Boultons are starting to suspect that Eunice's attitude might be only part of the problem. At this juncture they stop short of suggesting that she was able to overhear their discussion using magical means, though the implication is there.

7. Transcribed from *Massachusetts Archives Collection*, Massachusetts State Archives, Document 135: 3, 3.

8. David Hall attributes this testimony to Edward Rawson, but the original text suggests otherwise.

9. A witch's teat could show up anywhere, as in this case, under the left breast of an aging woman. Goody Cole could have been suffering from skin tags. Less important than identifying the skin eruptions from a modern medical standpoint is the fact that the search for the witch's teat on a suspected person creates the ideal set of circumstances for confirmation bias, in which evidence will only be gathered that reinforces a previously held position. If Eunice Cole was suspicious enough to warrant being searched for a witch's teat, then they were bound to find one—wherever and whatever it was.

10. The OED has the verb form of "flea" meaning "to remove fleas," with the earliest appearance being 1610. OED, 1896 edition.

11. Witches were typically suspected of interfering with such small-scale, yet personally devastating, situations as sick children and dead livestock. A confrontation about cows, and the question of their health and care, is what leads Abraham Drake to regard Eunice Cole's prediction about his cattle falling sick as a threat, which was then carried out by invisible means.

12. Eunice Cole was apparently convicted after this 1656 trial, and historian Carol Karlsen writes that she spent the better part of the next twelve to fifteen years in the Boston jail. See Carol F. Karlsen, *The Devil in the Shape of a Woman: Witchcraft in Colonial New England* (New York: Norton, 1987, 1998), 53.

13. Transcribed from Samuel Drake collection, *Trials for witchcraft in New-England: original manuscript records, including affadavits in the cases against Eunice Coles, 1656; John Godfrey, 1659, etc,* Houghton Library Special Collection, Harvard University, MS Am 1328.1-1.

14. Lost?

15. Eunice Cole appears in this account not just as an impoverished woman but as a grasping one who irritates her community with her need.

16. Transcribed from *Massachusetts Archives Collection*, Massachusetts State Archives, Document 135, 4.

17. Plums.

18. "Would you like some candy, little girl?" That line is enough of a trope in contemporary American culture that it shows up everywhere from ironic Internet come-ons to Faith No More song lyrics. In this instance, Eunice Cole—marginalized, widowed, and already tried once as a witch in 1656 and imprisoned, with her property seized by the colony, living in destitution—is charged with trying to tempt the child Ann Smith into living with her. She offers her plums—a sweet enticement in the days of seasonal fruit—and failing that, she tries to physically drag Ann Smith back home with her.

19. Transcribed from *Massachusetts Archives Collection*, Massachusetts State Archives, document 135, 5.

20. A pearmain is either a variety of pear or an heirloom variety of apple that grows shaped like a pear. OED, September 2005. Another deposition identifies the tree as a persimmon.

21. The spectacle of Eunice Cole's begging Ann Smith to come live with her, and then reacting with violence when turned down, is both horrifying and moving. John Demos, in conducting a thorough reconstruction of the respective circumstances and webs of relationship between Eunice Cole and Ann Smith, proposes that Eunice, having spent her entire life childless in a culture that valued women principally in their roles as mothers, and Ann, a foster child on her third family in nine years, who would have responded skittishly to any overture of this kind, were drawn together not at random. At no point does Demos read any more into Eunice's offer to "give [Ann] a baby," though the offer and the physicality of the violent engagement under the pearmain tree contain elements of sexual violence that are difficult to overlook. For more detail on Eunice and Ann and their relative positions in the Hampton community, see Demos, *Entertaining Satan*, 327–30.

22. Transcribed from *Massachusetts Archives Collection*, Massachusetts State Archives, Document 135, 6.

23. Hall transcribes this as "very."

24. Transcribed from *Massachusetts Archives Collection*, Massachusetts State Archives, Document 135, 9.

25. What became of Eunice Cole? Historians differ on whether she was ultimately convicted of witchcraft, with John Demos arguing that her lack of execution suggests that the community did not have enough evidence to convict her, while Carol Karlsen argues Eunice's lengthy and indeterminate jail sentence in Boston would only be for a serious crime on par with witchcraft. Karlsen suggests that the magistrates might have been hesitant to execute Eunice

Cole following the execution of Ann Hibbens in 1656. See Karlsen, *Devil in the Shape of a Woman*, 291, note 21. What is certain is that Eunice Cole lived out her days in the town of Hampton, a destitute and frightening creature on the outskirts of the community. Karlsen even points to Samuel Drake, *A Book of New England Legends and Folklore in Prose and Poetry* (Boston, 1901), 328–31, which holds that Eunice Cole was supplied with a hut along the river where she was feared until her death, and that when she died her body was dragged into a shallow grave and buried with a stake driven through it. Eunice Cole in that unverifiable folk tale begins to occupy a hazy middle ground between the historical witch and the mythical. The real woman behind the court records—poor, childless, widowed, publicly whipped, imprisoned, and who bashed a child's head with a rock—recedes behind the stories that were spun about her both in life and after her death.

MARY PHILIPS, CAMBRIDGE, MASSACHUSETTS, 1659

1. Transcribed from the unpublished notebook of George Lyman Kittredge, "*Witchcraft and Sorcery Curios, before 1927,*" Houghton Library Special Collections, Harvard University, MS Am 2585.
2. There is no Dinton in Massachusetts. There is a Clinton, though it is about forty miles away. There is a Dinton in Britain, so it's unclear if this apocryphal story was meant to take place in a town that has since been renamed or no longer exists, or if Kittredge noted the name down incorrectly.
3. "Galled" in this instance means "sore from chafing," that is, sore from having been spurred in her ribs. OED, 1898.

JOHN GODFREY, HAVERHILL, MASSACHUSETTS, 1659–1665

1. Demos, *Entertaining Satan*, 38.
2. Demos, *Entertaining Satan*, 42.
3. Transcribed from *Essex County Court Papers, Volume 5,* Massachusetts State Archives, Document 7-1.
4. Transcribed from *Essex County Court Papers, Volume 5,* Massachusetts State Archives, Documents 7-2 and 7-2A.
5. Transcribed from *Essex County Court Papers, Volume 5,* Massachusetts State Archives. Document 8-1.
6. Bumblebee.

7. Transcribed from *Essex County Court Papers, Volume 5,* Massachusetts State Archives, Document 8-2.

8. Charles Brown and his wife claimed that they saw John Godfrey yawn in church (shocking on the face of it), but even worse than that, they observed what they took to be a witch's teat under Godfrey's tongue while his mouth was open. It must have been a wide yawn indeed.

9. Transcribed from *Essex County Court Papers, Volume 5,* Massachusetts State Archives, Document 8-3.

10. William Osgood is complaining of something he remembers John Godfrey doing in 1640, almost twenty years in the past. Such long memories for slights and wrongs are not unusual in New England witch trials. John Demos discusses John Godfrey at length in *Entertaining Satan* and points out that Godfrey seemed to enjoy shocking his neighbors with exclamations such as this one. Godfrey was by all accounts a pretty weird guy. Clearly his unusual, quarrelsome, and provocative manner, to say nothing of his own admissions, contributed to his long-standing reputation as a witch.

11. "Ptesse" is rendered as a contraction in the manuscript. David Hall interprets it to mean "profess," but remarks in a footnote that it might instead be read as "protest." See Hall, *Witch-hunting in Seventeenth-Century New England,* 119.

12. Transcribed from *Essex County Court Papers, Volume 9,* Massachusetts State Archives, Document 82-5.

13. Ipswich.

14. Here John Godfrey is accused of sending his spirit out to visit Jonathan Singletary while he is in prison. Godfrey has sued Singletary for slander, presumably for calling Godfrey a witch. One of the surest ways for Singletary to defend himself was to prove that he had spoken the truth, which is why he enters spectral evidence of this kind against Godfrey.

15. Transcribed from *Essex County Court Papers, Volume 9,* Massachusetts State Archives, Document 83-1.

16. Jonathan Singletary is testifying that John Godfrey has sent his spectral image to blackmail Singletary into paying him in corn to drop the slander charges against him.

17. Probably cider. One wonders if Remington smelled the cider on himself, which would explain why it was so hard for him to stay seated on his horse.

18. Is it a real crow or a diabolical crow? Will it just hurt his body or will it hurt his soul too? The New England Puritans lived in a world of invisible wonders, which, in their belief system, could sometimes be made manifest. Was the crow Godfrey, or Godfrey's imp familiar? What's certain is that John Remington fell from his horse, an injury that was as common as it was serious, and which could easily have killed him.

That he was spared he would have owed to the grace of God. That he nearly wasn't, he would have owed to diabolical influence, especially of a man with a twenty-year-long reputation for witchcraft.

19. Four rods. A "rod" is defined as "A unit of length used esp. for land, fences, walls, etc., varying locally but later standardized at 5½ yards, 16½ feet (approx. 5.03 m)." OED, 2010.

20. Cripple; "to move or walk lamely; to hobble." OED, 1893.

21. Hall notes that this likely means "boastful" or "cocky," but that he can't be sure. See Hall, *Witch-hunting in Seventeenth-Century New England*, 126. More likely it is a phonetic spelling for "cockading," from "cockade," which the OED, 1891, defines as "a ribbon, knot of ribbons, rosette, or the like, worn in the hat as a badge of office or party, or as part of a livery dress." If a boy is "cockading," he's dressed up in livery for riding. In effect, Godfrey is calling Remington vain, in a manner that simultaneously insults his appearance, his horsemanship, and possibly his social class.

22. Slang for "victuals."

23. Yet another example of an accused witch's comportment causes something he says to be construed as having a greater meaning than it does. Godfrey is telling Remington—whose age we do not know, but who still lives at home with his parents—that if he had been thrown from a horse like that as a grown man he would have died. That could be true—children, even teenagers, are more flexible than adults. But Remington's mother, Abigail, upon hearing such a frightening pronouncement, suggests that Godfrey has unnatural knowledge. Godfrey could just have been expressing an opinion about the severity of the fall, and telling Remington he would have to be careful riding as he got older. But Godfrey's reputation clouds that message.

REBECCA AND NATHANIEL GREENSMITH, HARTFORD, CONNECTICUT, 1662

1. Hall, *Witch-hunting in Seventeenth-Century New England*, 151.

2. Transcribed from Increase Mather, *An Essay for the Recording of Illustrious Providences* (Boston, 1684) in George Lincoln Burr, ed., *Narratives of the Witchcraft Cases 1648–1706* (New York: C. Scribner's Sons, 1914), 3–38.

3. Samuel Stone, a minister in Hartford, Connecticut.

4. Hooker was a minister in Farmington, Connecticut.

5. Haynes was another minister in Hartford.

6. Rebecca Greensmith.

7. Puritans did not observe Christmas, believing it to be a pagan festival.

8. The same passage on the swim test appears in Hall, *Witch-hunting in Seventeenth-Century New England,* 151, only with the line about the swim-test victims' escape having been expunged. That Increase Mather mentions the subjects of the swim test making their escape suggests that they might not have been the Greensmiths, though it's hard to confirm.

A TRYAL OF WITCHES, BURY ST. EDMUNDS, ENGLAND, 1662

1. Keith Thomas, *Religion and the Decline of Magic* (New York: Scribner, 1971), 443.
2. Transcribed from *A tryal of witches at the assizes held at Bury St. Edmonds.* Originally published in London. Printed for William Shrewsbery, 1682. Images of the original document held at the Huntington Library may be viewed on Early English Books Online, http://gateway.proquest.com/openurl?ctx_ver=Z39.88-2003& res_id=xri:eebo&rft_id=xri:eebo:image:173121. An alternate site is https://archive.org/details/tryalofwitchesat00cull. The physical document is located at Huntington Library, San Marino, California, call number 148069.
3. The courts of assize were secular criminal courts established on a periodic schedule in the countryside of England and Wales. The assizes were occasions to hear the most serious charges, which were passed on to them by the quarterly courts, which met four times a year.
4. Ninth of Charles the Second, or the ninth year of Charles II's reign, 1657/8.
5. The Bury St. Edmunds trial offers another example of the interconnectedness between witchcraft, gender, and representations of motherhood.
6. Swooning. This trial follows a fairly typical relationship between cause and effect. A disagreement happens between two women around a matter of health and child care. One of the women has a poor reputation. Shortly after the disagreement, the child of one of the women falls ill. Correlation and causation are jumbled in the early modern mind, the one taken to imply the other.
7. This "Doctor Jacob" was most likely a cunning man. He offers a countercharm against the magic thought to be afflicting the swooning boy.
8. The suggestion of this anecdote is that Amy Denny had sent her spirit out in the shape of the toad. Because of the belief in correspondences, Amy's burn would be explained by the burning of the toad.
9. This slippage of opinion/prediction echoes the same kind of misunderstanding seen in John Godfrey's trial. Amy could be suggesting

that the child looks so sick it might die soon—that is, expressing an opinion or concern. But her reputation, combined with the heritage of ill feeling between Amy and her listener, turns the comment into a prediction, and therefore a suggestion of responsibility.

10. The court is asking if she was lame because of her menstrual period.

11. This is an example of the touch test, popularly used in English communities both to treat a bewitched person and to diagnose the witch responsible. A suffering person keeps his or her eyes closed, and then the suspected witch is brought to the afflicted's bedside. The act of bewitching someone was thought to create a correspondence between the bewitcher and the bewitchee, which could be broken by touching.

12. Begging and then going away grumbling or muttering will reappear in North American witch trials. It was bad enough to beg alms from one's neighbors, but to do so with insufficient humility or an excess of anger was much worse. See Karlsen, *Devil in the Shape of a Woman*, 108–10.

13. A young dog or puppy. See OED, 1923.

14. Defined as a historic term for "a medicinal substance; *spec.* a cathartic, a purgative. Also: medicines generally." OED, 2006. A doctor of physick is a medical doctor.

15. This kind of spectral evidence is a common feature of early modern witch trials and will play a large role in the Salem panic a century later.

16. Pin vomiting is a phenomenon in early modern witch trials that is hard to explain. Malingering and fraud is the most likely cause. However, a mental illness exists called "pica," which describes the tendency to consume inedible objects, most commonly dirt or pins. See "Section II, Diagnostic Criteria and Codes, Feeding and Eating Disorders: Pica," DSM V.

17. This physical acting-out of the afflicted children would also resonate with the Puritan theologians at the beginning of the Salem panic, when trying to understand the fits that seized the girls in that situation.

KATHERINE HARRISON, WEYERSFIELD, CONNECTICUT, AND WESTCHESTER, NEW YORK, 1669

1. Demos, *Entertaining Satan*, 87.

2. Transcribed from a document in Witchcraft Collection, unbound manuscripts, #4620. Division of Rare and Manuscript Collections, Cornell University Library.

3. Pleurisy, an inflammation of the lungs, or possibly pneumonia.

4. That is, refusing to give her charity.

5. Possibly an archaic use of "loving," which in this context is a figurative reference to the sticky qualities of mud, so "clinging, adhesive." See OED, 2008.

6. Testimonies.

7. Mary Haile has likely testified that she saw Katherine Harrison's head on a dog.

8. It's not clear what William Warren accused Katherine Harrison of, but here she is calling him out for accusing her of something she is supposed to have done seventeen years in the past.

POSSESSION OF ELIZABETH KNAPP, GROTON, MASSACHUSETTS, 1671–1672

1. Demos, *Entertaining Satan*, 102.

2. Transcribed from Samuel Willard, *A briefe account of a strange & unusuall Providence of God befallen to Elizabeth Knap of Groton*, in Samuel A. Green, ed., *Groton in the Witchcraft Times* (Groton, MA, 1883). Full text available via the Hanover Historical Texts Project, http://history.hanover.edu/texts/Willard-Knap.html.

3. Most colonists shared their sleeping arrangements. Even men stopping at an inn for the night would often sleep two or three to a bed.

4. Elizabeth accuses a neighbor of bewitching her in this instance, even going so far as to identify her distinct riding hood. It's rather remarkable that this accusation didn't flower into a witch trial. However, Willard explains why not by saying that Elizabeth and the neighbor prayed together, and Elizabeth admitted that the Devil must have deluded her. One wonders what would have happened if the neighbor had been a quarrelsome or irritating person, rather than a woman of "sincere uprightness before God."

5. Tergiversation is defined as "the action of turning one's back on, i.e. forsaking, something in which one was previously engaged, interested, or concerned; apostasy, renegation." OED, 1911.

6. A servant girl's desires poignantly appear in this account of what the Devil promised Elizabeth if she would sign his covenant: money, clothes that sumptuary laws would have held as being above her station, "ease from labor," and "to show her the whole world."

7. The Devil tempting Elizabeth to drown herself in the well by showing her beautiful images in the water echoes the myth of Narcissus, who was so drawn to his own reflection in a pool of water that he couldn't tear himself away and so he died.

8. By "a solemn day," Willard probably means that a company of people prayed with Elizabeth for her recovery.

9. The Devil.

10. Conversation or negotiation.

11. Elizabeth's actions with the stick are curious. They certainly allude to the common folk belief at the time (scientifically explained by King James I, in fact) that witches were able, with the Devil's help, to fly up a chimney while riding on the back of a stick. But Willard's description, and even the imagery of the folk practice, is decidedly sexual.

12. Again an attempt to identify the witch responsible is undertaken, including a variation on the touch test, whereby the afflicted girl is asked to identify her tormentor by touch alone. Elizabeth makes a mistake in her identification, however, and so her potential witch is spared suspicion.

13. The onlookers have decided that Elizabeth is truly possessed by Satan and not by a lesser demon.

14. Puritan belief held that Satan was most certainly real, but was made and permitted to exist by God. Therefore, no matter how great his power seemed, it was less than the power of God. One of Elizabeth's onlookers is reminding Satan that God is more powerful than he is.

15. The first question about Elizabeth Knapp, considered here, is whether she was faking her symptoms for attention. Minister Samuel Willard, her closest chronicler, judges her feats of strength to be beyond what she would be capable of if she were not truly afflicted by possession.

16. Assuming she isn't faking, Willard posits, is the cause of her behavior organic or diabolical? Is Elizabeth suffering from a physical illness or a spiritual one? He inclines to believe the latter.

17. Willard notes that she didn't seem ill, as her body isn't wasting, and in fact seems to be "gathering flesh." Of course, if she had been employed as a servant and was now being put to bed, fed well, and relieved of hard chores, her health and weight might improve. Important to note, however, is Willard's reasoned evaluation of Knapp's situation. He is operating within an intellectual and spiritual system that holds demonic possession to be a legitimate explanation for Knapp's suffering.

18. Ultimately, Willard despairs of being able to know for sure whether Elizabeth has signed her soul away to the Devil. Instead, he offers her as an example of God's might, in the hope that apprehension of the spectacle of her suffering might inspire greater fervor of belief in his audience.

REBECCA FOWLER, CALVERT COUNTY, MARYLAND, 1685

1. Debra Meyers, *Common Whores, Vertuous Women, and Loveing Wives: Free Will Christian Women in Colonial Maryland* (Bloomington: Indiana University Press, 2003), 35.

2. Excerpted from Raphael Semmes, *Crime and Punishment in Early Maryland* (Baltimore: Johns Hopkins Press, 1938), 168.

3. Mount Calvert Hundred refers to the original tract of land surveyed in 1657, and which served as the original county seat of Prince George's County, Charles Town, beginning in 1683. Rebecca Fowler lived on this manor during her witch trial, though occasional sources call her Elizabeth. See Earl Arnett et al., *Maryland: A New Guide to the Old Line State* (Baltimore: Johns Hopkins Press, 1999), 108.

GOODWIFE GLOVER, BOSTON, MASSACHUSETTS, 1688

1. Demos, *Entertaining Satan*, 71.

2. Excerpted from Cotton Mather, *Memorable Providences, Relating to Witchcrafts and Possessions*. Originally published in Boston in 1689. Images of the original document held at the Harvard University Library may be viewed on Early English Books Online, http://gateway. proquest.com/openurl?ctx_ver=Z39.88-2003&res_id=xri:eebo&rft _id=xri:eebo:image:49306. An alternate site is https://archive.org/ details/narrativesofwitooburriala.

3. Accusations of witchcraft often cropped up across the generations. Goody Glover the laundress had a mother who had been spoken of as a witch in their community, even by her own husband.

4. Catalepsy is defined as "a disease characterized by a seizure or trance, lasting for hours or days, with suspension of sensation and consciousness." OED, 1889.

5. Astonishment in this usage is defined as "loss of physical sensation, insensibility; paralysis, numbness, deadness." OED, 1885.

6. Goody Glover was Irish, and English would not have been her first language. Also, she would have been Catholic in a predominantly Protestant community that regarded Catholicism as diabolical and perverse. That she could not recite the Lord's Prayer in English might then not have been much of a surprise. But then again, neither would the reactions of her Puritan examiners.

7. The court endeavors to make sure that Goody Glover isn't insane.

8. Upon examination they determine that Goody Glover does know the Lord's Prayer—she has just memorized it in Latin.

9. Goody Glover apparently doesn't deny the accusations of witchcraft levied against her. And yet she had to have men present at the trial to translate the Irish for her. Her questioner admits that he doesn't understand what she's saying, and his lack of comprehension is perhaps the most important detail. It's not his job to understand her. It's *her* job to be identified as different and to be punished for it.

10. The account of Goody Glover's guilt admits a slippage between the idea of "saints" and "spirits." Puritan theology rejected the intercession of saints, instead encouraging a believer's personal relationship with Christ. Mather is encouraging Glover to repent and, as he sees it, to reject the Devil. But in her understanding, he is urging her to convert from Catholicism to Protestantism, which she says she cannot do without the leave of the saints to whom she prays.

11. Defined as "a mischievous, tricksy imp or sprite; another name for Puck or Robin Goodfellow; hence, a terrifying apparition, a bogy." OED, 1898.

SALEM

1. Robert Calef, *More Wonders of the Invisible World* (London: 1700).
2. Charles Upham, *Salem Witchcraft, with an Account of Salem Village and a History of Opinions on Witchcraft and Kindred Subjects* (Boston: Wiggin and Lunt, 1867).
3. Linnda R. Corporael, "Ergotism: The Satan Loosed in Salem?" *Science* 192, no. 4234 (Apr. 2, 1976): 21–26; Mary K. Matossian, "Views: Ergot and the Salem Witchcraft Affair: An Outbreak of a Type of Food Poisoning Known as Convulsive Ergotism May Have Led to the 1692 Accusations of Witchcraft," *American Scientist* 70, no. 4 (July–August 1982): 355–57.
4. Cotton Mather, *The Wonders of the Invisible World* (Boston: 1693), 13.
5. Benjamin Ray, "They Did Eat Red Bread Like Man's Flesh," www.common-place.org, vol. 9, no. 4 (July 2009); accessed September 1, 2012.

WARRANT FOR THE APPREHENSION OF SARAH GOOD, AND OFFICER'S RETURN, MONDAY, FEBRUARY 29, 1692

1. Transcribed from an image of the original document in the University of Virginia's online Salem Witch Trials Documentary Archive and Transcription Project. http://salem.lib.virginia.edu/archives/ecca/large/ecca1004r.jpg.
2. One interesting side note about Sarah Good is that she was a typical witch in that she was an impoverished woman of middle age. Yet she is also typical of mythological witches, in that her representation in popular culture is often as a hag. Bernard Rosenthal quotes several early historical sources that characterize Sarah Good as a "crone," "an old [woman] of dubious reputation," and so forth,

often in the same breath as they mention that she was condemned along with her four-year-old daughter and with a "sucking child" who died in prison. Sarah Good, like Eunice Cole, is an example of myth colliding with historical fact. See Bernard Rosenthal, *Salem Story*, 87–88.

3. The Salem episode took place before the Julian calendar was replaced by the Gregorian in the English Atlantic world in 1752. The Gregorian system was a Catholic reform, and Protestant nations hesitated to adopt a papal scheme. Under the Julian system the new year began on March 25, which means that dates for the first three months of the year are often denoted as they are here, with a slash.

4. Abbreviation for "masters."

5. Thomas Putnam was a wealthy landowner in Salem Village, father of afflicted girl Ann Putnam Jr. and husband of afflicted woman Ann Putnam Sr. Edward was his brother. Bother and Nissenbaum identify Thomas Putnam as being at the center of the affiliation group of powerful village men who were on the side of Samuel Parris, the beleaguered minister in town. See Paul Boyer and Stephen Nissenbaum, *Salem Possessed: The Social Origins of Witchcraft* (Cambridge: Harvard University Press, 1974).

6. Elizabeth Parris was about nine years old, the daughter of village minister Samuel Parris, and the first girl who was "afflicted." Abigail Williams, rather than being the nubile seventeen-year-old minx of Arthur Miller's fevered imagination, was a kinswoman of Parris's (she is often described as his niece, though such a term had more general use in the seventeenth century), eleven years old, and working as a servant in the Parris household. Elizabeth Hubbard, however, was seventeen and an indentured servant of Dr. William Griggs, the man whom most historians agree was the first to diagnose the girls as being under an evil hand rather than suffering from a physical disease. See Mary Beth Norton, *In the Devil's Snare* (New York: Knopf, 2003), 22.

WARRANT FOR THE APPREHENSION OF SARAH OSBURN AND TITUBA, AND OFFICER'S RETURN, MONDAY, FEBRUARY 29, 1692

1. Transcribed from an image of the original document in the University of Virginia's online Salem Witch Trials Documentary Archive and Transcription Project. http://salem.lib.virginia.edu/archives/ecca.xml.

2. Tituba's ethnicity has been the subject of much debate and analysis, particularly given that since the advent of Arthur Miller she has

morphed from being "an Indian woman," as she was described in the primary sources, to a woman commonly represented as African American in popular culture. Marion Starkey further racializes Tituba by alluding to her (entirely made up) expertise in "voodoo." See Marion Starkey, *The Devil in Massachusetts* (New York: Knopf, 1949), 30. In some respects Tituba's constantly changing physiognomy is a perfect approximation for the use of Salem as a prism through which historians view their own times.

3. Masters.

4. Sarah Osburn was about forty-nine when the witch trials began. Alexander was her second husband, and her marriage had scandalized her community, as he was a young servant whose indenture she had purchased. See Norton, *In the Devil's Snare*, 22.

5. Elizabeth Hubbard.

6. Sarah Good was imprisoned overnight at the constable's house. Watchers reported the following morning that she had disappeared from the room for a time "both bare foot and bare legde," and so was thought to have sent her spirit out in the night to accost the afflicted girls. See Norton, *In the Devil's Snare*, 29.

EXAMINATIONS OF SARAH GOOD, SARAH OSBURN, AND TITUBA, TUESDAY, MARCH 1, 1692

1. Transcribed from an image of the original document in the University of Virginia's online Salem Witch Trials Documentary Archive and Transcription Project. http://salem.lib.virginia.edu/archives/ecca/medium/ecca1011r.jpg.

2. Norton, *In the Devil's Snare*, 27.

3. A common belief about witchcraft involved the use of spirit familiars to do evil works. Accounts vary as to whether the familiars are devilish imps that attend on the witch, or whether the witch is able to transform herself into the form of an animal; examples of both metamorphoses appear in the historical record. In either case, the question of craft and technique remains at the center of early modern assumptions about how witchcraft works.

4. Sarah Good was a beggar. Good would have approached the parsonage hoping to be given something to eat for herself and her child, but in a culture that examined every turn of personal fortune for signs of God's approval or disfavor, begging for sustenance would have been shameful not only from an economic standpoint but from a social one. Good received something for her child and went away with thanks—but her thanks may not have been sincere,

or the Parrises may have found her thanks insufficiently humble for their taste.

5. The afflicted girls are asked to identify if it is Sarah Good who is hurting them, and they identify her not only by sight, but by acting out their torments for the benefit of the onlookers.

6. So far Sarah Good's crime is one of attitude rather than commission. She is pressed to explain her muttering when she goes away from someone's house, but this time instead of claiming she was saying thanks, she dismisses the question by saying she was speaking her commandments, or a psalm. It is tempting to regard this answer as the Puritan equivalent of "it's none of your business."

7. Worshipful.

8. Hathorne.

9. In 1710, William Good would file for restitution for the death of his wife, but in this instance he appears as a witness against her, again with complaints of her attitude toward him. If she isn't a witch yet, he fears she will "be one very quickly."

10. Sarah Osburn posits that the Devil might be doing harm in her shape, but if so it's nothing to do with her.

11. The children are all saying that they know Sarah Osburn and that they recognize her clothes.

12. "A thing like an Indian all black"—this example supports Mary Beth Norton's persuasive thesis that much of the volatility of the social world that coalesced in the Salem panic can be attributed to lingering fears connected to the Indian wars along the Maine frontier. The slippage of language used to describe Indians with that used to describe the Devil, together with the recognition that Puritan New Englanders would have regarded any unconverted people as devilish apostates, suggests a tangling of these concepts in the Salem Village mind. See Norton, *In the Devil's Snare,* 58–59.

13. A signal element of Osburn's suspicion is that she has not been present at church services for over a year. Parris was an unpopular minister, and Bother and Nissenbaum point out that a faction of villagers preferred to travel to Salem Town for meeting rather than stay in the village. In neighboring Marblehead, more villagers skipped church than not. But in the village, skipping out on meeting was sufficient to draw suspicion, particularly from a minister who felt as beleaguered as Samuel Parris.

14. OED, 1901, defines "ken" as an archaic word meaning "to (be able to) distinguish (one person or thing *from* another)."

15. Tituba and the two Sarahs were initially imprisoned in Boston rather than in Salem Town.

16. Original document reads "hure," which could be either "her" or "here," depending on the accent.

17. In the transitional handwriting of this time period distinguishing a "c" from an "r" can be difficult. Most transcriptions agree that Tituba is talking about having seen cats of various colors, rather than rats.

18. Ann Putnam Jr.

19. Lieutenant.

20. To "ride upon sticks" (either branches or brooms) shows up frequently in woodcuts and other descriptions of witches flying in the medieval and early modern period. It is an example of witchly behavior drawn from the English tradition rather than the African, yet another error of attribution in later characterizations of Tituba as practicing Caribbean magic.

21. Tituba says that a wolf was set upon Elizabeth Hubbard, and upon hearing that suggestion, members of the audience agree that yes, sure enough, Elizabeth Hubbard complained yesterday of a wolf. The spectacle feeds upon itself.

22. A man in black clothes, as distinct from "a black man." Norton points out the differences between attribution of whether the blackness refers to raiment, to skin, or possibly to moral character. The black clothes and white hair in this instance could suggest Samuel Parris or any number of powerful Puritan men.

TWO EXAMINATIONS OF TITUBA, AS RECORDED BY JONATHAN CORWIN

1. Transcribed from an image of the original document in the University of Virginia's online Salem Witch Trials Documentary Archive and Transcription Project. http://salem.lib.virginia.edu/archives/ NYPL/LARGE/NYPL03A.jpg.

2. A lentoe is a lean-to, the term for a low-ceilinged add-on room, commonly used to enlarge living space in early North American houses. The lean-to often became the kitchen or storage area. See David Freeman Hawke, *Everyday Life in Early America* (New York: Harper and Row, 1988), 53.

3. Earlier Tituba had only identified two other witches, but now her account has raised the number to four.

4. At this point Tituba suggests that the witch conspiracy extends beyond the bounds of Salem Village, for the other people she does not recognize, coming as they do from Boston. Tituba actually lived in Boston with Samuel Parris before his household moved to the village parsonage, so her reference to that town comes as no surprise.

5. The yellow bird appears frequently in Tituba's account, often offered as a present or as part of a selection of "pretty things." Though the usual interpretation of the yellow bird is as another incarnation of the

devilish spirit familiar, traditions in early and mid-eighteenth-century American portraiture use delicate animal pets, such as hummingbirds and squirrels, to denote refinement in the portrait sitter. It's possible that the "yellow bird" is a goldfinch or canary, and a coveted class signifier, though such an interpretation is difficult to prove.

6. Mr. Griggs's maid is Elizabeth Hubbard, the eldest so far of the afflicted girls.

7. The testimony shifts between first and third person. This passage describes Tituba saying that Sarah Good came to her while Samuel Parris was praying and would not let Tituba hear the prayers.

8. Marion Starkey and her "slave voodoo" assertion would have done well to review this testimony. Though Tituba is being figured as other in the course of this testimony, as someone who belongs to another country, Tituba is confessing here to practicing English witchcraft, which she learned only upon her arrival in New England.

9. The Proctors, John and Elizabeth, lionized in *The Crucible*, whose servant Mary Warren would shortly join the ranks of the afflicted, and who later would be accused themselves.

10. Another shift in point of view as Jonathan Corwin slips into his own voice to describe the behavior of the afflicted girls while Tituba is talking. Tituba is asked who is hurting them, and she accuses Sarah Good, which the children confirm.

11. Transcribed from an image of the original document in the University of Virginia's online Salem Witch Trials Documentary Archive and Transcription Project. http://salem.lib.virginia.edu/archives/NYPL/LARGE/NYPL04A.jpg.

12. The two examinations taken down by Jonathan Corwin occur one day apart. The first will strike a reader as largely similar, with only a few shifts in descriptive detail, to the foregoing account by court reporter Ezekiel Cheever. Many of the examinations were recorded simultaneously by different people, usually Cheever or Samuel Parris himself. The difference between the two examinations transcribed by Corwin will at first appear subtle, but on closer examination the substance of Tituba's confession, and the opening that it creates for a conspiracy, will become clear. Jonathan Corwin's house is still standing, and is operated as a museum in Salem. Called the Witch House, even though no accused witches lived there, Corwin's house is the only extant physical structure in modern-day Salem with a legitimate tie to the witch trials.

13. Tituba's seeming pining for fine things is a poignant detail. One is reminded of Reginald Scot's complaint that too many of the people accused as witches, whom one would expect to have bartered away their souls in exchange for fine things and ease from labor, are instead impoverished people with nothing to show for their supposed diabolical covenant.

14. Already in the span of one night the supposed witch conspiracy has grown from four people (Tituba, the two Sarahs, and the "black man" from Boston), to five, to nine.

15. Tituba concludes her dramatic confession, which involves riding through the night on a stick and making her mark in blood in the Devil's book, by claiming that there are nine witches total, but she knows only a few of them. Some of them live in Boston, but some of them live "here in this town." Recall that Perkins asserts that the identification of a witch by another confessed witch is very strong, nearly conclusive, evidence of guilt. Tituba has confessed, has confirmed the guilt of accused suspects, and has opened up speculation about the other members of the invisible diabolical conspiracy in their midst. The Puritans believed in "worlds of wonder," invisible realms of spirit that cannot be perceived. It would come as no surprise to frustrated and scared Salem Villagers that evil spirits were operating in their midst. The accusations had come about only after careful consideration of all other possibilities, including prayers, fasting, and the consultation of medical professionals. Instead of creating circumstances by which the witch trials might be contained, such as the examination of suspects in private, the community has inadvertently crafted a scenario in which fears will be heightened.

THE SUSPICION OF MARTHA CORY,
MONDAY, MARCH 21, 1692

1. Transcribed from an image of the original document in the University of Virginia's online Salem Witch Trials Documentary Archive and Transcription Project, http://salem.lib.virginia.edu/archives/essex/eia/large/eia01-1.jpg.

2. Martha Cory seems to believe that her church membership, or her being a "Gospel woman," should suffice to prove that she couldn't possibly be a witch.

3. The direct transcription of testimony is occasionally interrupted by marginal comments on the goings-on in the examination room. In this case, the court reporter Ezekiel Cheever has interrupted her by calling her a liar, and Edward Putnam has chimed in as well.

4. Cheever and Putnam break into the proceedings again. From such interruptions we can glean to some extent the uncontrolled and combustible atmosphere that surrounded the examinations.

5. "All this assembly" is a vague assertion, but nevertheless creates a strong impression of a crowd being present for Martha Cory's examination. At the very least John Hathorne, Ezekiel Cheever,

Edward Putnam, Giles Cory, and several others who either sign the document or are named therein are present.

6. Martha Cory's sarcasm! She's saying that if one of the children knew what clothes she was wearing without having seen her, it must be because the child "was wiser than anybody."

7. The collected assembly here also includes the afflicted little girls, who testify to a spirit seen whispering in Martha Cory's ear.

8. Martha Cory urges the magistrates not to give credence to what "distracted children" say.

9. In response to Martha's dismissal of them, the afflicted girls act out even more strongly.

10. "Improve" in this usage means "to disapprove as bad; to disallow; to reprove, rebuke; to blame, censure, condemn." OED, 1899.

11. "Crossly" might be Henry Crosby, husband of Deliverance Cory, Giles Cory's daughter by his first marriage. See Rosenthal, *Records*, 148.

12. Just the number of people referenced by name in this examination adds up to thirteen people. It wouldn't take many more to make a small crowd.

13. Part of the spiritual trap confronted by accused witches during the Salem episode is that lying is a mortal sin. If Cory bows to the pressure being applied to her, she will have endangered her immortal soul. This steadfastness would lead many of the Salem accused who went to their deaths without confessing to be lionized as Christian martyrs by nineteenth-century dramatists. See Rosenthal, *Salem Story*.

14. Hathorne points out that inconstancy of opinions is a "note of distraction," and that the girls' very consistency in accusing her should give weight to their accusations.

15. Martha Cory laughs at the magistrates and ministers, having publicly questioned their authority. In doing so she is upending the social hierarchy in place in her culture. Like Sarah Good, Martha Cory's error here is of attitude. Her unconcealed contempt renders her threatening, and in a symbol-ridden society such as hers, could itself be taken for a sign of diabolical influence.

16. An uncredited member of the assembly has suggested that Martha Cory should do as Tituba has done, that is, confess and then help them discover her confederates.

17. Tituba's confession is explicitly alluded to as a rationale for the spread of accusations to others.

18. John Hathorne is being sneaky in his questioning. He has asked her how long she agreed to serve the Devil. Was it ten years? If she says no, then he can catch her out by saying, "Ah! So if it wasn't ten years, how long was it?" By denying the question she will inevitably be answering the question in the affirmative.

THE ACCUSATION OF REBECCA NURSE, THURSDAY, MARCH 24, 1692

1. Norton, *In the Devil's Snare*, 47.
2. Norton, *In the Devil's Snare*, 61.
3. Transcribed from an image of the original document in the University of Virginia's online Salem Witch Trials Documentary Archive and Transcription Project. http://salem.lib.virginia.edu/archives/ecca/medium/ecca1072r.jpg.
4. An obsolete usage of "amazed," defined by the OED as "driven stupid; stunned or stupefied, as by a blow; out of one's wits." OED, 1884.
5. Demon?
6. Though the accusations against Rebecca Nurse stemmed from children, Ann Putnam Jr. and Abigail Williams, it is the subsequent accusations from girls in their late teens like Elizabeth Hubbard and Mary Walcott that draw the serious attention of the court. See Norton, *In the Devil's Snare*, 63.
7. "Professor" can be understood to mean a professor of the faith. Rebecca Nurse was a covenanted church member in Salem Town, though she attended meetings in Salem Village because it was closer to her home. The Rebecca Nurse homestead in Danvers, Massachusetts, remains extant and is open for tours in the summertime.
8. Hathorne wants to know if Rebecca Nurse could be a witch without knowing it.
9. And.
10. In the aftermath of the Salem panic, apologists would insist that the girls had indeed been bewitched but were mistaken in their attribution of who was responsible.
11. Belie, that is, tell a lie against myself.
12. Shorthand.
13. "Praetermitted" means "passed by, disregarded, overlooked; omitted." OED, 2007. The recorder is remarking that the scene of Rebecca Nurse's examination was so wild and noisy that much of the commentary was impossible to hear, and therefore left out of the court record.

WARRANT FOR THE APPREHENSION OF RACHEL CLINTON, WITH SUMMONS FOR WITNESSES, AND OFFICER'S RETURN, TUESDAY, MARCH 29, 1692

1. Rachel Clinton's earlier witch trials and overall unfortunate life receive thorough treatment in John Putnam Demos's *Entertaining*

Satan. She is notable not only for her dramatic plunge down the class hierarchy but also for her tendency to express her anger in physical confrontation.

2. Transcribed from an image of the original document in the University of Virginia's online Salem Witch Trials Documentary Archive and Transcription Project. http://salem.lib.virginia.edu/archives/Suffolk/small/S001A.jpg.

3. "Unlike the Salem Village arrest warrants, bond ('recognizance') for prosecution is posted here. Such bonds were a normal part of the legal process in Massachusetts Bay, and why bond was not required in the original cases is a matter of speculation. However, it may be that if bond had been required at the outset there would have been fewer complaints and the spread of the episode might not have occurred." See Rosenthal, *Records*, 164.

DEPOSITION OF THOMAS KNOWLTON JR. VERSUS RACHEL CLINTON

1. Transcribed from a document in Witchcraft Collection, unbound manuscripts, #4620, Division of Rare and Manuscript Collections, Cornell University Library.
2. Probably "scolding."
3. Pricked? Pinched? The subsequent use of "pins" suggests "pricked."
4. Probably "Rachel."

BRIDGET BISHOP, TUESDAY, APRIL 19, 1692

1. Norton, *In the Devil's Snare*, 112–13.
2. Transcribed from an image of the original document in the University of Virginia's online Salem Witch Trials Documentary Archive and Transcription Project. http://salem.lib.virginia.edu/archives/ecca/medium/ecca1125r.jpg.
3. Bridget Bishop sustained a conviction years earlier for arguing with her second husband, Thomas Oliver. See Norton, *In the Devil's Snare*, 359, note 2. Norton also notes that previous accounts of the Salem crisis conflate Bridget Bishop of Salem Town with another "Goody Bishop," whose first name was Sarah, and who lived in Salem Village. Reportedly, the two are unconnected.
4. Hathorne is challenging the accused to prove she isn't a witch without her own knowledge.
5. Parris makes careful note of additional commentary interjected into the testimony by bystanders.

THE NOTORIOUS GILES CORY,
TUESDAY, APRIL 19, 1692

1. Norton, *In the Devil's Snare*, 277.
2. Ibid.
3. Robert Calef, *More Wonders of the Invisible World*, quoted in Samuel Drake, ed., *The Witchcraft Delusion in New England, vol. 3* (Roxbury, MA, 1866), 45.
4. Excerpted from Robert Calef, *Salem Witchcraft* (Salem: Cushing and Appleton, 1823), 310–12. The original documents have since been lost, and the spelling was modernized by the 1823 publication.
5. Another tricky question, probably from Hathorne. He's suggesting that Giles Cory signed his soul over to the Devil willingly, without the Devil's even having to tempt him.
6. The recorder has slipped into third person here. Thomas Gold is saying that he heard Giles Cory say that he knew enough against his wife, Martha Cory, "that would do her business." Martha was Giles's third, and much younger, wife, and had already been jailed as a witch.
7. "Hipped," that is, "having the hip injured or dislocated; lamed in the hip; hip-shot." OED, 1898.
8. To kill himself, which Hathorne goes on to point out is a mortal sin, and therefore indicative that Cory was open to such sins.

EXAMINATIONS OF ABIGAIL HOBBS IN PRISON,
WEDNESDAY, APRIL 20, 1692

1. Though George Burroughs was respected, that's not to say he was liked. One of the other previous ministers of Salem Village, Deodat Lawson, who returned when he heard about the outbreak of witchcraft, wrote in his account of the trials, "Glad I should have been if had never known the name of this man [George Burroughs]; or never had this occasion to mention so much as the first letters of his name. But the government requiring some account, of his trial, to be inserted in this book, it becomes me with all obedience, to submit unto the order." Deodat Lawson, *A Brief and True Narrative of Some Remarkable Passages Relating to Sundry Persons Afflicted by Witchcraft* (1692), quoted in Hall, *Witch-hunting in Seventeenth-Century New England*, 291.
2. Transcribed from an image of the original document in the University of Virginia's online Salem Witch Trials Documentary Archive and Transcription Project. http://salem.lib.virginia.edu/archives/ecca/medium/ecca1155r.jpg.
3. In this obsolete usage, when describing an appearance, "sad" means "dignified, grave, serious." OED, 2008.

4. Medieval and early modern Europeans actually followed a rational system in their understanding of how magic worked. Just as the holy trinity in the Bible provided a template by which both the universe and the human body were organized, so too were like objects thought to affect like, and for small parts to stand in for a whole. This regression and expansion of scale appears in astrology, in fortune-telling, in folk medical remedies, and in many other realms of nondoctrinaire thought. For elaboration on poppet image magic, see Richard Kieckhefer, "The Specific Rationality of Medieval Magic," *The American Historical Review*, vol. 99, no. 3 (June 1994), 813–36.

5. This account of the witches' Sabbath, a perversion of the Christian sacrament of communion, appears frequently in witch-hunting manuals of the time, including James I's *Daemonologie*.

6. Though the two examinations of Abigail Hobbs in prison are dated a month apart, they appear on the same document. Further, George Burroughs is not mentioned until the second examination, which takes place after the minister is arrested in Maine on May 4 and transferred back to Salem to stand trial.

7. The inquiry about whether George Burroughs used magic to bewitch the failed eastward military campaigns against the French and the Wabanaki further suggests that the authorities trying the Salem witches saw an explicit connection between the two phenomena. The Devil was trying to lay waste to their godly purpose and he was doing so from multiple different angles.

8. Abigail Hobbs provides a further connection between malefic witchcraft at Salem and the Indian wars in Maine. The Puritans believed that they were living by a divine mandate. Therefore, any opposition to the success of their settlements would have been seen, in their worldview, as a challenge to God's will, and therefore a mark of diabolical influence. One possible reason for the public performance of the examinations, which so likely led to the growth and expansion of the trials rather than their swift containment, was for the religious edification of the community. Satan was subject to God's will, and a common interpretation for why God permitted the Devil to interfere with the lives of people and to recruit them as witches was as a challenge to spur them on to greater faith.

SUSANNAH MARTIN AND HER POOR REPUTATION, MONDAY, MAY 2, 1692

1. Norton, *In the Devil's Snare*, 146.

2. 1 Samuel 28:7–8, "Then said Saul unto his servants, Seek me a woman that hath a familiar spirit, that I may go to her, and enquire

of her. And his servants said to him, Behold, there is a woman that hath a familiar spirit at Endor. And Saul disguised himself, and put on other raiment, and he went, and two men with him, and they came to the woman by night: and he said, I pray thee, divine unto me by the familiar spirit, and bring me him up, whom I shall name unto thee."

3. Transcribed from an image of the original document in the University of Virginia's online Salem Witch Trials Documentary Archive and Transcription Project. http://salem.lib.virginia.edu/archives/ecca/medium/ecca1174r.jpg.

4. By this is meant, did Susannah Martin not give the Devil permission to go about in her shape.

5. Martin is attempting to turn the tables on her accusers, suggesting that if they are bewitched, then it could be because the Devil is their master.

6. Martin references 1 Samuel 28:14–20, in which the witch of Endor raises a spirit for Saul that seems to be Samuel. In quoting this passage, Martin is appealing to the chief theological controversy of the Salem episode, namely, whether or not the Devil could assume the shape of an innocent person. If he could, then spectral evidence should not be admitted against accused witches.

7. It's easy to wonder after the fact why more accused witches at Salem hadn't confessed, since none of the confessing witches were put to death. However, such an outcome was unusual. By giving a false confession, Martin would both damn her immortal soul, and if the experience of previous witch trials was any example, could expect to be put to death as well.

8. Lying, Martin is saying, will not make her guilty of witchcraft.

9. Mercy Lewis is one of the afflicted teenage girls, a servant of the Putnams and a refugee from Maine. She is sassing Susannah Martin, suggesting that she took her time getting to court, but she flies on sticks and torments her in the night.

10. Probably an attempt at the touch test. The idea behind the touch test was that if a suspected witch touched the afflicted, then the afflicted person would be relieved of the bewitchment. It was used both as a means of relief for the afflicted and as a diagnostic tool. Occasionally the touch test was administered blind, with the afflicted having to guess the guilty party among several different suspects. Use of the touch test was controversial, however, as Cotton Mather suggested that it was a method liable to be "abused by the Devil's legerdemains." For that reason it is not often used in New England witch trials. That could be why, when none of the afflicted were able to approach Susannah Martin in the courtroom, she suggests that the Devil "bears [her] more malice than another."

See Richard Latner, "'Here Are No Newters': Witchcraft and Religious Discord in Salem Village and Andover," *The New England Quarterly*, vol. 79, no. 1 (March 2006): 109–10.

STATEMENT OF ELIZABETH HUBBARD VERSUS GEORGE BURROUGHS, MONDAY, MAY 9, 1692

1. Transcribed from an image of the original document in the University of Virginia's online Salem Witch Trials Documentary Archive and Transcription Project. http://salem.lib.virginia.edu/archives/ecca/medium/ecca2030r.jpg.

ESTABLISHING THE COURT OF OYER AND TERMINER FOR SUFFOLK, ESSEX, AND MIDDLESEX COUNTIES, FRIDAY, MAY 27, 1692

1. In 1688 the Catholic English King James II was overthrown by the Protestant William of Orange to secure the succession rights of his wife, Mary, over James II's Catholic son; this permanently ended the possibility of a return to Catholicism in England.
2. Excerpted from *Governor's Council Executive Records (1692)*, vol. 2, pp. 176–77, Massachusetts State Archives.

MARTHA CARRIER, QUEEN OF HELL

1. Transcribed from an image of the original document in the University of Virginia's online Salem Witch Trials Documentary Archive and Transcription Project. http://salem.lib.virginia.edu/archives/ecca/medium/ecca1311r.jpg.
2. Here is a slippage of what is meant by "black." The afflicted girls who claim to see a "black man" whispering in Carrier's ear could be referring to his moral self or to his literal skin color. But Carrier turns the inquiry on the tribunal, referencing the clothing of her interrogators. A similar slippage occurs in Tituba's account of the "black man," when she specifies that the man who visited her wore black clothes and had silver hair.
3. Carrier suggests that the afflicted girls are faking their symptoms, and that they will worsen if she looks at them.

4. It's unclear if Carrier thinks that the afflicted are playacting, or if she thinks they are legitimately ill, but the implication that she thinks they are faking is strong.

STATEMENT OF SARAH INGERSOLL AND ANN ANDREWS REGARDING SARAH CHURCHILL, JUNE 1, 1692

1. Transcribed from an image of the original document in the University of Virginia's online Salem Witch Trials Documentary Archive and Transcription Project. http://salem.lib.virginia.edu/archives/ecca/medium/ecca2113r.jpg.

AFTER SALEM

1. Frances Hill, *Hunting for Witches* (Beverly, MA: Commonwealth Editions, 2002), 65.
2. John Demos, *The Enemy Within: 2000 Years of Witch-Hunting in the Western World* (New York: Viking, 2008), 59–61.

THE APOLOGY OF SAMUEL SEWALL, JANUARY 14, 1697

1. Norton, *In the Devil's Snare,* 198.
2. A full account of Sewall's apology and evolving political positions on such prescient issues as slavery and the equality of the sexes can be found in Richard Francis, *Judge Sewall's Apology: The Salem Witch Trials and the Forming of an American Conscience* (New York: Harper, 2005).
3. Transcribed from the University of Virginia's online Salem Witch Trials Documentary Archive and Transcription Project. http://salem.lib.virginia.edu/diaries/sewall_diary.html.

THE APOLOGY OF THE SALEM JURY, 1697

1. Excerpted from George Lincoln Burr, *Narratives of the Witchcraft Cases, 1648–1706* (New York: Charles Scribner's Sons, 1914), 387–88.
2. Satan.

3. Deuteronomy 17:6, "At the mouth of two witnesses, or three witnesses, shall he that is worthy of death be put to death; but at the mouth of one witness he shall not be put to death."

4. 2 Kings 24:4, "And also for the innocent blood that he shed: for he filled Jerusalem with innocent blood; which the Lord would not pardon."

5. The word "delusion" would appear often in the aftermath of the Salem crisis. All individuals involved who ought to bear the brunt of blame instead disavowed their responsibility by claiming to have been deluded by Satan. At no point is there doubt that the Devil lay at the heart of the panic. The only question was how, precisely, he was able to work his will.

ROBERT CALEF, *MORE WONDERS OF THE INVISIBLE WORLD*, 1700

1. Excerpted from George Lincoln Burr, *Narratives of the Witchcraft Cases, 1648–1706* (New York: Charles Scribner's Sons, 1914). Full text available from the University of Virginia's online Salem Witch Trials Documentary Archive and Transcription Project. http://xtf .lib.virginia.edu/xtf/view?docId=modern_english/uvaGenText/tei/ BurNarr.xml;chunk.id=d57;toc.depth=1;toc.id=d57;brand=default.

2. Even Calef recognizes the relationship between the Salem panic and the Indian wars, though his interpretation of the significance will differ from that of the court.

3. Cotton Mather's published account of the trials, which came out in 1693.

4. Jean Bodin, a sixteenth-century French jurist who wrote widely on demonology. His 1580 work "On the Demon-Worship of Sorcerers" advanced the theory of a pact being drawn up between a practicing witch and the Devil, and advocated loosened expectations for evidence in sorcery trials, on the grounds that rumors of sorcery were almost always true.

5. By "pagan and popish," Calef does not mean pagan in the contemporary sense. Calef, like many religious Puritans, identified Catholicism with magic, as a false version of unreformed Christianity. He is not suggesting that witchcraft is a remnant of a pre-Christian religion; he is being critical of what he sees as the delusional, superstitious beliefs inherent in Catholic practice.

6. Calef spends much of his treatise exposing what he sees to be the logical inconsistencies of contemporary witch trials. He cites first the relative paucity of detail on the nature and mechanics of witchcraft found in the Bible, and goes on to say that an individual's strength

should be credited to God. Yet the accusations levied against George
Burroughs, former minister of Salem Village, alluded to his suppos-
edly preternatural strength. Calef points out that Burroughs had
been known for unusual strength since he was in school, and as such
his strength should be regarded as a gift from God, rather than a
sign of his pact with the Devil.

7. Icarian, for Icarus, the young man of Greek mythology who flew
   too close to the sun on wings of wax and then plunged to his death.
8. Increase Mather.
9. William Perkins.

A CASE OF POISONING IN ALBANY, NEW YORK, 1700

1. A further account of English colonial thinking about Native American magic can be found in Alfred Cave, "Indian Shamans and English Witches," *Essex Institute Historical Collections* 128 (October
   1992): 241–54. This account is excerpted from Samuel Drake, *Annals
   of Witchcraft in New England and Elsewhere in the United States
   from their First Settlement* (Boston: WE Woodward, 1869), 208–10.
2. A "sachem" is a term for the head of some North American tribes,
   especially the Algonquian. OED, 1909.
3. A seventeenth-century term for the Indian tribes in New England,
   New York, Quebec, and Ontario who converted to Christianity.
4. In this account, fear of the native population continues to be bound
   up in a fear of Catholicism along the New York frontier.

JOHN HALE, *A MODEST ENQUIRY INTO THE NATURE OF WITCHCRAFT*, 1702

1. Excerpted from John Hale, *A Modest Enquiry into the Nature of
   Witchcraft*. Originally published in Boston by B. Green and J. Alten
   for Benjamin Eliot under the Town House. Images of the original
   text available from the University of Virginia's online Salem Witch
   Trials Documentary Archive and Transcription Project, http://salem
   .lib.virginia.edu/archives/ModestEnquiry/index.html.
2. John and Tituba Indian had made a "witch cake" at the behest of
   Mary Sibley, an intriguing example of the use of so-called white magic
   in the discovery of devilish doings. The witch-cake episode represents
   an instance of English folk-magical belief that stopped short of being
   considered witchcraft. Episodes like this indicate that the Puritan

worldview was one heavily inflected with, and even understood by, magical principles, which should be taken on their own historically contingent terms.

3. Hale references not only witch-hunting manuals that were in wide circulation during the Salem panic, but also the guides for jurymen that were used to ensure that the trials proceeded appropriately. Hale is struggling with the fact that the Salem trials were conducted legally, and in accordance with established precedent. The Salem trial was a failure both of faith and of system, and Hale, like others of his generation, is at pains to determine how such a tragedy could have come to pass.

4. Witchcraft historian George Lincoln Burr identifies "D. H." as Deliverance Hobbs. See Burr, *Narratives of the Witchcraft Cases 1648–1706*, 417.

5. George Burroughs preaching at a witches' Sabbath.

6. Burr identifies Goody F. as Ann Foster, who later died in prison. Burr, *Narratives of the Witchcraft Cases 1648–1706*, 418.

7. Among other things.

8. There is something rather sweet and quotidian about this witches' picnic, with bread and cheese wrapped up in a cloth for convenience while flying about on a stick.

9. Martha Carrier.

THE TRIAL OF GRACE SHERWOOD, PRINCESS ANNE COUNTY, VIRGINIA, 1705–1706

1. Ducking stools were most often used in England and Scotland as punishment and humiliation, primarily for women accused of being scolds. They were infrequently used to determine whether someone was a witch. English witches were more frequently identified using the touch test. The ducking stool has more in common with the pillory or the stocks as a punishment, rather than as a diagnostic tool. Interestingly, the ducking stool persists in contemporary carnival settings as the dunk tank, in which a person sits over a tank of water, scolding and jeering at the carnival goer who tries to hit a lever with baseballs that will release the jeerer into the water.

2. Excerpted from Henry Howe, *Historical Collections of Virginia*. Originally published in Charleston, S.C., by Babcock and Co, 1845.

3. Howe falls victim to a commonly voiced curiosity about Salem; namely, if everyone who confessed was let off, why didn't everyone just confess, whether guilty or not? The editor concedes that strength of character might have had something to do with it, though more likely was the fact that the accused at Salem consid-

ered lying to be a mortal sin. Mostly likely of all was that it was hardly a foregone conclusion that confession would lead to leniency. In witch trials leading up to Salem, confession was more expected to contribute to a death sentence. Salem was an exception because of the necessity of identifying all the other presumed witches in the conspiracy, who could only be reliably identified by another confessed confederate.

4. There is a Witchduck Lane off Lynnhaven Bay in Princess Anne County, Virginia, and a nearby neighborhood is referred to on Google Maps as Salem. Data retrieved March 10, 2012.

5. "Uxor" is Latin for "wife."

6. Original document reads "Differr," and might imply that the jury of women is to ascertain if Grace Sherwood's body has any marked differences from what is expected, which might determine that she is a witch.

7. Anew, that is, to have Grace Sherwood examined again.

8. To look for "images and such like things" suggests that the court wanted Sherwood's house searched for poppets and other examples of image magic.

9. The first jury of women assembled to search Grace Sherwood for teats actually refused to do so and were then charged with contempt.

10. Grace is to be tossed into water "above a man's depth" and have her ability to float gauged. However, care is to be taken to keep her from drowning.

11. Grace Sherwood is ducked and searched and found guilty, but instead of being hanged, is committed to prison. By 1705/6 witches were no longer the mortal threat that they had been a mere decade earlier.

MOB JUSTICE IN THE SOUTH, 1712

1. Excerpted from Samuel G. Drake, *Annals of Witchcraft in New England and Elsewhere in the United States from Their First Settlement*. Originally published in New York, 1869, 215–16.

LITTLETON, MASSACHUSETTS, 1720

1. Excerpted from Thomas Hutchinson, *History of Massachusetts-Bay,* vol. II. Originally published in Boston, 1767, 20–22.

2. Proverbs 19:5, "A false witness shall not be unpunished, and he that speaketh lies shall not escape."

3. The key word here being credulity, not only of the girls' parents, but also of the neighbors who diagnosed witchcraft in the first place. As an explanatory category, witchcraft has persisted to 1720, even though Hutchinson would have his readers see this account as an example of the fallacy of belief in it.

BOSTON, MASSACHUSETTS, 1728

1. The First Great Awakening was a period of religious revival that took place in the North American colonies from the 1730s until the early 1740s. Whereas ministers of Samuel Parris's generation delivered intellectual sermons that were dense in their theological underpinnings and argumentation, the leaders of the First Great Awakening emphasized an emotional experience of faith for their congregations.
2. Excerpted from *The Weekly News-Letter*, Boston, MA, no. 97, October 31, 1728, 1–2.
3. The most popular contemporary representation of the diagnosis of witchcraft via weight doubtless occurs in a scene in *Monty Python and the Holy Grail* (1975), in which a suspected witch is weighed against a duck, which, if they weigh the same, would mean she floats in water, and is therefore guilty of witchcraft. She is found guilty and hauled away to her death, commenting, "It's a fair cop."

NEW YORK, NEW YORK, 1737

1. Excerpted from *The New-York Weekly Journal*, New York, NY, no. 214, December 12, 1737, 1.

NEW YORK, NEW YORK, 1741

1. The best account of this grim episode in the history of colonial New York is found in Jill Lepore, *New York Burning: Liberty, Slavery, and Conspiracy in Eighteenth Century Manhattan* (New York: Vintage, 2006).
2. Excerpted from *The New England Weekly Journal*, September 29, 1741, 1–2.
3. Latin for "Though the name changes, the moral stays the same."
4. The idea of witchcraft as an impossible act underscores what the writer sees as the unreason of the position that a group of con-spirators should be responsible for burning the city. Witchcraft has

transformed into a rhetorical device, one that will persist well into the twenty-first century, to denote unreason, paranoia, and irrational fear.

PHILADELPHIA, PENNSYLVANIA, 1787

1. Excerpted from Old Whig, *From the Independent Gazetteer, &c.* (Philadelphia, 1787).
2. Exodus 22:18, "Thou shalt not suffer a witch to live."

MOLL PITCHER, LYNN, MASSACHUSETTS, 1738–1813

1. For more on the consumer revolution of the eighteenth century, see Richard Bushman, *The Refinement of America: Persons, Houses, Cities* (New York: Vintage, 1992).
2. Excerpted from Samuel G. Drake, *Annals of Witchcraft in New England and Elsewhere in the United States from Their First Settlement*. Originally published in New York, 1869, xliv–xlvii.
3. High Rock is now marked by a tower within a state park in Lynn, Massachusetts.

Index